To Dear Dad

We hope you get much
pleasure from the

love Gillian & Robert.
May 94.

# SAILORS
## IN THE RAF

Patrick Stephens Limited, a member of the Haynes Publishing Group, has published authoritative, quality books for enthusiasts for a quarter of a century. During that time the company has established a reputation as one of the world's leading publishers of books on aviation, maritime, military, model-making, motor cycling, motoring, motor racing, railway and railway modelling subjects. Readers or authors with suggestions for books they would like to see published are invited to write to: The Editorial Director, Patrick Stephens Limited, Sparkford, Nr Yeovil, Somerset, BA22 7JJ.

# SAILORS
## IN THE RAF

## The story of the Marine Branch of the Royal Air Force

## Keith Beardow

**Foreword by Air Vice-Marshal J.E. (Johnnie) Johnson
CB, CBE, DSO and Bars, DFC and Bar**

Patrick Stephens Limited

Dedication
To Sarah, James A. Ducarreaux
and Stephanie J. Ash

First published in 1993

British Library Cataloguing-in-Publication Data:
A catalogue record for this book is available
from the British Library

ISBN 1 85260 407 7

Library of Congress catalog card no 93-78067

Patrick Stephens Limited is a member of the
Haynes Publishing Group P.L.C.,
Sparkford, Nr Yeovil, Somerset, BA22 7JJ.

Typeset by BPCC Techset, Exeter
Printed and bound in Great Britain by
Butler & Tanner Ltd, Frome and London

# Contents

# Foreword

*Air Vice-Marshal J. E. (Johnnie) Johnson, CB, CBE, DSO and Bars, DFC and Bar*

In the early 1960s the author and I were serving together in Aden. Keith was the senior Marine Fitter on the crew of one of our air-sea rescue launches, and I was the Air Officer Commanding, Air Forces Middle East.

It was one of my jobs to make sure that we got the maximum serviceability from all our equipment, and from time to time I would put to sea to check on the efficiency of the launch crews and especially their navigation skills, since they could be called out at any time to help a ship or aeroplane in distress in the Indian Ocean or the Red Sea. Thus, on one occasion we made the voyage from Perim Island, once a flourishing coaling station but then derelict and abandoned, to a group of rocks near the African coast known as the Seven Brothers.

Apart from the crew we had on board Doctor Colin McCance, son of the renowned Professor R. A. McCance, who was advising on survival at sea and in the desert, two RAF doctors, and Val Hinds, a civil servant and a very knowledgeable fisherman who was trying to establish a Government-sponsored fishing industry in Aden.

When we saw the Brothers we reduced our speed to about five knots, set up a couple of outriggers and trailed four fishing lines behind the launch. We soon had enough barracuda for our supper, and the remainder were cut up for bait on a 24-hook long shark line which we laid between two buoys at last light.

Early the next morning we made for the shark line and began to haul it aboard. The first few hooks were empty. Then we got just a big head — the rest had been devoured by its mates. Then another head, but cruising round it an enormous tiger shark which Val estimated at between 700 and 800 lb and which was dispatched with my FN rifle. The line held one more dead shark with its tail sheared off as if by a circular saw.

We all took turns at trolling for the rest of the day, packed the barracuda (the biggest was 37 lb), horse mackerel, garfish and sharks into ice, and as the light faded made for home accompanied by a dozen dolphins and a few frigate birds.

A few days later, my ADC said the Financial Controller — a senior civil servant who was there to uphold the principles of public accountability — would like a few minutes, and I had an uneasy feeling we would not see eye to eye on the recent trip to the Brothers. However, it was about something else but as he turned to go he said, 'My staff tell me, Air Marshal, that the airmen at Steamer Point really enjoyed the fresh fish you brought them yesterday!'

On a more serious note I commend Keith Beardow's splendid, well-researched narrative about the brave men who managed the rescue boats and, sometimes at great risk, brought airmen back from the sea to fight again.

# Introduction

'The sea shall not have them' was the motto of the RAF Air Sea Rescue Service during and after the Second World War. When the Marine Branch was disbanded on 1 April 1986 it was the longest surviving branch of the service, having been inaugurated as the Marine Craft Section on 12 April 1918, just 11 days after the Royal Air Force was founded. Among those who served were many who achieved fame in other fields, including racing driver Sir Algernon Guinness, novelist Alistair Maclean, writer John Harris, mast-maker Ian Proctor, marine photographer Beken of Cowes and, by association, Lawrence of Arabia.

Air-sea rescue was a purely British invention and, like so many others, it was born of necessity. When in 1939 the small and overcrowded Kingdom became the last bastion of freedom in an oppressed Europe, every operation by land, sea or air required the islanders and their allies to traverse treacherous waters.

There were no precedents for the founders of the ASR Service: large scale air warfare was new. Mistakes were made and demand under-estimated, but like all good inventions, the product was honed and developed to near perfection. When Britain was later transformed into a launching pad for vast air armadas, the RAF sailors were more than ready to fulfil their role of mercy. The RAF had acquired the mantle of sea rescue almost by chance.

The wartime Marine Craft crews were as unique as their flying colleagues. They set out regularly from the relative normality of their home bases to defy and often fight the enemy in his own territories, but with a different motivation. They saw their task as one of saving lives when all about them were hell-bent on killing. To this day, the veterans are justly proud of it. Their other contributions included aircrew survival training and waterborne support for the flying boats of Coastal and Overseas Commands. At the final reckoning after VE day, the RAF sailors had played their part in saving almost 14,000 lives at sea.

It is said that history is a matter of interpretation. Even with the well documented evidence available for such an epic event as the Battle of Britain, historians and archaeologists are still uncovering facts which add to or detract from the myriad written accounts. When investigating the Air Sea Rescue and Marine Craft Section history, needlepoint accuracy was impossible.

During the war, ASR units were under Royal Navy control while Marine support bases remained within RAF Command structures, although their activities often overlapped. For the most part, RAF vessels at sea operated alone where few events were witnessed and fewer were recorded accurately. ASR units did not enjoy the comparatively sophisticated debriefing system which was standard practice for all operational aircrew, and even had they done so, it was no guarantee of veracity. Thus, if the knowledgeable should find any specific errors in the text, then I ask for their forgiveness, for such are unintentional. Where an element of doubt has occurred, I make no excuses for erring on the side of the RAF sailors.

Those ex-aircrew who have cause to recall the Marine Craft Section and those of other ground trades who never quite understood 'web-foot' practices, are instantly alerted and start nodding knowingly as soon as the words 'High Speed Launch' or 'Air Sea Rescue' are offered in explanation. In fact, the ASR function spanned many more years than the conflict of 1939–45 and a much wider spectrum than is generally understood.

The RAF sailors were present in Malaya, Suez, Cyprus and Aden, in addition to a multitude of less troublesome locations throughout the Commonwealth and Empire. Wherever British aircrews operated over the sea, the RAF provided rescue cover for them, but it did not stop there. Many yachtsmen, holiday-makers and merchant seamen owed their lives to the skills of the men who sailed under the RAF ensign. By the late 1950s this global network, along with some 30 Marine Craft Units around the UK, was still the biggest lifeboat service in the world.

The sailors had their own traditions, language and mode of dress which was as remote from the general concept of airmen as were aircrew from infantry. They worked in an exciting and, to the layman, glamorous environment, which concealed all the lurking dangers that are inherent with seafaring. In their strange admixture of Senior and Junior Service disciplines, they were an élite, but unlike other special forces not by prior selection. In war or peace, it was the very nature of the job and the ever constant trial by wind and water that sorted out the weaker spirits.

As the ubiquitous helicopter was gradually developed in terms of speed, range and all-weather reliability, and the big flying boats were phased out, the nature of the seagoing job changed. The fleets of seaplane support and high-speed surface craft were replaced by larger, long-range craft which continued to serve the Air Force into the 1990s.

This book does not set out to be a definitive history. It is an overview of which little will be revelationary to the ex-sailors themselves, but it is intended to introduce the story of RAF seafaring to a relatively unaware public. It is also my tribute to all ex-shipmates; the Webfoot Brigade; the Sailors In The Royal Air Force.

# Acknowledgements

The biggest accolade must go to all the airmen, the matelots, the civilians and most of all, the ex-RAF sailors whose deeds have contributed to this book, either knowingly or unknowingly. Prominent among those who helped directly was Mervyn Manson who, having once embarked on a Marine Branch history himself, made his material available. Photographs, letters and verbal assistance came from the following: Bob Moore, John Philbin, Jack Hill, Harry Field, Tom Carroll, John Crouch, Bob Symons, Peter Bettesworth, Mike Lawrence, Les Flower, Jim Burchall, Eddie Pow, John Mills, Spencer Capper, Dave Morgan, Alan Alker, George Selman, Alan Thorne, Geoff McGuire, Denis Winstone, Ralph Ashton, and Bob West, and many others who helped via the ASR/MCS Club newsletters and the Marine Craft newsletters. Special thanks are due to ex-Coxwain John Blagg, and to the only Parachutist/WOp to serve on RAF boats, Chris Allen.

The RAF Museum, Hendon, provided most of the photographs and masses of documents and information. All photographs and illustrations are courtesy of the RAF Museum unless otherwise stated. Mr Ken Hunter of the Archives Department has given special attention to marine memorabilia for several years and was unstinting in his efforts to assist. I am also immensely grateful to my one time AOC, Johnnie Johnson, for the foreword.

Finally, a standing ovation to my wife who has allowed her home life to be disrupted, yet has been supportive in every conceivable way.

# Prologue

A 'Whaleback' crew from Dover were directed to search for the crew of one of the then new Lancaster bombers, which had relayed its position before splashing down off Holland. The aircrew made a perfect exit to their dinghy before the aircraft sank, but were still undiscovered when a dawn mist began to shroud the sea. The HSL searched for several hours in freezing fog, until the skipper decided to cut the engines and drift until the fog cleared, reasoning that their position relative to the dinghy would remain more or less constant. A few minutes later, the sense of total isolation which fog-bound seafarers know so well was disrupted by the sound of loud voices close by. The surprised sailors called out and received welcome replies from the seven men in the dinghy. It had been a lucky fluke.

Soon the survivors were aboard, dry and warm, but getting wetter on the inside as copious tots of rum were shared with the crew. Before the celebrations were over and the launch engines restarted, one of the deckhands heard more unseen voices and the sound of diesel engines. This time the language was German. The HSL was in the midst of a flotilla of E-boats. For several hours the sailors played a cat and mouse game with the enemy. The HSL would run for a few minutes, then stop engines and listen, then repeat the process again and again, all the time edging in the direction of the English coast. Once, they came under fire, tracer appearing from the fog and passing over their heads.

Eventually they were able to make a dash for it, and after lying alongside an anchored freighter, the fog lifted and they finally entered Lowestoft harbour having spent some 40 hours at sea.

## Chapter 1

# Dark blue plus khaki equals a blueish-grey

*The RAF motto* Per Ardua Ad Astra *was adopted by the Royal Flying Corps in March 1913. It is claimed that two Royal Engineer Lieutenants were discussing a request for ideas, when one of them remembered the line in H. Rider Haggard's book,* The People of the Mist. *The motto has no literal translation, although according to Haggard it is 'Through Struggle to The Stars.'*

T he RAF was the first air force in the world. It is still the only one that does not have the country of its origin incorporated in its title. At the time of its inauguration the concept of an independent air force was not only unprecedented, but also highly controversial. That the RAF should find itself operating its own 'private navy' was stranger still, and it reflected how the Air Force evolved from a combination of early maritime and terrestrial aviation.

During the First World War the Royal Navy was the most powerful in the world, whilst the Army was committed to a static war of attrition. Both forces operated primitive aircraft in the roles of gunnery spotting and observing enemy movements. The respective High Commands saw little prospect in using heavier-than-air machines beyond these purposes.

The first military unit to utilize the aeroplane had been No 2 Company of the Air Battalion of the Royal Engineers, formed on 1 April 1911. Shortly afterwards, a sub-committee of the Imperial Defence Committee was set up under the chairmanship of Lord Haldane to examine aviation issues. It recommended the pooling of all aviation resources to create a Flying Corps containing a military wing, a naval wing, and a central flying school.

To co-ordinate the naval and army requirements and to exercise control over the new corps, an Air Committee was suggested. A sub-committee was given the task of working out the details and presenting the plan to the IDC. As a result, the Royal Flying Corps was established on 13 April 1912 by Royal Warrant. Acting Major Fred Sykes was given command of the Corps, but immediately found himself in conflict with the all-powerful Admiralty.

The Navy strongly resented the Army's incorporation of the naval wing, believing that naval matters were for their Lordships alone. Even at wing level, the personnel saw themselves as a separate entity and began to refer to themselves as the Royal Naval Air Service instead of the officially designated RFC Naval Wing.

In defiance of the principles of the Central Flying School, the RN set up its own facilities for flying training at Eastchurch in Hampshire. Between 1912 and 1914, the Naval Wing opened seaplane bases independently at the Isle of Grain in Kent, Felixstowe in Suffolk, Cromarty on the Moray Firth, and Calshot on the Solent, the future home of the RAF sailors. Eventually the might of the Admiralty prevailed and the RNAS received official approval as a separate force on 26 June 1914, only 39 days before the declaration of war with Germany.

With the outbreak of the Great War, military aviation was divided into two main activities. The RFC, being now completely Army orientated, followed the Expeditionary Force to France and concentrated on aerial reconnaissance and artillery support. As the technology of war progressed, landplanes were at first adapted, then purpose built, for offensive use, that is air fighting and bombing. The War Office created a basic plan that encouraged and supported the expansion of the Flying Corps.

The RNAS, tasked mainly with the air defence of the home islands, was largely ignored by the Admiralty and left to operate defensive landplanes and seaplanes without any real directives. The development of aerial torpedoes, aircraft carriers, air to sea gunnery etc, was only explored in a haphazard manner by enterprising middle-rank officers.

The RFC built upon the Squadron system, mobile units which, complete with their own ground support staff, followed the land battles, while the Navy placed its seaplane Wings in permanent 'stone frigates', along with their attendant marine craft and personnel.

On 15 August 1914, command of the RFC went to Brigadier-General Sir David Henderson. He in turn was succeeded by Hugh Montague Trenchard on 19 August of the following year. It was Trenchard who nurtured the aggressive spirit of the flyers and lobbied the government of the day for an air power to transcend the operational limitations of army support and coastal defence.

The main problem which the new commander had to face was the shortage of aircraft, equipment and personnel. The Admiralty was monopolizing all three, leaving the Military Wing to take second place in the queue. In 1916, a special committee under the leadership of Lord Derby was established to investigate ways of ending the inter-service wrangling for men and equipment. The Naval delegate opposed even the smallest compromise and after only six weeks, Lord Derby resigned in despair. In a statement, he warned of the impossibility of bringing the two Wings closer together unless they were amalgamated into a single service.

Around the coasts of the UK, the Navy continued to expand its maritime air activities. The convoys required protection from the growing menace of German submarines and regular patrols were carried out to deter attacks. In support, the numbers of small marine craft and crews increased accordingly. The RFC operated a few waterborne aircraft, but where boats were needed they were usually on loan from the Navy.

Meanwhile, the RNAS pursued the theory that in order to protect warships at sea efficiently, the fleets should take their aircraft with them. As early as 1911 an American, Eugene Ely, had successfully flown a Curtiss biplane from a platform erected aboard USS *Birmingham*. Two months later he had landed on a similarly equipped USS *Pennsylvania* with the aid of a rope stretched between sandbags as a crude arrester. Both ships had been tethered to a dockside during the experiments. Within a year, on 10 January 1912, Lieutenant Charles Samson RN flew a Short S 27 from an improvized flight deck on HMS *Africa*.

These events did not lead immediately to the concept of the aircraft carrier, but they did stimulate the introduction of the seaplane carrier, whereby aircraft were launched by wheeled trolley or derricked into the sea for take-off. The cross-Channel steamers *Empress*, *Engadine* and *Riviera* were the first of these, carrying four seaplanes each, whilst the Cunarder *Campania* was adapted to deploy 10 aircraft.

In 1917, Flight Commander F. J. Rutland, RNAS, demonstrated that a wheeled Sopwith Pup could be flown from a small seaplane deck. The take-off run was a mere 15 ft and the aircraft lifted at an indicated speed of 23 mph. As a result, 22 light battle cruisers were fitted with 20 ft platforms and furbished with fighter aeroplanes. The first of these was HMS *Yarmouth* and it was from her deck that Flight Sub-Lieutenant B. A. Smart flew to shoot down Zeppelin L 23. A further development by Rutland obviated the need for the ship to turn up-wind to enable the aircraft to take off. Platforms were erected on the top of the massive gun turrets which were then swivelled as required.

In 1918, Charles Samson evolved a system whereby flat-topped barges were towed behind fast warships. On 11 August 1918, Zeppelin L 53 fell to the guns of Flt Sub Lt Stuart Culley, who coaxed his Sopwith Camel to 18,000 ft from a barge towed by HMS *Redoubt*. Several of these barges were later converted to seaplane lighters and used by the RAF Marine Craft Section.

The shortcomings of these methods were manifold. Seaplanes were slow compared with their landplane equivalents and both types of aircraft had to alight on the sea to facilitate recovery. This in turn meant that the mother ship was required to heave to, an often vulnerable and dangerous circumstance.

In parallel to the above experiments, HMS *Furious* was fitted with an unusually long 228 ft flying-off deck forward of the superstructure.

Determined to solve the problem of the ship having to stop, Squadron Commander E. H. Dunning side-slipped his Sopwith and stalled it on to *Furious*'s deck in August 1917. A party of matelots stood by to grab the aircraft and prevent it from kiting. A few days later he tried it again without the deck team and was killed. HMS *Furious* returned to port for an additional deck to be fitted aft of the superstructure. Although arrester hooks and wires were still six years away, by late 1918 the aircraft carrier had arrived.

Whilst the RFC was suffering huge losses in offensive operations over the Western Front, the defence of the British Isles was found to be sorely lacking in quality. The rift between the War Office and the Admiralty deepened and even the remotest possibility of a co-ordinated effort receded.

The catalyst for a new review of the situation came from an unexpected source: the German Imperial Air Service. Zeppelin attacks on Britain had peaked in 1916, but between November and the beginning of June 1917 only two night raids had taken place. In the same period twin engined Gotha bombers attacked the south-east on seven separate dates. On the morning of 13 June 1917, a formation of 14 Gothas flew over London and dropped 4 tons of high explosives in the docks area, and three weeks later, a flight of 22 Gothas bombed the city again. The public cried out for vengeance and protection. Britain had neither the long-range aircraft to retaliate nor the infrastructure for effective defence.

Prime Minister David Lloyd George intervened by appointing the South African General Jan Smuts to head a board of enquiry. Within two months, Smuts reported with a résumé of defence requirements (and a plan for the strategic bombing of Germany). His aspirations were optimistic, but in presenting his strategy he advocated a separate, single air service. He went even further by proposing that the Air Committee should be replaced by a new Air Ministry with all the status and power that such an office implied.

The War Office and the Admiralty were incensed. They were fiercely opposed to the proposals, but the matter had widened into an important parliamentary debate which embraced both public and political interests. The recommendations were bulldozed through parliament, with the result that by the end of 1917 the Air Force Act was approved.

Bitter clashes arose between serving commanders and politicians in the new Ministry. Appointments and resignations became an almost weekly occurrence. The highly revered land commander Field Marshal Earl Douglas Haig expressed vociferous opposition and even Hugh Trenchard, who was the first appointed Chief of Air Staff, found cause to resign before the new Air Force was inaugurated.

Despite all this, on 7 March 1918, King George V gave his assent. On 1 April, the Royal Flying Corps and the Royal Naval Air Service became the Royal Air Force.

The Marine Craft Section was inaugurated a few days later, on 12

April. Lieutenant Colonel G. Holmes was appointed Senior Staff Officer for Marine Equipment with four other officers in his department, the most notable of whom was Captain W. E. G. Beauforte-Greenwood*. To the men and women of the defunct RFC and RNAS there were no immediate perceptible changes. While the brass hats and politicians jockeyed for position, there was a war to finish.

For many months the embryo Royal Air Force did not outwardly appear to exist. Officially, the old RFC rank structure applied to all personnel but some historians and contemporary reporters still quoted Naval ranks well into 1919. The RNAS already sported uniforms of navy blue or khaki, both with naval insignia. To these, the RFC and Royal Engineer versions were added, complete with their respective army badges. The High Command confused the situation even further by being unable to establish an exact shade for the new RAF blue-grey. In the interests of economy, they had been obliged to adopt an existing material from a cancelled export order. The word 'uniform' was an outstanding misnomer.

When the RAF uniform pattern was finalized, the officers' rig was clearly of RFC origin, but without the Sam Browne belt, epaulettes and knee boots. The new cap badge was taken directly from the RNAS but with greater emphasis given to the eagle. (For many years, some referred to it as an albatross, but in 1947 it was officially stated to be an eagle.) Pilots and Observers wore the full and half wings of the RFC.

For the Other Ranks, uniforms were manufactured from an uncomfortable serge. To the ex-Navy personnel who found themselves in the newly formed RAF Marine Craft Section, the new uniforms were a painfully retrogressive step. They soon discovered that the material was hot and itchy in the warmer months and stiff and itchy in the cooler ones. The collar abrased the neck like the emery cloth both its colour and texture resembled, and in all seasons of the year it soaked up sea spray, dew and fog damp like a sponge. The brass accoutrements quickly tarnished in the sea air before turning green with verdigris and the 'cheesecutter' peaked cap had to be held on by its chin-strap in the lightest of airs.

Sir Hugh Trenchard, 'Father of the RAF', returned to the post of Chief of Air Staff on 11 January 1919 and immediately took action to secure a separate identity for the new service despite renewed efforts by the War Office and the Admiralty to have it disbanded. In the post-war financial constraints, the complement of RAF officers was reduced from 27,333 to

---

*Formerly a Lieutenant in the Royal Navy Volunteer Reserve, Beauforte-Greenwood became a RFC Captain. When the new RAF ranks were introduced in August 1919, his automatically changed to Flight Lieutenant. Like many others, in the course of barely a year he had held Navy, Army and Air Force rank! Before leaving RAF service, he adopted the title of Captain yet again — this time as a Marine Civilian Supplementary Officer.

a mere 1,246 and the total of other ranks fell from 263,837 to 36,608. Trenchard, however, adopted a philosophy of building on the quality and not the quantity of his resources. He was denied the opportunity to establish an Air Force on a scale fit to fight another war, but he set out to create a nucleus from which a powerful force could rapidly be created. He called it 'building a cottage on the foundations of a castle'.

On 1 August 1919 a new rank structure was introduced which helped to confirm the individuality of the RAF. Flight Lieutenant, Squadron Leader, Wing Commander, Group Captain and Air Commodore were of naval origin, while Pilot Officer, Flying Officer and the higher echelon of 'Air' ranks were newly promulgated. Warrant Officer was taken from the RN and Corporal, Sergeant and Flight Sergeant were derived from army equivalents. In the lower ranks a new Aircraftman status replaced the army title of Private.

The post-war exodus of RAF officers left only five Motor Boat Officers in 1919, a drop to a fifth of the former establishment. The low number of wartime Motor Boat Officers was due to the fact that they did not 'skipper' a wide range of marine craft as they were to do in later years.

The main cause for concern was that the RAF, who had inherited a miscellany of floatplanes, flying boats and coastal stations from the RNAS, had no idea how many or what types of marine craft had been transferred with them. There was difficulty too in determining the exact numbers of personnel. In the last months of the war there had been many transfers in and out of various units. Recruiting for Motor Boat Crew (MBC) was still being actively pursued and some RAF men were serving overseas and on HM ships. In many cases, the paperwork lagged behind actual events, causing demobilization lists to show a mix of RFC and naval trades and ranks. The foundations for administrative chaos were firmly laid.

The challenge that faced Holmes and his staff was firstly to determine the number, type and condition of the boats they had inherited; secondly, to adjust the inventory to suit the requirements of the new RAF; and thirdly, to ensure that there were sufficient numbers of trained personnel to meet those needs.

The first of these tasks proved complicated. Estimates of powered boats varied between 300 and almost 500. It transpired that although the majority of the boats now belonged to the RAF, 50 had formerly been loaned to the RNAS from the Admiralty. Just over half of these 20–40 ft motor boats were transferred back to their original owners. The remainder, which included such unlikely vessels as coaling lighters, stayed on loan to the Air Force.

To add even more confusion, there were a number of motor boats carried aboard HM ships which became the property of the RAF. The Admiralty, in one of its more obtuse moments, insisted that these should be manned by Air Force personnel. Eventually the matter was resolved with the return of the boats to the Navy.

The second part of Holmes' brief might at first glance seem to have been his easiest task, but in the absence of accurate numbers and disposition of aircraft, it was impossible to be specific about requirements for support vessels. A compromise was reached in June 1919 with a provisional figure for a fleet of 191 boats, including non-powered craft, but the condition and serviceability of those that were to be retained had yet to be assessed.

Flight Lieutenant Beauforte-Greenwood was given the unenviable task of touring all the marine craft bases to collect and collate the information. It took the best part of eight months before a report was submitted in the autumn of 1920. The situation was dismal. Barely half the boats were serviceable, and at the larger bases serviceability was as low as 10 per cent. Although neglect and uncertainty had contributed to this state of affairs, the principal cause was the shortage of trained men.

Several Air Ministry orders were issued during 1920 which were to establish the work pattern of the MCS, which was mostly concerned with the handling of seaplanes afloat and policing their landing zones. The majority of contemporary seaplanes were of the floatplane variety, land planes which had been converted by fitting hollow floats constructed from wood and fabric. Flying boats, on the other hand, were purpose designed with the lower part of the fuselage constructed in the form of a boat hull and the upper section specially strengthened. Both types were unwieldy under their own power, and it was neither prudent nor economical for them to taxi in confined waters. Being lightweight and perched delicately on the surface like mosquitoes, they were highly susceptible to the wind. At frequent intervals, they had to be slipped for servicing or moved between moorings and, sometimes, harbours. Because of their fabric and timber construction, early seaplanes were not left afloat any longer than necessary, for the floats or hulls soon soaked up water, thereby critically increasing their weight.

When seaplanes were embarked on HM ships, RAF personnel stayed aboard with the aircraft and their attendant launches while the ships were at sea. Marine craft crews were posted to the first aircraft carriers, HMS's *Furious*, *Argus* and *Hermes* and continued serving with what was to be the Fleet Air Arm of the RAF and later the RN, until as late as 1940.

The 1920 orders also specified that the MCS held the responsibility for both the laying and six-monthly servicing of all seaplane and marine craft buoys and moorings. Coupled with this was an instruction to complete quarterly returns of the marine craft inventory and their serviceability states. To aid identification a method of numbering boats according to hull length was devised, but it was to be many years before the sequence of numbers complied with the individual boat types. However, a systematic approach was beginning to emerge.

Inadvertently, the orders contained a few short paragraphs that anticipated air-sea rescue by almost 20 years. The first of these was to the effect that units operating motor boats where *any over-sea flying* was carried out should ensure that a motor boat is standing by, either underway or ready for immediate start up, in case of accident. Further to this, the instructions specified that a tool kit be carried aboard all stand-by boats. The kit to include metal and woods saws, axes, wire-cutters, grappling irons and crowbars. 'Stand By Flying' or 'SBF' and 'Crash Kit' were still familiar terms to boat's crews over 60 years later.

More significant was an order that contained details of alterations to 35 ft and 40 ft motorboats to provide for two 6 ft 1½ in stretchers in each craft. This was the first reference to RAF launches fulfilling an ambulance role.

The list compiled by Beauforte-Greenwood showed a jumble of power craft of almost every foot length between 16 ft runabouts and 80 ft ex-Navy ML's, but the very diversity of boat and engine types had in part contributed to the difficulties of maintenance. A clear need for rationalization was indicated. Thirty-two 35–40 ft boats known as 'Brookes' or 'Thornycrofts', after their builders, Brooke Marine of Lowestoft and J. I. Thornycroft of Southampton, were selected as the principal types. The sailors adopted the habit of referring to some vessels by the type of engine installed. Thus, 50 ft boats were known as 'Kelvins' or 'De Jinns' and refuelling boats as 'Pelepones' or 'Asters'. With others, type descriptions were adhered to, such as seaplane tenders, docking lighters and pinnaces. One anomaly was the Bolinder-powered concrete lighter, in which the description refers neither to the Swedish engine nor the application, but to the hull material where concrete had been utilized in place of steel during the war.

The Brooke boats had fine lines, were slender of beam and built much in the style of Thames slipper launches. The coxswain stood aft of the long coach roof where a coaming swept down in a graceful curve to the stern. A low freeboard on the quarters made reaching overside easy, if somewhat wet, in choppy conditions. The boats were fitted with 65 hp, six-cylinder petrol engines, and could achieve a speed of 15 knots. Samson posts for towing were fitted near the transom and in inclement or rough conditions, removable canvas dodgers and canopies were provided. These boats were the subject of the ambulance modifications outlined above and many of them were listed as seaplane tenders. They were durable and performed well in many operational theatres until replaced from 1931 onwards.

The 50 ft launches were fewer but more varied. Several Kelvins had been inherited from the RNAS in 1918. These were numbered from 1 to 12 and a further six, numbers 81 to 86, were on the stocks at Cox and King's yard at Wivenhoe in Essex, for delivery from March 1921. These craft were slab-sided, boxy, and gave nothing to aesthetics. The 45 hp engine was a temperamental petrol/paraffin unit which propelled the launch at up to 10 knots. Some of the Kelvins were equipped with aft cabins, while others sported open and very spacious well-decks. They were all fitted with a towing bar or horse at the aft end and were mainly employed in moorings inspection, towing larger seaplanes and ferrying stores or personnel. Eventually they were superseded by 56 ft pinnaces.

For handling aircraft, seaplane docking lighters proved invaluable. The majority of them were small, dumb craft (ie not self-propelling) consisting of a series of compartments in a 'U' configuration with catwalks along the hulls and a winch at the apex. The compartments could be flooded to lower the vessel until a seaplane was able to be winched into the dock through the open end. When the water ballast was pumped out or displaced by compressed air, the lighter rose in the water bringing the aircraft with it. Larger versions of these were adapted from the flat-topped barges such as that used by Culley for his Zeppelin attack during the war.

With their frequency of slipping, early seaplanes seldom required refuelling afloat. It was more common to top up their small capacity tanks by means of a can and a funnel. As the range and power of aircraft increased so did the size of their fuel tanks, and special refuelling boats were needed. These were similar in appearance to the Brookes, but an open well deck held four interlinked supply tanks and a 'Zwicky' semi-rotary handpump for transferring the petrol. Purpose-built, high-capacity refuellers entered the service when the transition from float-planes to flying boats took place at the end of the decade.

The 120 ft concrete lighters were the first of many larger craft operated by the RAF. In profile, they resembled late nineteenth-century coasters or drifters. 'Drifter' is the most apt description because their lamp-start, semi-diesel engines coaxed them along at only 4 knots, thus for much of their lives they had to lie at anchor waiting for favourable tides. Mainly used for recovering crashed or immobilized seaplanes from around the Solent and Isle of Wight, they were also utilized for stores and personnel carrying. Numbered 109 and 110, they were based at Calshot and Haslar respectively, but their slow speed was their biggest drawback and they were eventually replaced by civilian manned auxiliary ships.

In addition to these mainstream craft, there were some 140 'pulling' boats which embraced rowing boats, pram dinghies, skiffs and 27 ft sailing/oared whalers.

The Air Force also inherited compass barges and kite balloon vessels. The former were used for seaplane compass adjusting. The aircraft would be swung through all the cardinal points of the compass circle while a comparison of each indicated bearing was made against a hand-bearing compass held outside the range of local magnetic influences. Kite balloon vessels had been used to good effect by the Royal Navy for fleet gunnery spotting during the hostilities. In the days before radar, kite balloons, with their air-to-surface telephone links, proved invaluable. These vessels remained with the RAF for some years and were still being operated by the Navy in the Second World War.

Increasingly, the RAF sailors became involved in training both Royal

Navy and RAF aircrew. To save expense, some aircrew received navigation training aboard RAF launches. The navigation principles were about the same, but the pace was slower and the trainees were often hampered by seasickness. Bases such as Smoogroo in the Shetlands, and Marske in Yorkshire were training stations and Calshot and Lee-on-Solent were RAF/Naval co-operation units. At Gosport in Hampshire, the Torpedo Development Squadron introduced the Marine Craft Section to what was to become an ongoing task of torpedo recovery. RAF marine training was also carried out at Gosport and a reserve of boats was held at nearby Haslar.

On the Isle of Grain in Kent, the Marine Aircraft Experimental Establishment (MAEE) used four motor boats, a seaplane lighter, a refueller and a number of pulling boats. There were seven UK seaplane stations at Dover, Portland, Felixstowe, Plymouth, Leuchers, Donibristle and Dundee and a further three abroad, in Malta and Alexandria. One 50 ft Kelvin was attached to the airship station at Pulham in Norfolk and there were several detachments to HM ships at sea.

Throughout the 1920s the duties of the RAF boat crews kept them mostly in protected or sheltered waters. Seaplane and training stations were, by their very nature, in safe areas. The hazards of the open sea were rarely experienced, and extended coastal passage-making virtually unknown. Night flying was in its infancy and aircraft were restricted to operating in conditions of good visibility and moderate winds. Nevertheless, the boat crews had to learn to cope with inshore shoals and skerries, shipping movements, buoyed channels and the dangers of flotsam and tidal currents. In fog or gales, ice and snow the sailors were required to regularly check their swinging and pitching charges. Occasionally, it was necessary to board, perhaps to secure a line or rekindle an anchor light. A moment of inattention or misjudgement going alongside could end in rent fabric, shattered timbers, torn flesh or broken limbs.

The essentially high standards of boat handling skills had been acquired by the RAF when it absorbed the personnel of the RNAS, whereas the Royal Navy lost virtually all of its small boat expertise overnight and resented it profoundly. But even with this nucleus of trained and efficient crews, manpower was well below the 2,086 men that Holmes had recommended in his 1919 estimates. Recruiting and training were urgently needed.

From civilian sources came fishermen, deckhands, stokers, engineers and boatwrights, who felt that the regular pay and conditions within the RAF were more attractive than the risks of a fast approaching economic depression. As the decade progressed, other members of the RAF chose to remuster to the marine craft trades. Many were ex-Merchant Service cadets or seamen who for a variety of reasons found themselves in the Air Force. Yet others were aircraft fitters, mechanics, and 'Trenchard Brats' to whom a life afloat had some appeal. From the skilled ranks of the motor transport trades came the F/DPs (Fitter/Drivers/Petrol) who, with their specialist knowledge of internal combustion engines and workshop practices, found it relatively easy to adjust to the idiosyncrasies of marine engineering. These men were very much the advanced technologists of the age, for petrol and diesel engines were inventions of only twenty years previously. Carpenter/Boatbuilders were drawn from the 'chippies' and riggers of general workshops and aircraft repair.

On such resources, the RAF developed its nautical service. It was a broad platform from which seamanship, technical knowledge and experience helped to form the castle foundations on which Trenchard's cottage was rapidly taking shape. All that the men needed was indoctrination into the Marine Craft Section 'style'. All the Section needed was the right boats to do the job.

The style came very quickly via the Marine Craft Training schemes; the boats took considerably longer.

## Chapter 2

# You look like a bleedin' centipede

*An instructor's observation after watching recruits trying to row a whaler.*

When Royal Naval Air Service squadrons became part of the RAF they retained their old squadron numbers prefixed by the figure 2. One of these was 210 Squadron, based at RAF Gosport, and it was here that the first Marine Craft Training Section was established. Firstly, the new recruit was required to attend RAF Uxbridge for basic training or 'square-bashing' as it was universally known. For some of the ex-merchant seamen and civilian candidates, it was a culture shock. The whole thing was pure nineteenth-century army, a constant round of drill, PT, inspections, fatigues and parades, interspersed with infantry weapons training and instruction in RAF structures and procedures.

The Corporal Drill Instructors were only once removed from God, but far from god-like. God himself was the Regimental Sergeant Major, later re-titled Station Warrant Officer. From Uxbridge and other recruit camps came all the expressions so beloved of Ealing Studios and a multitude of television programmes which delighted later generations.

'On the double — you 'orrible little man.'

'Get some in.'

'The ablutions look like a shithouse.'

'When I say jump, you JUMP — and you don't come down 'til I tell you.'

'Don't walk; MARCH!' and many, many more.

All orders were bawled eyeball to eyeball, in a sonorous cadence that was peculiar to the DIs. Remarkably, or perhaps not, basic training concepts have changed little to the present day.

Discipline at the Marine Training Section was also strict, but priority was given to imparting the skills and knowledge that would enable the recruit to perform his duties both ashore and afloat. The courses were divided into separate stages, each stage covering a particular aspect of the job. At the end of every stage the trainee sat a written and/or practical test. If he passed, he continued on to the following subject; if not, he was either relegated to start again with a later group or, if he was not able to make the grade generally, he reverted to Aircraft Hand and departed for other duties.

Normally, at the end of training, the men would be promoted to Aircraftman 1st Class, but ex-'Brats' passed out as Leading Aircraftman as part of their pre-ordained career programme. This led to resentment among some of their more experienced seamen colleagues. Ultimately, direct entry graduates of outstanding ability were also promoted to LAC, a highly revered rank in the early years of the RAF.

Of the three MCS trades, the MBCs, who were the backbone of the Marine Section, were in the lowest paid category, and were at times the most neglected in terms of career prospects. The usual path of promotion was via Corporal 2nd Class Coxswain, through Sergeant, Flight Sergeant and Warrant Officer 1st Class Coxswain. Promotion was entirely subject to vacancies in the establishment level and could take many years to attain.

In the 1930s the system was changed. All candidates for the RAF were required to pass an education test and subsequent elevation to NCO status was linked to the individual's technical ability. The new boats that were planned for the service were larger, faster and designed for offshore work and passage-making, so a high level of proficiency in navigation and handling was essential. As a result, the seamanship standards of the 1st Class Cox'ns became very high indeed, but some of the 2nd Class Corporal Cox'ns and MBCs, who were of a more practical than academic bent, were condemned to promotional stagnation.

The training of MBCs embraced small boat handling, rowing and sailing, supplemented by procedures for lifting moorings, going along-side and seaplane towing. A great deal of emphasis was placed on morse, semaphore and flag signalling of the 'England Expects' variety, for this was before the introduction of marine wireless sets. The Admiralty Manual of Seamanship was the main source of reference and from this the sailors were required to learn by rote the International Rules of the Road for proceeding at sea and on leaving or entering harbour.

The recognition of types of buoys by day or night and the identification of vessels by their lights was also part of the syllabus. Emergency drills had to be understood as did the rudiments of first aid and makeshift hull repairs at sea. Many of the trainees became highly adept at rope and wire work. Swimming and life-saving were eventually added to the programme, but it was not until 1932 that the ability to swim became mandatory.

MBCs were universally known within the branch as 'deckhands' or 'webfeet'.

The courses for 2nd and 1st Class Coxswains expanded on the basic subjects to include construction and handling of the larger craft and terrestrial/astro navigation. Torpedo recovery, target-towing and towing disabled craft were soon a part of the learning process, along with the use of specialized equipment for the handling and treatment of survivors.

As post World War 2 RAF launches became more sophisticated, the Cox'ns had to assimilate a basic knowledge of radio, radar and eventually, satellite navigation aids. Working in co-operation with search aircraft and helicopters demanded special techniques. A few found themselves on the bridge of RAF ships, performing the tasks of Coxswain or Bosun.

The day to day administration of Marine Craft Sections and Air Sea Rescue Units was also a part of the SNCO Cox'n's brief, especially during the 1920s and '30s when there were no officers with a marine trade background. The tradition of appointing the senior Flight Sergeant Cox'n to the role of 2nd in Command of smaller Marine Craft Units was carried through until well into the late 1950s. In a few cases even the CO might be a Flight Sergeant or Warrant Officer Cox'n. (The in-house title for Coxswain was 'Dickie,' and it is not difficult to figure out why!)

For the fitters, the first training courses were shorter than the three months of the MBCs. Most marine engines then, as now, were built from an automotive base and the FD/Ps did not need instruction in the basic principles of the four-stroke internal combustion engine. Magneto ignition, carburation and diesel injection systems were identical with automotive versions while hot-bulb and petrol/paraffin engines were widely used in tractors and their derivatives. The two main areas which differed were the water cooling and transmission systems. Marine gearboxes were much simpler and more accessible than those of cars and lorries, and the method of propulsion via shafts, glands, bearings and propellers was easy to learn. However, the *principles* of propellers, the effects of torque, paddle-wheeling, slip and cavitation, must have been mind-blowing to fitters whose previous thinking was based on the logic that if you make the wheel go round the vehicle goes along the road.

FD/Ps were given a knowledge of boat electrics and the maintenance of equipment as diverse as rudder steering systems, auxiliary generators, winches, bilge pumps, sea toilets and cooking stoves. FD/Ps served aboard the early types of motor boats in the capacity of gear changer and general hand. Cox'ns used a series of bell signals to the engineer in a similar manner to the Navy's whistles. In later years, the fitters had to handle telegraph and other engine room signals on a variety of much bigger craft.

The introduction of new boats and engines in the 1930s left many of the FD/Ps swamped by technical advance. Ignition, fuel and cooling systems became extremely complex and the gearboxes, Vee-drives, steering and control systems equally so. By this time too, the RAF was carrying out its own major repair and overhaul programmes and no longer relied on dockyards. The build-up of the high speed launch fleet caused a serious engineering manpower problem. The solution came from within the RAF itself when Aircraft Engine Fitters were encouraged to change to marine craft. Batches of Fitter 2Es, as they were known, received conversion courses.

During the 1939–45 war, the MCS and its component ASR Service trained their own engineers from scratch in highly intensive courses lasting nine months. The training was extremely thorough and high standards were achieved by the 'pass and continue' format.

When new post-war trade structures for technicians were announced, marine engineering training was divided into two elements at the Marine Craft Training Schools. The first element comprised teaching recruits the fundamentals of the subject to a level whereby they could crew up to 41½ ft seaplane tenders, refuellers etc, or act as second engineer on larger craft. Alternatively, they could be usefully employed ashore in workshops. Trainees passed out with the rank of AC1 as Marine Mechanics. Private study and two boards took them through Leading and Senior Aircraftman ranks until they were selected to return to the MCTS for an advanced course in the trade of Marine Fitter.

On qualifying, Marine Fitters were allocated the rank of Junior Technician and until the scheme was abandoned in the mid-1960s, they had a choice of ascending either a 'Command' or 'Technician' ladder to higher promotion. The 'Command' ladder, ie Corporal, Sergeant, Flight Sergeant and Warrant Officer, depended on trade tests and vacancies as before, but in the 'Technical' ladder promotion was guaranteed on passing a series of trade tests and serving a minimum specified time in each rank. The technician ranks were Junior Technician (depicted by a single chevron), Corporal Technician, Senior Technician, Chief Technician and Master Technician. These new ranks were easily distinguished by inverted chevrons for the NCOs and revised 'Tate and Lyle' insignia for the Masters. The Technicians enjoyed all the privileges and authority of their command equals and a higher pay level.

The Technician ladder was open to all technical tradesmen in Marine Craft except MBCs. The Deckhands and Cox'ns were categorized as 'skilled tradesmen' and were not eligible for the structure which applied to the 'advanced' trades of Marine Fitter and Boatwright. It would seem that the Air Ministry definition of an advanced trade was based on wielding a spanner, a soldering iron or brace and bit! Standards of engineering competence were very high indeed and were recognized outside the service by entitlement to an equivalent Board of Trade Certificate for seagoing engineers. All Marine Fitters, Mechanics, FD/Ps or Fitter 2Es enjoyed the distinctive nickname of 'Grease Monkey'.

The Carpenter/Boatbuilder story followed a similar pattern to that of the Marine Fitters. At the time of the formation of the Marine Craft Section a large number of craftsmen were inherited from the RNAS. General Carpenters were also encouraged to remuster to C/B and many others were drawn from civilian apprenticeships and boatbuilding companies. The new title for the 'advanced' tradesmen was a resurrected naval term, Boatwright. Trade training courses were of approximately the same duration as those for Mechanic/Fitter and promotion via time-serving, 'homework', and exams was identical. The Carpenters, Boat Repairers and Boatwrights were the only marine tradesmen who did not serve on boats' crews, although they were frequently responsible for the running of trials after a repair or rebuild. Those who were based on the larger Marine Craft Maintenance Units also provided a kind of 'Para-boatbuilder' emergency service which was equipped to go anywhere in the world where repair jobs were beyond the capacity of local resources.

It is no surprise that all the boatwrights and affiliated tradesmen were called 'Chippies', but they were also endowed with the less complimentary title of 'Wood Butchers'.

In the late 1930s a few RAF Wireless Operators were seconded to marine craft. They were required to attend a conversion course which increased their ability to carry out repairs. Once aboard a motor boat at sea, the W/Op was very much on his own. Wireless Telegraphy (key operated morse code) was the main method of communication between launches, bases, and other air or surface craft. During the 1940s, short range Radio Telephony (voice) sets were introduced on high speed launches and other craft, but these were mainly used by the Launch Masters and Coxswains.

In many ways, a W/Op (or W/OM, Wireless Operator Marine) had a most unenviable job. W/Ops would have to spend many hours confined in gyrating, claustrophobic cabins, striving for precise tuning and accurate key work on wildly vibrating transmitter/receivers. When not working the sets, many W/Ops were excellent extra hands for deck crews and were invaluable on the bridge or in the wheelhouse when morse lamps were being used.

After the war, a substantial number of National Servicemen became W/Ops alongside their Regular Service colleagues. By the jet age of the 1950s, they had to un-learn much of their more modern technology, for marine craft continued to use the R1154/T1155 receiver/transmitters that had equipped Second World War bombers such as the Lancaster and Halifax. They were probably disenchanted at being referred to as 'The Wop' or 'Sparks' as well.

Nursing Orderlies were co-opted into the Marine Section with the expansion of the Air Sea Rescue Service during the Second World War. Every ASR launch crew included one of these highly skilled tradesmen who were instrumental in saving many lives at sea. A lurching, pitching boat was not conducive to administering precision medical treatment, but somehow the N/Os succeeded, often under enemy attack.

At the end of the hostilities, when the Air Sea Rescue Service was disbanded in favour of RAF Coastal Command Search and Rescue, the inclusion of a N/O on every crew was abandoned in all but a few cases. The majority of peacetime Marine Craft Units retained a rudimentary sick bay ashore with a newly titled Medical Orderly in attendance, but first aid training for MBCs had to be intensified to cope with emergencies at sea. Nursing Orderlies were known collectively as 'Medics' and individually as 'Doc'.

One slang word applied to the element which brought all the marine craft men together. The sea was always referred to as the 'Oggin'.

In 1921 the Marine Craft Training Section at Gosport was moved to nearby Haslar after only a few months. In 1922, the location changed yet again to RAF Calshot, a spit of land where Southampton Water meets the Solent. During the 1939–45 war, the base was considered too exposed and vulnerable to enemy attack and too small for the enlarged throughput of tradesmen. After several moves the Marine Craft Training School returned to Calshot and remained there until 1953 when it was transferred to RAF Mount Batten on Plymouth Sound. There it was to stay, until the Marine Branch was disbanded in 1986.

Both before and after the Second World War, all Marine tradesmen except W/Ops, or those with a civilian nautical background, were Regulars, ie they had to be prepared to enlist for several years. The Marine Branch was a 'closed shop' to novices, difficult enough to enter as a Regular, but almost impossible for National Servicemen. However, as in many other aspects of service life, there were the exceptions and loopholes. One recruit was accepted by the Careers Office at his basic training camp on the strength of his Yacht Club Fixture list!

The majority of the trainees that were sent to operational units after their first session at a MCTS were only 18 or 19 years of age. They had yet to earn their standing among the more experienced hands. Neither sprockets nor cogs in the machinery of things, they were invariably called 'sprogs'.

Following an uncertain and nomadic start, the training schools were always regarded with warm affection by the RAF sailors. They provided a central point whereby scores of tradesmen got to know each other, perhaps to meet again on the various active units and return together once more to the MCTS for further training. The number of personnel in the Marine Branch was never very great, which made it both easy and pleasurable to retain the 'family' spirit that was engendered by the schools.

*Chapter 3*

# So much from the Schneider?

---

*Participation in the Schneider Trophy air races benefited the RAF both in terms of prestige and international standing. They became a springboard for the development of advanced fighter aircraft and lightweight, high-powered engines — engines which made high speed rescue launches possible.*

After the Great War the RAF did not have a job to do that was not in some way connected with either naval or ground forces' operations and many people believed that the tyro RAF should be disbanded and absorbed back into the two services that had spawned it. This was an objection which was constantly raised by anti-Air Force lobbyists, but Winston Churchill, newly appointed as Secretary of State for both the War Office and the Air Force, was a firm supporter of the separate air arm, and of its chief, Hugh Trenchard. Two contrasting events, both involving the Army, radically changed the negative attitudes in 1919.

The majority of squadrons, some 25½ of them, were stationed overseas. There were eight squadrons in India and a seaplane squadron in Malta. Seven more were based in Egypt, one of these being for naval co-operation. A further three were in Mesopotamia, where Kurdish tribesmen were rebelling in the Northern Territories. At home, there were two fighter squadrons, two army co-operation squadrons and two-and-a-half seaplane units.

The first object lesson was from India, where the RAF contingents were firmly under the boot of Army command. The squadrons were ill-equipped, under-manned and totally overlooked by the controllers of Army finances. Outdated, ex-wartime Bristol F2b aircraft and their strained aircrews were expected to support army activities throughout the whole country. Along the North-West Frontier Province, some ten million fiercely aggressive tribesmen were ranged against the White Raj and control was impossible.

By contrast, the Army Camel Corps in Somaliland had been trying for some 20 years to suppress the legendary Mad Mullah when a small Flight of de Havilland bombers under RAF command, were deployed to assist the ground forces. Due to the effective use of well-equipped tactical air power, the objectives were achieved in only three weeks.

The outcome was a series of government proposals to use the RAF more extensively for such operations, thus relieving the Army of heavy commitments in both manpower and expense. The scheme was finalized at the Cairo Peace Conference of March 1921, and for the first time an airman, Air Vice-Marshal Sir John Salmond, became overall commander of all three services in Mesopotamia (now known as Iraq). At the same conference were Sir Hugh Trenchard and Winston Churchill. Lieutenant Colonel T. E. Lawrence participated as an assistant to Churchill and specialist in Arab affairs.

The Air Force quickly earned a reputation for efficient and economical counter rebellion actions in both the Middle East and India, thereby establishing its essential *raison d'être*. But while the politicians and the service chiefs were convinced, the RAF had yet to convert the general public. To that end, the High Speed Flight was set up to challenge for the Schneider Trophy, in which role it was unsurpassed. The trophy events had everything; danger, speed, courage, technology, glamour, and a wide international following. Newspapers headlined the triumphs, the tragedies and the trivia, while cinemas showed newsreels to packed houses. The Schneider Trophy races kept the Air Force in the public eye at a time when it was most needed.

Created in 1912 by French Under-Secretary for Air, Jacques Schneider, the competition was primarily intended to promote the development of flying boats for passenger travel. He visualized a transcontinental network of flying boat airliners carrying the wealthy, the influential and the adventurous to every corner of the earth where water provided a natural runway, but in the competition series, long range and reliability soon became secondary. Ultimately, the contest became a circuit race over a fixed distance, where speed was of the essence.

Before his death in 1928, Schneider saw contesting aircraft evolve from fast, single-seat, biplane fighters of the First World War via flying boats to streamlined record-breaking monoplanes. These finely honed racing floatplanes of the late 1920s, with their high-powered engines enclosed in slender, low drag fuselages, barely gave room for the pilots. Weight was kept to a minimum and, in the floats, there was just enough fuel to complete each course. The trophy stimulated technical advances in both airframes and engines which were to prove invaluable, especially for Britain. It is well known that R. J. Mitchell's Supermarine S6B racer was the design foundation from which the Spitfire emerged five years later. Similarly, a lower stressed derivative of the supercharged Rolls-Royce 'R' racing engine was to become the famous Merlin.

Less well known is the fact that the Schneider races brought together two elements and one man that were to prove instrumental in establishing an effective high-speed rescue launch capability for the RAF. Firstly, recognition by the Air Ministry of the need for fast surface craft; secondly the concentrated development of lightweight, liquid-cooled aero engines which could be marinized; and thirdly, the chance attachment of Lieutenant Colonel T. E. Lawrence, in the guise of Aircraftman Shaw.

By the time of the inauguration of the High Speed Flight under the command of Squadron Leader L. Slater, AFC, in 1926, the Americans were dominating the series and were poised to win the trophy outright the following year. In Italy, Mussolini had pledged unlimited government support for the Macchi floatplanes. The British Schneider team, gearing up for the 1927 races in Venice, were working hard on the Napier Lion powered Supermarine S5 aircraft. They drew upon the readily available facilities of the Marine Craft Sections at Felixstowe, Cattewater, Lee-on-Solent and Calshot.

During the practice sessions and the preparations for the race, 56 ft seaplane lighters and the various ferry and servicing boats were indispensable. From the rescue point of view, the 35 ft ex-naval Brooke seaplane tenders, the Kelvins and the small Brooke seacars were clearly inadequate. They carried 'crash kits', but were severely hampered by lack of speed and limited stretcher space. In the preceding 10 years, racing aircraft speeds had doubled to over 250 mph. Engines and airframes had been extended to fragile safety limits and the lives of the pilots were being exposed to escalating risks. A potential need for fast ambulance launches was evident, but as yet neither the Air Ministry nor the Marine Craft Section had formed any firm ideas for the concept.

As an interim measure, the RAF borrowed three coastal motor boats from the Royal Navy. The CMBs were 56 ft long, with a pencil-slim beam and a stepped planing hull. Originally designed and built by Thornycroft as fast attack boats, they were capable of over 35 knots in calm weather. In practical use, the CMBs had several undesirable features. Their Thornycroft Y 12 petrol engines had a knack of catching fire on starting, a quirk that was subsequently to write off one of the boats. They were also very difficult to handle in confined waters as they were not fitted with any form of astern gearbox. Not only did this make manoeuvring uncertain, but when slowing down from high speeds, a drogue had to be streamed to create drag.

In the air, only the S5s survived the gruelling 1927 race, Flight Lieutenant Webster and Flight Lieutenant Worsley finishing first and second at 281 mph and 275 mph respectively. After the event, it was agreed by all competing nations that more time was required for development work between races. A two-year gap was settled upon and it was the prerogative of the British to host the next series at Calshot in 1929.

While the marine crews who were engaged in High Speed Flight support roles persevered with the CMBs, a new type of launch was introduced. It was yet another design to an Admiralty interpretation of RAF requirements, but the letters HSL (High Speed Launch) were used for the first time, and the boats did provide stretcher access and cabin accommodation for six casualties. When the engines worked, the attainable speed was 25 knots. The launches were 62 ft in length, of hard chine configuration, and powered by twin Thornycroft Y12 engines of 375 hp. The engines continued to be troublesome and only four of the type entered service numbered 150, 151, 152 and 162. One of them was seconded to the High Speed Flight in time for the 1929 races and subsequent air speed record attempts.

The next round of the Schneider Trophy was an exclusive Anglo-Italian match. The Napier Lion engines had been fully extended to produce 875 hp in the S5s, so Mitchell's latest Supermarine S6 seaplane was built around the new supercharged Rolls-Royce 'R' engine of 1,920 hp. Flight Lieutenant H. Waghorn won in one of these at an average speed of 328 mph. An early model Macchi M52 flew into second place, with a Napier-powered S5 a very close third. An S6 flown by Flight Lieutenant Stainforth suddenly dived when on landing approach and the pilot was rescued by Corporal C. H. Rider, the Cox'n of a Brooke seacar, who was on SBF patrol.

One of the RAF personnel involved in the High Speed Flight racing and record attempts was Wing Commander Sydney Smith, Commanding Officer of RAF Cattewater. This officer had tried to smuggle Aircraftman Shaw (T. E. Lawrence) from the SS *Rajputana* when Shaw was sent home from India in a blaze of unwanted publicity (see next chapter). After disembarkation leave, Shaw had been posted to Cattewater as clerk to Wing Commander Smith, and it was in this capacity that he was first introduced to the maritime operations of the RAF. By the time of the 1931 Schneider Trophy race, Aircraftman Shaw was fully engaged in the prototype trials of the RAF's first purpose-designed inshore fast seaplane tender, a design which, in terms of hull form and construction, established the way ahead for all future RAF high-speed motor boats.

The positive moves towards defining a format for future rescue craft proved to be prophetic in the light of the events leading up to the 1931 Schneider Trophy. The Italians and French paid dearly for trying to prevent the trophy from staying permanently in British hands. The Italians had produced a viciously unstable aeroplane, the Macchi M72. They had taken two 12-cylinder Fiat engines and linked them in tandem in a strikingly elongated nose cowling. The torque reaction, in opposition to the powerful rotating mass, made the aircraft veer dramatically on take-off and extremely hard to handle in the air. Macchi solved the problem by fitting two contra-rotating propellers. Whilst over Lake Garda on a test flight the two propellers touched and the aircraft crashed, killing Giuseppe Monti. Shortly before the Italian team were due to embark for Calshot, a second M 72 blew up in mid air.

Meanwhile, France fared no better. Back in the contest for the first time since 1923, the French had developed a very fast seaplane specifically for the race, but this too crashed, killing the pilot.

Both unfortunate nations asked for a postponement until 1932, but the British team were in no position to agree. With Government prompting, a sceptical Hugh Trenchard withdrew funds for the High Speed Flight during the build up to the race. After a public outcry, the Cabinet conceded that the RAF could continue if sponsorship could be found. On this, the last chance for Britain to secure the Schneider trophy for all time, Lady Lucy Houston put up £100,000 and saved the day.

With the Rolls-Royce V 12 engine boosted to 2,350 hp, Flight Lieutenant John H. Boothman flew the Supermarine S 6B around the course unopposed, at a mean speed of 340 mph. Flight Lieutenant Stainforth, flying a second S 6B, set a new world speed record at 379 mph on the same day. Two weeks later, on 29 September, he raised it to 407.5 mph using a specially tuned 2,550 hp version of the 'R' engine. The Schneider Trophy competition was finally over.

Four years and five months afterwards, on 5 March 1936, Reginald Mitchell watched test pilot Jeffrey Quill take off in the first of over 20,000 Supermarine Spitfires to be built.

In June of the same year, the RAF Marine Craft Section received a prototype 64 ft HSL designed by the British Power Boat Company of Hythe and constructed to a method based on Shaw's seaplane tender. With accommodation for crew and survivors, a maximum speed of 38 knots (42 mph) and a range of approximately 400 nautical miles, HSL 100 was the forerunner of a class of 22 similar craft and a whole series of offshore rescue launches. She was powered by three marinized versions of the Napier Lion aero engine that had reached its peak of development as a result of the remarkable competitiveness of the Schneider Trophy races.

Much as the sailors dreamed of twin Merlins for their HSLs, it was not to be. The fast-approaching conflict in Europe ensured that all the Merlins being produced were allocated to the aircraft of the day. Thus did the triple Napier Sea Lion layout remain in service until a post-war generation of high-speed rescue launches were fitted with a Merlin derivative, the Sea Griffon, in the late 1950s.

# Chapter 4

# Out of the desert

*'I went into the RAF to serve a mechanical purpose, not as a leader but as a cog of the machine...I leave it to others to say whether I chose well or not.' Extract from letter to Robert Graves from Lieutenant Colonel Lawrence of Arabia writing as Aircraftman T. E. Shaw, 4 February 1935.*

In the same letter to Graves, Lawrence wrote:
'Since 1850 ships have merely got bigger. When I first went into RAF boats in 1929, every type was an Admiralty design. All were round-bottomed, derived from the first hollow tree, with only a fin, called a keel, to delay their rolling about and over... Now, not one type of RAF boat is naval... We have found, chosen, selected or derived our own sorts: they have (power for power) three times the speed of their predecessors, less weight, less cost, more room, more safety, more seaworthiness. As their speed increases, they rise out of the water and run over its face. They cannot roll nor pitch, having no pendulum nor period, but a subtly modelled planing bottom and sharp edges.

'Now I do not claim to have made these boats. They have grown out of the joint experience, skill and imagination of many men. But I can (secretly) feel that they owe to me their opportunity and their acceptance. The pundits met them with a fierce hostility: all the RAF sailors, and all the Navy, said that they would break, sink, wear out, be unmanageable... In inventing them we have had to make new engines, new auxiliaries, use new timbers, new metals, new materials... Nothing now hinders the application of our design... except the conservatism of man of course. Patience. It cannot be stopped now.'

There is an element of over-statement in the above extract, possibly a concession to the nautically lay mind of Graves, but in essence Lawrence's influence on this and many other RAF matters was profound, especially for a self-proclaimed 'cog'.

Lawrence, who claimed that his was an adopted name, adopted yet another on his first entering the RAF as John Hume Ross in August 1922.

He had written to Sir Hugh Trenchard, Chief of Air Staff, in January, asking the CAS to assert his influence to get him accepted. Lawrence was not in good health and was 33 years old. He planned to leave Winston Churchill and his work at the Colonial Office in March, but was unable to resign until July. His declared aim at that time was to immerse himself in anonymity within the ranks.

Eventually, with the agreement of Churchill and the Secretary of State for Air, Lawrence presented himself as 'architects clerk, J. H. Ross, aged 28, no previous military service', to a pre-warned RAF recruiting officer at Covent Garden. At the subsequent medical examination, the severe scarring on his buttocks, from a flogging by the Turks in 1917, took some explaining, but he failed the medical anyway. To his acute embarrassment, he once more had to call upon influential superior officers to cover for him.

He found his basic training period at RAF Uxbridge unsettling and painfully rigorous. However, the discomforts of which Lawrence complained were somewhat masochistic, as he was free to leave the service whenever he chose.

After Uxbridge, Lawrence was posted to RAF Farnborough to join a photographic course, but he missed the beginning and was told he had to wait for the next one. At this early point, Lawrence drew attention to himself thereby giving a lie to his claimed wish for obscurity. By soliciting the intervention of Air Vice-Marshal Sir Oliver Swann, he prompted the Commanding Officer of the photographic school to investigate him. The CO soon established the real identity of A/C Ross, and Lawrence himself revealed his whereabouts in letters to various people including, incredibly, the editor of the *Daily Express*. Moreover, he went out of his way to be 'different' among his peers and he mocked and abused some of the junior officers whom, he was later to write to Trenchard, were in his opinion not as able as the men they commanded.

Not suprisingly, the story emerged in the *Daily Express* and by early 1923 Lawrence was once again a civilian. Lawrence responded by appealing to Trenchard and Air Minister Sir Samuel Hoare. He was offered a Commission in the RAF and the task of writing its history, but re-entering in the ranks was denied to him. The RAF was then only four years old and many of the Senior Commanders were ex-Army traditionalists. It was impossible for them to accept that an Oxford scholar, a war hero with a DSO (a VC had been recommended for him, but his actions had not been witnessed by a serving officer), and post-war diplomat should wish to lose himself among the lowest ranks of the Empire's most junior service. More confounding still was his subsequent carelessness over maintaining the masquerade.

Once again a highly placed acquaintance came to his rescue and he was offered a place as a private soldier in the Tank Corps. He saw this as an opportunity to transfer to the Air Force at a later date and duly reported for training at Bovington Camp. It was here that he adopted the name

'Shaw', picked at random from the Army List.

He soon discovered that the life of an Army Private was a completely different matter from that of Aircraftman in the RAF. He made the comparison:

'There [in the RAF] we were excited about our coming service. We talked and wondered of the future almost exclusively... The fellows were decent, but so wrought up by hope that they were carried out of themselves... There was a sparkle round the squad. Here every man has joined because he was down and out: and no-one talks of the Army or of promotion, or of trades and accomplishments. We are all here unavoidably, in a last resort, and we assume this world's failure in one-another... We are social bedrock, those unfit for life by competition...'

In order to escape from the barrack-room existence, he rented what was to become his permanent home, Clouds Hill cottage, near the camp. During this period he would occasionally visit the nearby cottage of Thomas and Mrs Hardy, and he also found time to strike up a lasting friendship with George Bernard Shaw and his wife Charlotte.

As his Army service dragged on, Lawrence became more and more morose and by 1925 he was dropping suicidal hints. Following a meeting with Trenchard, Lawrence was allowed to re-enter the RAF in August 1925, as 338171 Aircraftman 2nd Class Shaw, T. E., at the age of 37.

After induction at Uxbridge, basic training was waived and Shaw was posted to the Cranwell Cadet College in Lincolnshire to work with aircraft ground handling and servicing teams. He settled into the life quickly and this time made no secret of his real identity, possibly a wise course of action because his novelty and notoriety soon wore off and he was accepted as an equal by his colleagues.

Early in 1927, Shaw saw some virtue in a five-year posting to Karachi, for he would be well away from any arousal of public interest. Later, he was moved up to the North-west Frontier at Miranshah and although he could have reasonably assumed that his presence there was innocuous and remote from the point of view of the media, it was not so. In September 1928 the London Evening News published a highly inventive article under the headline: 'Lawrence of Arabia's Secret Mission. Countering Red Activities in The Punjab. Posing as a Saint. Warding Off The Evil Eye and Curing Illnesses.' The Sunday Express followed a few days later with a fantasy about secret Afghan missions. By the end of the year both home and international press were making even wilder assertions almost daily. Although Shaw was for some while unaware of the furore, he was delighted, in December, to find that the RAF had decided to kill the rumours and withdraw him from India immediately, three years before his overseas tour was due to expire.

He boarded the SS Rajputana on 12 January 1929. It was pre-arranged that the liner would make an unscheduled stop in Plymouth. The naval launch which customarily visited ships in Plymouth harbour would be utilized to smuggle him ashore and away from the press. The plan did not quite work, for pictures of Shaw disembarking were published, but certainly most of the army of journalists were fooled. Wing Commander Sydney Smith, Commanding Officer of the nearby station at RAF Cattewater, was given the task of meeting Shaw and whisking him away to London. Whatever means were adopted to avoid discovery by the press, they were to no avail and various newspapers printed stories of Lawrence of Arabia's return.

Shaw's landing at Plymouth and his meeting with Sydney Smith again (they had met before in Cairo) prompted the idea that he would be removed from the mainstream of publicity if he were to be returned to Cattewater. He wrote to E. M. Forster: '…It is a decent little camp… A spine of rocks and grass, like a fossil lizard, swimming out from the Devon shore towards the Hoe…' The station had been closed down after the war but was now re-equipping and building up to become a flying boat base. Shaw was assigned to Headquarters as clerk to the CO and, because of his standing perhaps, was given much more responsibility and freedom of action than would normally be enjoyed by an Orderly Room Clerk. He forged a firm friendship with Smith and his wife, spending many of his off-duty hours with them.

Meanwhile, the unprecedented correspondence between airman Shaw and Commander-in-Chief Trenchard, continued on a familiar basis.

'I heard about your lecture… He [Wing Commander Smith] called it the most severely practical speech he had ever heard. So if you tried to be Winstonianly eloquent, you didn't succeed! Winston's speaking is never severe… The RAF would be happier as it knew your aims better. It is extremely hard, in a big show, to get through to the rank and file a clear knowledge of where they are going. You've got a lot through but not enough to satisfy me, your very particular subordinate.

'I enclose a separate sheet of pure pearls. If you find them too pure and pearly for your Deportment Department, then put them in the fire. They are trifles. It is the trifles that do most harm…'

The 'pearls' were criticisms which included the irksome carrying of walking-out canes; the wearing of bayonets on church parades; the frequency of kit inspections; the ban on carrying pillion passengers on motor cycles; weekend passes that expired at midnight on Sundays instead of turn-to on Mondays; the practice of officers wearing caps in the men's mess; and the inconsistent ruling covering the wearing of civilian clothes when off-duty. Shaw's proposals were all adopted by the RAF in time.

On a more local level, he suggested that the rather ugly name of RAF Cattewater be changed to RAF Mount Batten. The Air Ministry approved the letter that Shaw drafted to this effect for Sydney Smith. He helped Smith in his capacity as RAF representative to the Royal Aero Club for the Schneider Trophy races and, in addition to his clerical work, he found time to become involved in the preparation of the boats which were to be used during the races. For relaxation, he worked on a de Havilland Moth seaplane which was jointly owned by Sydney Smith and a Major A. Nathan. Shaw enjoyed flying and planned to tour Europe with the Major during his leave.

Shaw was detached to RAF Calshot for the period of the 1929 Schneider challenge and worked close by the side of Sydney Smith at the hub of all the activity. The control boat, *Karen,* had been lent by a Major Colin Cooper and one of the tenders was an American built Biscayne Baby speedboat, which was suffering some sort of performance problem. Shaw offered to sort it out, and to his delight after he had done so the little launch was presented jointly to him and Smith by Major Cooper.

This pleasant eventuality was offset, however, by the probability of Shaw being ousted from the RAF again. The Secretary of State for Air, Lord Thompson of Cardington, observed Shaw issuing orders and directives to visiting VIPs. Trenchard summoned Shaw to the Air Ministry once again and instructed him to isolate himself, in person and in correspondence, from all influential and political friends. Furthermore, he was banned from private flying, including his proposed flight to Europe with Nathan.

When he returned to Plymouth, these enforced constraints were to have the effect of concentrating Shaw's mind into narrower channels. Unable to pursue his love of aircraft, his focus was directed to motor boats. At the end of 1930, he peevishly stated to Charlotte Shaw, 'I have only flown once this year, against a 100 times last year. That was Lord Thompson's doing...' He turned down invitations to meet various dignitaries and declined an offer of an Honorary Doctorate from St Andrew's University. Instead, he worked hard on his RAF duties and on a translation of the *Odyssey.* He also spent many hours restoring the Biscayne Baby, which he and Smith named *Biscuit.* When the work on the boat was finally completed in April 1930, he spent most of his leisure time driving it around the bays and estuaries that fringed Plymouth Sound. At this time, Shaw acquired a great deal of nautical knowledge, not only in boat handling, but in trade nomenclature and technicalities, for he was able to call upon the expertise of the marine tradesmen he worked among.

Notwithstanding his former associations, as confidant and friend of Sydney Smith, he obtained an insight into the plans and philosophies of the Higher Command. His placement was unique, in that he daily experienced the grass root operations of the MCS as well as involvement in high level policy-making. It was a dual position to which no other officer or airman could possibly have aspired.

It is difficult to determine from contemporary records precisely when Shaw officially began to work on RAF marine craft. At the beginning of October 1930, he referred to being on 'Duty Crew' when he received news of the R 101 crash and the death of 47 souls, including Lord

Thompson. Shaw's claim to have been 'partly responsible for the craft at moorings in the Cattewater' on the night of the airship disaster, indicates that he had by then become part of the webfooted establishment.

Both Shaw and Sydney Smith held strong views in favour of faster boats for the RAF, and had expressed them to the Air Ministry on numerous occasions. The abortive efforts with the Admiralty allocated HSLs and the loaned CMBs during the Schneider Cup races had sown the seed of conviction that the RAF should have its own boats to a purpose-built design.

These beliefs received a graphic and tragic illustration on 4 February 1931, when a Blackburn Iris seaplane plummeted into Plymouth Sound a few hundred yards from the Mount Batten foreshore. Shaw witnessed the crash and was aboard one of the first launches to reach the wreck. He dived into the water and helped to save six lives, but another six were lost. Shaw attended both the Court of Enquiry and the painful Public Inquest which followed. The cause of the crash had been pilot error, where a Wing Commander pupil had over-ruled his more junior instructor. Subsequently, Shaw and others campaigned for pilots to be aircraft commanders regardless of rank, and eventually this principle was adopted throughout the Air Force.

The Iris disaster highlighted the inadequacies of the Brooke motor boats, Kelvins and 56 ft pinnaces as rescue craft. They were slow getting to the scene, there was difficulty in pulling saturated, semi-comatose survivors aboard and there were shortcomings in stretcher handling and first aid provision.

Unbeknown to the majority of sailors, the lobbying by Hubert Scott-Paine of the British Power Boat Company and the perpetual pleas of Beauforte-Greenwood, Smith and Shaw had worn down Admiralty and Air Ministry opposition at last. When the Iris crashed, the Marine Craft Section was only days away from a radical breakthrough, in the shape of Seaplane Tender RAF 200. A great deal of high level scepticism surrounded what, at the time, was a revolutionary design, but the initial trials at Stokes Bay on 19 February were an outstanding success.

In deference to Scott-Paine's wishes to continue tests away from the eyes of his Solent based competitors, it was agreed that the boat should be transferred to Mount Batten. This was fortuitous, and not entirely coincidental, for Beauforte-Greenwood was well aware that an influential group of advocates for the new design, comprising Flight Lieutenant Jinman (an Engineering Officer with 209 Flying Boat Squadron who had attended the Solent trials), Wing Commander Smith, and A/C Shaw were there already.

Beauforte-Greenwood specifically asked for Shaw to be on the trials crew, for although he was not a marine tradesman *per se*, he had knowledge of high-speed boat handling and was an accomplished self-taught mechanic with a high literary ability. Most important of all, he was enthusiastic for the concept. The pro faction knew that Shaw's reputation and tenacity would help to secure the boat's approval.

Three other men from Mount Batten were selected for the trials crew, Corporals Heward and Staines, both Coxswains, and Corporal W. Bradbury, a Fitter. Although outranked by the other three there is evidence to confirm that Shaw was in charge of the operation. The four men were detached to the British Power Boat Company yard at Hythe for a week of instruction on the handling and maintenance of RAF 200. Here, Shaw met Hubert Scott-Paine for the first time and discovered an immediate rapport. The extrovert, innovative boat builder found a perfect match in the meticulous, contemplative airman.

With his full-time appointment to the testing of RAF 200, a change in Shaw's attitude towards the RAF became evident. Probably for the first time in his nine years in the ranks of Air Force and Army, he found his work totally absorbing, almost to the exclusion of all other activities. He wrote to Charlotte Shaw about the testing.

'We run her for hours daily and try all sorts of things... She is very good... Picture me just as a sailor, now-a-days, working so hard all the bright hours that in the evening I just bath and bed. No Homer: and no letters.'

By early April the first 50 hours running of the Seaplane Tender had been completed. In his report, Shaw said:

'The boat has been found to behave extremely well in all weathers including broken 19 ft seas. In one run up-channel from Falmouth to Plymouth against a strong south-east wind and in breaking water she only shipped solid sea once; an average of 12 mph was achieved... She does not roll and is an exceptionally clean sea boat. In winds of up to 20 mph the deck can be kept dry by careful steering. The very deep Vee-section below the wheelhouse prevents the boat from hammering into every wave like the ordinary hard chine speed boat. She is lively and dances, but seldom knocks and is therefore comfortable across a chop. She runs excellently before a sea and is not difficult even then to keep steady. She has been tried in all the duties normally performed by Marine Craft at this station and can be pronounced a cleaner sea boat than anything yet...'

When the tests had been completed, it was apparent that alternative engines to the old-fashioned and inaccessible Brooke 100 hp petrol units were desirable. Scott-Paine had already approached the Midland company of Henry Meadows, who were the builders of the 100 hp engines supplied for the Vickers tank and the Invicta car. An agreement was reached whereby the BPBC would marinize the engine and sell it under the name of Power-Meadows.

A/C Shaw and Corporal Bradbury were assigned to the yard in Hythe to work with the BPBC on the new engine which, in terms of power/weight ratio, was considered very advanced. The new power units worked well and when installed in the production run of seaplane tenders, were a credit to the thoroughness of the two men.

Shaw was being a little self-aggrandizing when he wrote to his biographer Liddell-Hart:

'My two-year war with the Air Ministry over the type of motor boats suited to attend seaplanes is bearing results now, and experimental boats are being offered by the contractors. I've become a marine expert, and test the things for them...'

Shaw's contribution was outstanding, but he was not, as he implied, the leader of a 'two-year war' with the Air Ministry. The credit for that belonged jointly to Scott-Paine and Beauforte-Greenwood. Jinman, Smith and Shaw were in the support column. It was true that Shaw had no intellectual equal among his peers and none could approach his record of previous accomplishments, but other RAF sailors were just as competent. Many achieved success without the advantages of familiarity with their superiors, their suggestions being accepted as 'pearls' and their written words being kept for posterity. After Shaw departed from the RAF, his job was taken over, at a time of rapid development, by Bill Bradbury, who later became the General Manager of the BPBC factory in Poole.

None the less, Shaw did an exemplary job. RAF 200 was very close to the hearts of the MCS directorate and one can speculate on how much their choice of project leader was coloured by his influence in high places. Shaw himself was the one who drew his biographer's attention to the importance of his position, and in due course it was focused on by the national press, not because of the task at hand, but because it was Lawrence of Arabia doing it.

When all the Southampton trials of the re-engined seaplane tender were finished in June 1931 and eight more craft had been ordered, Shaw supervised further tests of RAF 200 at Mount Batten before it was moved back to Calshot for the Marine Craft Training Section. A part of this testing included analysing boat performance when towing water-borne targets for practice bombing. Hitherto, boat speeds had been too low to simulate accurately a fast-moving enemy warship. RAF 200 was eminently successful, but Shaw found that the targets themselves were less so. After the seaplane tender had departed for Calshot, he continued the tests using *Biscuit* as the prime mover. The eventual outcome of this research was the adoption by the RAF of simple, cheap, but effective 'Splash' targets which remained in service for many years.

In early October 1931, Sydney Smith was promoted to Group Captain and posted to RAF Manston in Kent. Expecting to find a breathing space to catch up with his correspondence and literary work, Shaw found that it was not to be. Although he managed to grab a month's leave, he was assigned to Hythe to liaise with the British Power Boat Company during the production and trials of the next eight seaplane tenders, but this plan was seriously delayed by a fire at the boatyard. All the boats under construction, except ST 201, were destroyed. On completion, she was transported to Mount Batten where Shaw filled in his time by teaching Coxswains how to handle her. In November, he was back in Hythe testing a new engine, the Power-Meadows 8/28 which was installed in the RAFs new 16 ft planing dinghy.

By January 1932, he was once again involved with the seaplane tenders. ST 202, completed after the fire, was retained at the builders for trials with a new throttle and gearshift control system. Shaw was deeply embroiled in the development of this over many weeks. At the same time, he worked on an instruction booklet entitled *The 200 Class Royal Air Force Seaplane Tender – Provisional Issue of Notes*. This document was printed in March and received wide acclaim from the RAF sailors, despite its quaint literary style and a few unusual synonyms for regular nautical words.

Once again, the press threatened his continuance in the service, but Shaw had become much more adroit at deflecting their overtures. When in April *The Times* published a story about a hazardous voyage Shaw had made in ST 210 from Calshot to RAF Donibristle in Scotland, he co-operated by providing notes, although later implied that he had not. In this way, he avoided the story being coloured by fanciful exaggeration.

His work at Hythe continued apace. By mid-summer he was testing a flying boat refueller version of the 16 ft fast dinghy. On a passage to Dover from the Solent in company with a pinnace escort, he came very near to sinking. The bottom of the boat was holed by heavy pounding in the steep sea.

'...the water was up to the thwart, and running away over the two corners of the transom. It swilled in as fast, over either bow, as she wallowed in the following swell. There was no buoyancy in the hull of course, but she was navigating nicely, if sluggishly, on her tanks. The engine went on for nearly 90 minutes, the oil pressure rising slowly as the sump filled. It was an odd experience. Dampish too. The engine finally sputtered out in the mouth of Newhaven Harbour, and the pinnace towed me up river...'

These were productive times for the Marine Craft Section. Yet another new boat which would occupy Shaw was on the stocks at the British Power Boat Company.

A foursome comprising Scott-Paine, Beauforte-Greenwood, Shaw and Captain Nicholson from Hadfields armour plating company, had jointly evolved a high-speed armoured target boat (ATB) for aircrew training. The armour plate was required to withstand the impact of the light practice smoke bombs the RAF were using at the time, and the crews were kitted out with steel helmets and gas masks.

The ATB was an adaptation of the seaplane tender hull, but with a lower freeboard to reduce excessive top-hamper and a third engine to counteract the additonal weight of the plating. Two prototypes were built and initial trials on the Solent were successful, the launch attaining just over 30 knots. Shaw was detailed to accompany the two ATBs to RAF Bridlington in Yorkshire for futher evaluation trials. This time the press picked up the story without consulting him. Absurd headlines such as, 'Colonel Lawrence is Human Target' and 'Colonel Lawrence, The Man Behind Britain's Planes, Cars and Speedboats' infuriated the Air Ministry, and Shaw was hurriedly returned to Mount Batten to resume 'normal' duties.

At first, Shaw was philosophical about the event and even found solace in the fact that he could return to his reading and writing. At least the RAF had not sacked him, but gradually, overtones of gloom became detectable in his letters. His job with the boats had been both fascinating and fulfilling and he wrote with nostalgia of the transformation in boat types he had helped to achieve. By the beginning of January 1933 he was thinking either of leaving the RAF or transferring to a different station. He wrote to Sir Philip Sassoon, Under Secretary of State for Air, to enquire about moving to RAF Hendon as an Aircraft Hand. In the following month he was still wavering, but finally applied to purchase his release on 28 February. Sir Geoffrey Salmond, Chief of Air Staff elect, wrote to Shaw, saying:

'I do not know what's going on at Air Ministry but you have now become an institution in the RAF, it seems difficult to imagine you as anything else.'

A few days before his discharge was due, Shaw wrote to Sir Philip Sassoon again:

'My feeling was that I should do something more if I was to justify my staying on in the RAF… I will not go on at Batten, doing routine work. I want to do more boats…'

Beauforte-Greenwood intervened and even as Shaw was disposing of his kit and preparing for civilian life, he was offered a new job with the Marine Aircraft Experimental Establishment at RAF Felixstowe.

He was delighted to be back, a feeling that was enhanced when he found he would be working with his friend and ex-Flight Commander from Mount Batten, Flight Lieutenant W. Jinman. The new job was partly an extension of the testing work he had been engaged in earlier, but with a much broader brief. He was also formally instructed to assist with the development of high-speed rescue boats and salvage craft. To avoid the attention of the newspapers he was ordered to wear civilian clothes when outside the bounds of an RAF establishment.

During those last two years with the MAEE, Shaw travelled extensively on marine business and continued to contribute both in ideas and in practical terms to the modernization of the MCS. His tests covered the smallest of equipment to the largest. A film documentary of the time shows him aboard the RAF Auxiliary and Recovery steamship *Aquarius* and he stated in a letter that he had '…been a fortnight in Cheshire, Liverpool, the Irish Sea and Plymouth, testing a new ship.'

In 1934 he was influential in helping Scott-Paine in his efforts to convince a reluctant Royal Navy of the virtues of high-speed patrol boats. He also knew of plans to introduce the first true offshore rescue launch, HSL 100, and of the BPBC marinization of Napier Lion Aero engines.

His vision and foresight, as usual, roamed into other areas. In March 1934, in a letter to Lionel Curtis, editor of the *Round Table* he warned:

'When Germany wings herself — ah; that will be another matter, and our signal to reinforce: for the German kites will be new and formidable, not like that sorry French junk...'

This was at a time when no-one else, except Churchill, saw the embryo Third Reich as a threat.

Shaw was accredited with being joint designer of a revolutionary three-point, surface-effect craft for a world speed record attempt which was patented by Edward Spurr in 1938. The origin of the story appears to be an article by H. F. King in *Flight International* in 1966, but according to the authorized biography by Jeremy Wilson, there is no hard evidence to support the claim. Shaw met Spurr at the BPBC yard, and it is fairly safe to speculate that they would have discussed high-speed planing craft theory in some depth, but there is no record of any of the regular meetings which would have been necessary for the two men to produce such a revolutionary design. The fact that the boat, *Empire Day*, had the legend 'To L of A à compte' (To Lawrence of Arabia on account) on its nose, does nothing to either confirm or deny Shaw's involvement. *Empire Day* was not revealed to the public until over three years after Shaw's death and it is likely that Shaw's encouragement alone was sufficient to prompt the dedication. At that time, even the most nebulous connection with the Lawrence legend was guaranteed to attract attention.

In the run up to Shaw's demobilization in March 1935, he spent most of his time at Bridlington supervising the overhaul of several target boats. As his engagement drew to a close he felt some remorse at leaving his 'home' in the RAF, but also realized that he was extremely weary. He wrote:

'The wrench is this: I shall feel like a lost dog when I leave — or, when it leaves me, rather, for the RAF goes on. The strange attraction in the feel of the clothes, the work, the companionship. A direct touch with men, obtained no other way in life...'

After demobilization on 25 February 1935, he continued to suffer from the unwelcome attention of journalists, but returned to his cottage at Clouds Hill and picked up with his remarkable circle of influential friends. On 13 May whilst riding his Brough Superior motor cycle from Bovington Camp to Clouds Hill, he swerved to avoid two boys on bicycles and was thrown off the machine. As a result of head injuries, he remained in a coma for six days and died on 19 May. He was 46.

Among the Generals, Air Marshals, explorers, political leaders, artists, writers, and business tycoons who attended his funeral, was pallbearer Corporal W. Bradbury, of the RAF Marine Craft Section.

# Chapter 5

# Waves of contentment and bloody officers!

*The sailors were delighted with their new boats, but not so pleased with one of the ideas from the new Marine Craft Policy Committee.*

When boats were designed for the RAF or the RN in the 1920s, they were subject to the constraints of practicality and cost. Kelvins, Brookes and the early pinnaces could all have been made to go faster if they had been extended by 10 or 15 ft and given larger engines. They would, however, have had to sacrifice manoeuvrability, carry larger crews and would have cost far too much. Thus with these craft, there was always a compromise within the parameters of the boat's size and purpose.

Construction methods had changed little over the years. Small dinghies and whalers were of the 'clinker' type: a series of frames longitudinally planked in the overlapping style of rowing boats. (Later 16 ft and 18 ft planing dinghies were exceptions to the rule. They were built in 'reverse clinker', where the planks overlapped in an upward direction. They also, as their name implies, had a semi-planing bottom.) The larger Kelvins, Brookes and pinnaces were of 'carvel' construction. This was a stronger and more watertight method of planking in which the exterior planks were fitted and shaped so that they were butted one to another on the frames to give a smooth outer skin.

As flying boats and amphibians gradually replaced floatplanes, more powerful engines and the use of light alloys in aircraft construction enabled designers to create bigger, faster and longer-range seaplanes. The RAF sailors welcomed them. With their high wing monoplane configuration, they were easier to go alongside than floatplanes, and they were fitted with better mooring equipment. Most importantly, with their all-metal skins, they did not require the frequent and often hazardous slipping for the purpose of drying out. Against this, they were cumbersome and more windborne when under tow; they required substantial quantities of fuel, and they had the capability of flying at night and in bad weather. This meant the SBF duties became much more demanding.

To match these developments, new refuelling boats and bomb scows were added to the MCS inventory. A new class of general personnel boat, the 16 ft planing dinghy, entered service in 1931 and became an ideal water taxi for the aircrews and technicians. Night flying dictated a need for floating flarepaths to be streamed in the direction of the wind to indicate landing and take-off areas. At first, dan buoys, then a new series of pram dinghies with oil lamps and, later, battery-powered lights, were trailed like a string of lobster pots and then anchored. In exceptionally windy conditions, the towing vessel would sometimes dispense with the anchors and steam upwind to maintain the position of the string.

With the advent of the larger and faster aircraft, threshold speeds and the length of landing and take-off runs were far greater, but the designated areas still had to be checked for driftwood, flotsam or unwary small craft. As the reliability of seaplanes improved, accidents were less likely, but if a crash did occur, the rescue boats faced a much more difficult task in reaching and extricating survivors.

In 1930, the RAF's largest biplane flying boat, the Blackburn Iris, carried a crew of five with provision for seven or eight passengers. By the time the Short Sunderland entered service in 1937, the crew count had increased to 13 and the passenger capacity was into double figures. In Germany, a giant Dornier, the Do-X, had flown with 170 passengers as early as 1929. Although this was a publicity stunt, such an event provided a stimulating challenge for the planners of marine craft developments. The sailors were soon equipped to meet the demands of this expanding role with a revolutionary hard-chine planing boat, the '200 Class' seaplane tender.

As early as 1905 it had been discovered that a wide flat bottom near the stern of a boat helped to prevent the sucking down effect inherent in round bilge craft, but the improvement was not dramatic. Other developments had followed the line of the sea-sled floats which were fitted to early aircraft. These soon incorporated steps to break the suction effect during take-off. The Royal Navy's First World War CMB's were true stepped planing boats, but they were intended for quick forays across the Channel in favourable weather conditions, and were of very light construction in order to achieve high speeds with the engines then available.

Apart from military applications, British and American boatbuilders had experimented with hard-chine boats for leisure purposes and for racing. Lawrence's *Biscuit* was a production example of a small unstepped hard-chine speedboat.

The breakthrough, almost incomprehensible after several thousand years of traditional thinking, was in the ability of hard-chine hulls to rise in the water as speed increased until they were skimming over the surface. At first, the action was called hydroplaning or aquaplaning, but this was soon shortened to the universal 'planing'. As power was applied from rest, the bows rose while the point of the cutwater under the Vee-bottom gradually moved aft. The almost flat stern began to lift until the bows dropped and the entire hull came over the 'hump' and accelerated away on the surface. At speed, only the after part of the hull was in contact with the water, thus keeping the propellers and rudders immersed.

Planing boats banked into turns like aircraft instead of swaying outwards like destroyers. In any degree of chop, they were most uncomfortable, with a hard, noisy and unpredictable pounding motion. In a heavier sea they could be thrown around alarmingly and needed a great deal of skill, and a measure of courage, to keep them on the plane. When stopped and lying a'hull, they rolled sickeningly and invariably turned obliquely to the waves if not kept head-to-sea by engines or drogues. Whilst manoeuvring at low speeds, the engines had to be used for steering, as the rudders were small in order to reduce helm loading at high speed. Although these were alarming characteristics to the new-comer, the boats were extremely easy to handle once the special techniques had been acquired.

It was Scott-Paine of the British Power Boat Company who combined the hard-chine principle with a robust form of construction to create the fast crash boat that the RAF sailors had yearned for. Planing boat characteristics were new to everyone, not least the RAF sailors, who were the first group of people in the world to assimilate them *en masse*.

Seaplane tender 200 was 37 ft 6 in in length by 8 ft 8 in beam. With a dry weight of 3½ tons and a four-man crew, she was capable of just under 25 knots (29 mph). The fuel carried provided for five hours running at a cruising speed of around 22 knots. The keel, stem and main fore-and-aft members were carved from Columbia pine. All the main frames and the outer skin were made from African mahogany with the deck and chine strakes shaped in Canadian Rock Elm. The side planking was of single thickness but the bottom planking had to be strong yet flexible, and this was achieved by sandwiching oiled and doped calico between mahogany planks laid in diagonal opposition from chine to keel. It was a unique method of construction that Scott-Paine had drawn from the pioneering work of seaplane designer Linton Hope in 1916. The structure of the outer shell, known as 'double-diagonal' planking, lent itself to use in much larger craft, including Naval MTBs and RAF rescue launches, until well into the 1960s.

All the tenders were equipped with stretcher berths, crash kits and fire extinguishers, but crew comforts were minimal until the later boats were built, when cooking stoves, sea toilets and wirelesses were installed.

Generally, the RAF and the British Power Boat Company had got it right, and further modifications in the light of on-the-job experiences were in the nature of improvements rather than problem solving. For example, the wheelhouse was modified from an open sided cuddy to an enclosed version with side hatches, and the flat windscreens were redesigned in a vee-form with rotating Kent Clearview screens instead of wipers. Of the Mk I seaplane tenders which survived the Second World War, some were bought by the Thames Division of the Metropolitan Police, while many others became harbour launches or private yachts.

The last of the series, ST 324, left the Hythe yard in 1940. The trend-setter, ST 200, after service in many parts of the world with radio-controlled target floatplanes, was converted to a heavily equipped fire float in 1942. It was last heard of in South Africa.

Whilst flying boats were emerging as the main type of seaplane, other maritime activities were being undertaken by landplanes, notably air-to-sea bombing, gunnery and torpedo dropping. The sailors were not always able to meet the demands of these activities with their existing launches and recovery ships. They were conscious of a need for a specially designed craft that could combine all the towing and seaplane handling abilities of the Kelvins with deep sea torpedo recovery and the retrieving of static moored targets. The answer was found in the GP pinnace.

The concept of the general purpose pinnace had been bequeathed by the RNAS in 1918, when three steam pinnaces were taken over by the new Air Force. Experiences with these and the Kelvins led to the RAF's first 'own specification' boat, a 56 ft motor pinnace first introduced in 1926. The pinnace had a beam of 11 ft 9 in and a draft of just under 4 ft. It was fitted with a Gardner 4TS hot bulb, blowlamp start, semi-diesel of 96 hp and could steam at about 10 knots. The deck layout was unusual in that it had a large funnel containing the engine exhaust in front of the helm position. The helmsman had limited protection behind a canvas dodger and had to suffer not only from inclement and cold weather, but also from fumes and smuts streaming aft. Later versions were provided with an enclosed wheelhouse forward of the funnel.

The fitter also experienced an uncomfortable time on these pinnaces. The engine was fitted with an 'ahead' and 'neutral' gearbox only. When the coxswain rang the telegraph for 'astern,' the engineer had to stop the engine and, using a long steel bar, ease it over top dead centre on one cylinder and restart it in the opposite direction of rotation. Later 56 ft pinnaces were tried with 90 hp McLaren engines, but to everyone's relief, the last few boats had the admirable Gardner 6L2 diesels.

While the seaplane tenders established the reputation of double-diagonal construction, production of the round bilge 56 ft pinnace ceased at No P 31 in 1935 and a new prototype General Purpose pinnace, P 32, entered the service in the same year. Built by J. I. Thornycroft, the new 56 ft boat was of hard-chine/double-diagonal construction for strength, but was not designed for a planing performance. Twin Gardner engines provided a fair turn of speed at around 12 knots. Significantly, an officers' cabin was incorporated abaft the 'sunken' wheelhouse. The crews quarters for'ard included a galley and a sea toilet. The boat was fitted with a large aft hold which was for stowing mooring buoys, floating flarepaths, recovered torpedoes or seating for 80 passengers. A hydraulically operated derrick on a strong Samson post made overside lifting effortless.

The prototype was well received, but the next in line, pinnace P 33, did not appear until 1938. When it did, it had been extended to 60 ft and a third engine had been added, increasing the speed to 15 knots. The extra length also allowed for a larger wheelhouse with the officers' cabin relocated below decks. From P 40 onwards, the Gardners were substituted by Perkins S6M engines, which were by then being installed in the seaplane tenders.

The introduction of the new boats extended the activities of the sailors beyond the estuaries and protected waters which had been their domains. The ability to navigate by night and day in fair weather or foul became an essential skill for the cox'ns to acquire. As the number of boats in service increased, so did the number of crews with offshore experience. T. E. Shaw's voyage from the Solent to the east coast of Scotland had been exceptional in 1932, but within four years coastal passage-making was commonplace. The 200 Class seaplane tenders and 60 ft pinnaces never did achieve the legendary dash of the high speed launches, but with them the sailors acquired all the skills of seamanship that served them so well in the perilous years that followed.

These same coxswains and crews received an astonishing blow in July 1936, when it was announced by the Marine Craft Policy Committee that the new 64 ft HSLs which were about to enter the Service, were to be commanded by commissioned officers. There had been no seagoing Motor Boat Officers in the RAF for 13 years. The MCPC initiated a national advertising campaign for qualified applicants. Warrant Officer and Senior NCO Coxswains were not permitted to apply.

# Chapter 6

# All 2,000 engines ahead — 3 revs!

*An erroneous order from a newly recruited skipper to the helmsman aboard a high speed launch.*

In 1932, Hubert Scott-Paine was already thinking along the lines of large, powerful craft for offshore rescue, gunnery or torpedo firing. He tried desperately to persuade the Admiralty to order his high-speed planing hulls for the Royal Navy and made much reference to fast attack forces and the 'mosquito' boats that would equip them. He had lobbied and lectured, written to the press and knocked on the doors of the influential, all to little avail. The Navy was reluctant to accept his ideas, despite the glaring success of the RAF's seaplane tenders and armoured target boats. Although the Royal Navy Coastal Motor Boat Committee showed some support, Their Lordships turned a Nelsonian eye to the idea.

Several foreign operators, however, were far less steeped in 'ironclad' attitudes. Various representatives from European, Asian and South American maritime services showed interest. A 45 ft armed customs launch, for opposing piracy in the South China Sea, was ordered in 1934 and it performed very well, attaining 30 mph with three of the 100 hp Power-Meadows engines. The Government of Australia ordered a special adaptation of the same hull to carry out long-range rescue work in the Timor Sea for the flying boats of Qantas Empire Airways. Even the War Office placed an order for a Napier-powered target-towing launch, having been impressed with two fast boats that had been loaned to them by a sales-minded Scott-Paine.

At the end of 1934, the Admiralty's shield of prejudice began to crack when the BPBC secured an order for a fast Admiral's barge, based on the China station 45 ft hull. This order gave Scott-Paine an opportunity to make yet another presentation of his 'mosquito' boat theory to the board of the Admiralty. In it, he emphasized the possibilities of fitting guns and torpedo tubes to a larger version of the high performance barge. There was little reaction, but the ideas were not wasted on the RAF.

Flight Lieutenant Beauforte-Greenwood had helped 'Scotty' in his sales efforts with the Australians. Aided by his assistant, Flight Lieutenant Norrington, and by AC Shaw, he worked with Scotty on an idea for a 60–70 ft seaplane handling and rescue launch. One of the main advantages of this type of craft was that crews could live aboard for long periods as a self-sustaining unit. Although all Air Force marine purchasing was via the Admiralty, the Navy was finally cajoled into issuing a specification for a new high speed launch. It was put out to tender in June 1935.

Scott-Paine was highly displeased with the Admiralty's action in putting the HSL to general tender. His competitors, among them Vosper, J. S. White, Thornycroft and Saunders-Roe, had been highly critical of his much-publicized claims about the speed and durability of his hard-chine boats. Yet, here they were, openly invited to compete on a specification of which he himself had been the prime instigator. As it transpired, the other yards did not match up to the BPBC tender, and the Hythe company had a monopoly on the most favoured type of engine. Aero engines were ideal in terms of power/weight ratio, but there were few which were suitable for conversion to marine use.

Scott-Paine's experience with the Napier Lion engine in aircraft and racing boats, and his 'sole rights' agreement with Henry Meadows, had provided him with something of a head start in the required technology. He bought some used aero Lions from RAF surplus, carried out extensive modifications to them and developed a suitable marine gearbox. He then negotiated an exclusive agreement with Napier for manufacture and supply of the new marine variant, under the name of Power Napier Sea Lion.

Although the RAF team had been the first to recognize the potential of the 'mosquito' boats, the Navy ordered two experimental 60 ft coastal motor boats while the RAF were considering the tenders. During the autumn of 1935, the two boats were completed in the remarkably short time of four months. As these were of a different class to the old CMBs, they were given a new name. It was the first recorded use of the description 'Motor Torpedo Boat' (MTB).

Even as the yard were setting the jigs and laying the keels, Italian forces invaded Abyssinia, thereby creating a sudden requirement for a flotilla of small, fast boats to be based in Malta. Immediately, four more MTBs were ordered by the Admiralty.

A stretched version of the 60 ft MTB hull provided the format on which the RAF based their decision for a prototype high speed launch. To be known as RAF 100, the dimensions of the launch were 64 ft loa by 10 ft 6 in beam. Powered by a trio of Power Napier Sea Lion engines, the range was 500 miles at a speed of 35 knots. The two wing engines were inclined to drive directly to the outboard propeller shafts, while the centre engine faced the opposite way and transmitted via a vee-drive to the centre propeller. This arrangement allowed for 'cruising' on the centre engine only, a range extending economy measure which retained a high degree of manoeuvrability.

The accommodation included an officers' wardroom/sickbay for four and forecastle bunks for eight crew. A rather quaint part of the specification called for a cabin aft of the engine room with separate berths and toilet for Asiatic crewmen.

With target-towing in mind, an after well was incorporated above the tiller mechanism, but this feature was deleted from later models.

The scantlings were, in effect, a beefed-up version of the methods and materials used for the ST 200 series. Scott-Paine's revolutionary system of framing up and planking the hulls whilst inverted in rows had been pioneered with the seaplane tenders and was the first true boatbuilding production line. All the wooden components were prefabricated before being brought together in the main assembly shop. Thus, once the factory had swung into gear, the output of completed craft was staggering by contemporary standards.

The prototype HSL was launched at Hythe in May 1936, the month in which the Royal Navy received their first MTB. Whereas the Admiralty shrouded their high-speed boat programme in a blanket of secrecy, the same restrictions did not apply to the RAF launch. Beauforte-Greenwood had been appreciative of the goodwill that had resulted from Shaw's publicizing of the seaplane tender and was only too keen for the public to be informed about the new HSL.

On 23 May RAF 100 slipped her Southampton moorings and headed for the English Channel and the open North Sea, destination Grimsby on the East coast. Beauforte-Greenwood and Norrington were aboard, along with several staff from the yard. Mr L. R. Butters, a Civilian Substitution Officer and captain of the RAF trawler *Cawley,* was aboard for reasons which would not have pleased the NCO Cox'ns if they had known. Mr Butters was to become the first commissioned HSL Master.

Scott-Paine stayed at the helm for most of the 373 nautical miles. They met heavy weather in the Wash and Scotty exploited this in an interview with reporters later. 'I do not ever remember such confused sea conditions', he said. The 14-hour outward voyage and the 10 hours 45 minute return trip, at an average speed for the run of over 30 knots, was a trouble-free success. The press made much of it and a further spate of national publicity followed when the HSL was officially handed over to the RAF in July.

The acceptance trials took place in the Solent on 14 July 1936. The weather was ideal: cloudy, with bright periods, and a south westerly wind coursing over the Isle of Wight at a steady Force 4. The boat was crewed by five men from the BPBC under the direction of Scott-Paine, with help from representatives from Messrs Napier and the Patent Log Company. On behalf of the RAF, Beauforte-Greenwood, now entitled Captain, Squadron Leader Norrington and Sergeant Bill Bradbury, were accompanied by two senior officers from Manston and two representatives of the War Department.

The launch, in full service trim, exceeded the parameters which had been set by both the builders and the clients. The trial speed achieved was 36.06 knots, over 41 mph, but, in a demonstration to the press later the same day, the boat seemed to rise to the occasion and a speed of 45 mph was recorded.

The event was so significant that it made headline news. Here was a class of boat that was safe to operate in the open sea, was faster than a destroyer, and could maintain high averages over a distance. The Admiralty took notice at last, while the RAF sat smugly back and smiled on their acquisition. RAF 100 had set a new standard and emerged as the worthy forerunner of the fleets of HSLs, MTBs and MGBs that were to earn distinction with the Air Sea Rescue Service and Coastal Forces.

The Air Ministry immediately placed further orders. Numbers 101 to 114 were ordered in 1936 with deliveries commencing in 1937. Two more were laid down in 1938 and with the threat of a European war becoming more likely, numbers 117 to 132 were contracted in 1939 for delivery during the following two years. In the event, production of the '100 Class' HSLs was stopped at hull 121 when the remaining 11 boats, scheduled for completion in 1941, were switched to a later design.

In 1936 the RAF sailors were euphoric about their new craft, but they were far from enthralled by the plans to provide commanders for them. The new Launch Masters were all certificated Master Mariners, the majority in the 30–40 age group. Already part of the build-up of Reserve and Volunteer Reserve part-time officers in the RN, most of them held a RNR or RNVR rank higher than that being offered by the RAF. However, due to the economic slump of the 1930s, their occupations were insecure and the Air Force appeared to provide full-time career openings at a time of depression and uncertainty.

Experience of oceangoing ships and naval practices had not prepared them for either the cramped and informal conditions aboard RAF launches, or the different traditions and disciplines of the service. Warrant Officers and SNCOs to whom small craft handling was already second nature, found themselves instructing the new officers. Added to this was the Masters' natural ignorance of everyday Air Force procedures. It is not surprising that feelings ran high and these ex-deep sea sailors became the butt of many disparaging jokes and remarks. The order which is the title of this chapter was still being mimicked almost 50 years later. It should read, 'All three engines ahead — 2,000 revs'.

The Direct Entry officers were themselves treated badly by the RAF at first. They retained civilian status after joining the Service and were appointed to the Reserve of Air Force Officers. The RAFO scheme meant that they carried out the duties of a serving RAF officer, were granted the honorary rank of Flying Officer and wore the appropriate uniform, but they were not entitled to the protection, privileges and security of contract which applied to regular career officers. Their RAFO category was later changed to RAF reserve Class CC, which in essence invoked no improvements for them although they had been recruited on the understanding that their task was to skipper HSLs before being promoted to command Marine Craft Sections, implying that permanent commissions and promotions were part of their conditions of entry.

By 1938 and the time of the Munich crisis, it was clear that war with Germany was inevitable. Both the Royal Navy and the Merchant Service were gearing up for the conflict. Some HSL Masters, quite understandably, felt that they had made a crucial mistake in forsaking their former careers for service in this 'minor' branch of the RAF. A few of the Masters protested about the indifferent arrangements, but these were not revised until after the outbreak of war. Meanwhile, some very good officers left the branch and returned to the Naval Reserve to serve with the fleet. Others, who were perhaps too elderly or too inflexible for the Air Force, departed and were not missed.

In the main, the recruiting campaigns for HSL Masters attracted some fine seamen who brought a high standard of knowledge and practical ability with them. Most of the first batch of launch skippers stayed with the RAF for many years. Some of them achieved Senior Rank and went on to command various units and occupy high positions within the MCS.

When the Air Ministry relented under the pressures of wartime manning needs and eventually allowed the commissioning of former WOs and NCOs, the combination of RAFOs, ex-rankers and 'hostilities only' volunteers in the Marine Craft Officer Corps set standards of excellence that were to be maintained throughout the history of the Service.

In the three years preceding the declaration of war, there was little sense of urgency to expand the HSL fleet beyond the 33 boats that were already on order. When the RAF was reorganized into various functional Commands in 1936, Fighter Command became known as 'The World's Most Exclusive Flying Club'. The HSL crews could well have been dubbed 'The World's Most Exclusive Motor Boat Club'.

In the late 1930s, very few people had experienced the thrill of skimming across water at high speed. Racing boats and fast boats were in the exclusive domain of the wealthy. When the early HSLs and MTBs entered the two maritime services, they were the procreaters of a new generation of seafarers, each group of whom viewed the subject from opposing directions.

To the Royal Navy, 60–70 ft motor boats seemed very small indeed. Although their speed and manoeuvrability were appreciated, they continued to be viewed as insignificant toys until the effectiveness of RN Coastal Forces in the early days of the war changed this attitude. Conversely, to the RAF sailors, the 64 ft boats were the largest in the fleet (with the exception of the more pedestrian trawlers and lighters) and were therefore an upward extension of all that had been gleaned from their years with smaller craft.

The MBCs found their new HSLs relatively spacious and luxurious, while Naval crews thought of MTBs as cramped, damp and spartan. Whereas the MTB crews retained most of their 'big ship' routines and each craft carried up to four officers, the HSLs, with only one junior officer in command, still relied heavily on the NCOs and other ranks. The airmen were accustomed to the informality and close teamwork of small boat crews and they were used to working on their own initiative.

In the MCS there was no 'piping aboard' or saluting the quarter deck. HSL wardrooms were Officers' Messes in name only, for they doubled as sickbays. Some naval traditions did cross over to the Air Force, however. 'Lining the side' and 'Boathook drills' were observed on formal occasions and the verbal response of 'Aye, aye' was universal. Perhaps the most popular naval tradition adopted by the HSL crews was the carrying of a barrico of rum. This was not issued in watered down daily tots, but was doled out neat, at any time, at the skipper's discretion.

Unlike contemporary motor yachts, HSLs and their like had no stanchions and wires around the gunwhales and there was neither pulpit nor pushpit. The decks were plain and uncluttered in the interests of being able to move around and work overside when recovering torpedoes, buoys or survivors from the sea. Fore and aft man-ropes were rigged centrally for the crewmen to grab in bad weather, but there were no clip-on harnesses or lifelines in the modern sense.

In poor conditions no-one ventured outside the wheelhouse or cabins unless it was absolutely essential. Streaming, windswept decks with breaking seas and few hand holds were potentially lethal. A man falling overboard would find the surface of the sea glass-hard at high speed, and if he was uninjured he would see the launch vanish very quickly from his personal horizon. Should the other crew members fail to notice at the time, the possibility of finding their unfortunate shipmate before he succumbed to exposure or drowning were extremely remote.

In heavy seas, those in the fo'c'sle and the wheelhouse experienced negative gravity with almost every wave. Feet would leave the deck with each downward plunge, bodies would float in the air connected to the bucking craft by hand grip alone, until the hull hammered into the trough and slammed the crewmen back to the deck. All the crewmen acquired the technique of 'one hand for the ship and one for yourself'. With the exception of the W/Op, who spent most of his working life perched on a padded seat, the crew soon adopted permanent ape-like stances, arms swung loose ready to grab at the nearest support, legs braced apart for stability and bent at the knees to absorb the shocks of the pounding. Heads were stooped and shoulders hunched in readiness to avoid contact with the deckhead should the launch fall away from beneath their feet. It was a sight that contrasted starkly with the head up and shoulders back images of the parade ground.

The stresses on hull and machinery were immense. In HSLs and MTBs the engines were subjected to a continual usage that even Scott-Paine could not possibly have foreseen. The racking of the hull was transmitted directly to the crankcases and holding down bolts, all of which had to be specially strengthened. When the hulls leapt clear of the water the engines raced unless quickly throttled back. On re-entering again, the forward momentum of the launch caused the propellers to 'drive' the engines, reversing the torque and putting great torsional stresses on the transmission.

Constant vibration and slamming also strained mountings, pipe joints and control connections. The marine environment of salt-laden air and dampness was often the cause of electrical failures and air, fuel or oil filters could become contaminated with salt deposits or water. It was usually these ancillary fittings, if any, that failed first. The fitters had an uncomfortable time tending the machinery in normal conditions, but if things went wrong their task was unenviable. Besides the discomforts of heat, noise and fumes, HSL engine rooms were extremely confined. Whirling shafts and pulleys, hot fluids and metals and myriad sharp projections all combined to catch the clumsy and unwary. A minuscule bench with a vice was squeezed into a most inaccessible part of the engine room where hand tools were used to fabricate simple replacement parts. Components would have to be removed, stripped, repaired and replaced in these near impossible conditions.

Naturally, the sailors treated their launches with care and did not normally go charging about at full speed, irrespective of sea conditions. None the less, if they were on a 'Crash Call' and lives were at stake, caution and crew comfort were disregarded.

Sometimes the weather conditions were idyllic, and on such days nothing seemed to go wrong. In peacetime, emergencies were rare and fate's perversity saved most 'Crash Calls' for times when cold winds whined through the rigging and grey seas thundered on the foreshore.

The crews proved to be very tough indeed. Mostly they were young and fit and had the positive attitude and optimism of youth which they shared with their aircrew contemporaries. Many men spent their entire service careers with HSLs and an even greater number of 'hostilities only' crewmen were to spend all of the war years aboard them. There were exceptions, but it was accepted that 35 years was fringing on the upper age limit for the arduous lifestyle of an HSL crewman. Inevitably there were fatalities and injuries, but these were rare considering the risks that were taken on an almost daily basis.

The war brought greater risks, and although the need for sea rescue facilities had been well anticipated, no-one could have foreseen the scale of the demand which was to follow the rapid collapse of Hitler's opposition in Europe and the débâcle of the British Expeditionary Force's retreat from France.

The Battle of Britain was to show how Fighter Command, with its sophisticated system of fighter control, was just, and only just, able to meet the challenge of the Luftwaffe. The same battle also demonstrated how dismally ill-equipped and disorganized the air-sea rescue network was, despite the skill of the HSL crews.

But first, there was Dunkirk.

# Chapter 7

# Where in hell is the RAF?

*A plea said to have been on the lips of many of the troops at Dunkirk. However, on the aerial approaches to Dunkirk and farther inland, the RAF was fighting furiously. Four hundred and thirty-two Hurricanes and Spitfires were lost during Operation Dynamo. Meanwhile, the RAF sailors went to war.*

Early in May 1940, Royal Naval establishments were making up a list of small, privately owned craft. The Admiralty had already requisitioned scores of cross-Channel ferries, pleasure steamers, trawlers and other larger ships for war work. Many of them had been converted to escorts, minesweepers and hospital ships for the duration. The list was an inventory of boats which might be suitable for future use as harbour craft and picket boats, in order to release naval vessels for more important work. At the time, it had no connection with the subsequent Dunkirk operation. The probability of an evacuation was not even discussed by either War Office or Admiralty until 20 May. None the less, the appeal became part of the Dunkirk legend, and was a propitious coincidence.

On 10 May 1940, Winston Churchill became Prime Minister. On the same day, the 7th Panzer Division under the command of Major-General Erwin Rommel led a 54 division attack against the Allies through the Ardennes Forest. The Supreme Allied Commander, France's General Gamelin, had believed an assault from that direction impossible. In the north, Colonel-General Heinz Guderian's 19th Panzers spearheaded 32 Wehrmacht divisions in a breakthrough at Sedan, forcing the French and British Armies to yield.

Three days later, Churchill was telling the House of Commons that he had 'nothing to offer but blood, toil, tears and sweat'. On the following day, Holland fell to the advancing German army and the Allies were being squeezed into what became known as the Dunkirk pocket.

A meeting at the War Office was convened on 19 May to discuss the logistics of supplying the British Expeditionary Force in France. Lord

Gort, commander of the BEF, recommended that a withdrawal of forces towards the channel ports of Ostend, Dunkirk and Boulogne should be considered. The meeting agreed that non-essential personnel should be evacuated immediately to enable supplies to be priority-issued to combatant troops. Two thousand men per day were to be shipped out, with effect from 20 May, and a further 15,000 non-combatants were to prepare for embarkation from 22 May.

By the next meeting, only a day later, the situation in France had deteriorated to the point where Admiral Ramsey, C-in-C Dover, had to begin planning for a mass evacuation. His office was located in a labyrinth of tunnels hewn from the cliffs below Dover castle. The room overlooked the Straits and was called the Dynamo Room after the generating equipment that it had once held. The operation which was sketched out within its walls was entitled Operation Dynamo. The retreat began on Saturday 25 May.

Gort's disengagement from the fighting and subsequent fall back to the port was aided by the sudden halt of the opposing German forces. The German divisions paused for two whole days, while Hitler procrastinated. It was just long enough for the bulk of the British and French soldiers to retreat behind the defensive positions of the Dunkirk perimeter. Operation Dynamo officially began at 1857 hrs on Sunday 26 May.

By the morning of 27 May, the town of Dunkirk was already wrecked and burning. A black pall of smoke from blazing oil storage tanks hung over the ruins. The port's locks and quays were out of action, and the only place in the inner harbour suitable for berthing ships, was the long finger of the West Mole. During the first day, almost 8,000 troops were returned to Dover, adding to the 28,000 pulled out before 26 May.

On Tuesday, it was decided that troops would have to board the rescue ships from the vulnerable and relatively fragile structure of the East Mole which protected the other side of the harbour enclosure. Further still to the east, at Malo-les-Bains, Bray Dunes and La Panne, personnel ships used their boats to take men from the beaches. Progress was slow, as there were insufficient shallow draft boats, but despite the difficulties, almost 18,000 men were rescued, a third of them from the beaches. Back in Dover, an appeal went out to assemble the 'Little Ships' of the registry, with the result that fleets of small craft headed for the mustering point at Sheerness in the Thames Estuary.

Ramsey's fleet retrieved nearly 50,000 personnel during the Wednesday. While most of the ships were taking men from Dunkirk, others were delivering essential food, fuel and ammunition to the beleaguered troops. Many of these supply ships were beached and left to act as embarkation platforms.

On Thursday 30 May, the perimeter closed in until the BEF, no longer able to use the beach at La Panne, was concentrated in the town and on the beaches adjacent to the East Mole. French troops held back the

German advance while the evacuations were stepped up. A stiffening onshore wind made beach work impossible for a time and the Luftwaffe bombed and strafed the crowded troops continuously. Between dawn and dusk, nearly 54,000 men were safely transported to Dover. Ramsey called in his last reserves of small craft on this desperate day, among them an RAF pinnace and five seaplane tenders.

The RAF sailors received their baptism of fire on the morning of Friday 31 May, when six launches were ordered to assist the evacuation. The prototype pinnace No 32, and seaplane tenders 243, 254, 291, 276 and AMC 3 had arrived from Calshot in response to Admiral Ramsey's call. (AMC 3 was in all respects identical to the other boats, but belonged to the Civil Aviation Authority.) Pilot Officer E. Page was in command of the Pinnace, with P/O Collings responsible for the five STs.

Pinnace 32, which due to her lower speed had arrived independently, was sent to Ramsgate and thence to Dunkirk. On the outward passage P 32's propellers were fouled and she returned to Ramsgate unable to take further part in the operation.

To conserve fuel, the five seaplane tenders were towed from Dover by *Sun 7*, one of the well-known Thames tugs which had been requisitioned by the Navy in 1939. (The log of *Sun 7* records towing all five STs, but eye-witness accounts claim that two tugs were utilized.) Leaving at dawn on Friday 31 May, they met strong winds and a heavy swell which made towing difficult. After the tow had parted several times, P/O Collings aboard ST 291, ordered the boats to proceed independently to the beaches from 12 miles offshore.

Before leaving Dover, Collings had pointed out the vulnerability of the seaplane tenders' unprotected propellers, shafts and rudders, but the Navy was desperate, and the order to sail was upheld. During the day, the STs succeeded in ferrying some 500 men to the waiting vessels, thus vindicating the Navy's decision to use them. However, it was not without loss. On the first run to the beach the STs were on a lee shore with both wind and waves trying to push them aground. ST 254 was overwhelmed by the press of bodies trying to board and she hit the bottom. The underwater fittings were destroyed and the launch had to be abandoned. AMC 3 found a more disciplined queue under the control of an Army Major, but he caught his clothing in the propellers, which were still turning to help keep the boat head to sea. When the Coxswain, Corporal C. Webster realized, he cut the engines to prevent further injury, but the breakers picked up the boat and spun it around, whereupon it broached on to the beach and was holed.

The other three boats continued to ferry troops back and forth until both ST 291 and ST 276 had sustained so much damage that they were almost unable to make way or to steer. They obtained permission to return to Dover, one of them, ST 291, having to be towed by a French boat. Pilot Officer Collings remained with the last tender, ST 243, which returned late in the evening, almost out of fuel. The crews of the two STs which had foundered were later picked up. They were the lucky ones, for their colleagues were unwittingly heading for a nightmare of horror and self-sacrifice.

On the following day, the RAF contingent were advised that there would be no further need for them, but the crews stayed in Dover and carried out repairs to the three boats. By means of cannibalizing and improvisation, two of the launches were serviceable by the morning of Sunday 2 June. Despite the earlier assurance to the contrary, Collings received orders to take two naval berthing parties to Dunkirk that afternoon. With only two boats and three crews to choose from, Collings asked for volunteers. All of the men offered to go.

The final crew lists comprised: ST 243, Pilot Officer Collings (O.C.), Corporal R. Lawson (Cox'n), Leading Aircraftman L. Hunt (MBC), Aircraftman B. Kernohan (MBC) and Leading Aircraftman Lockwood (Fitter); ST 276, Corporal L. Flower (Cox'n), Leading Aircraftman F. Clarke (MBC), Aircraftman J. White (MBC) and Leading Aircraftman G. Wooton (Fitter). The two RN berthing parties each comprised a dozen officers and ratings, the Senior RN Officer embarking with Pilot Officer Collings aboard ST 243. Before leaving, the crews took aboard extra cans of fuel and two Lewis guns which they had scrounged.

The boats cast off at 1430 hrs and motored towards France. As they hove-to for a final briefing eight miles from the shore, three Ju 87 Stuka dive-bombers howled down upon them, releasing sticks of bombs and a fusillade of machine-gun fire.

The Cox'ns opened the throttles to take avoiding action, but with the extra weight of the passengers and the additional fuel, the boats were sluggish and slow to accelerate. A second attack followed immediately and bombs erupted all around. On each of the STs, the Fitters had grabbed the Lewis guns. ST 276 had the advantage, where Leading Aircraftman Wooton, aided by the deckhands, had improvised a swivel mounting. Aboard ST 243, Leading Aircraftman Lockwood hand-held the heavy gun and, wedging himself between the aft cabin bulkhead and the engine casing, blazed away at the attacking aircraft as they dived straight at the launch. Lockwood continued firing after a near-miss split ST 243 from stem to stern. He carried on blasting away as the boat careered on, settling deeper and deeper into the water and he did not stop until all way was lost, and the launch sank from under him.

Meanwhile, Corporal Flower was taking evasive action by violently swerving ST 276 at her best laden speed of 18 knots. After the second dive-bomb attack, the Stukas made five more strafing passes with machine guns. The second pass disabled the starboard engine and shot away the throttle controls. ST 276 was reduced to a crawl of only 6 or 7 knots. The best that Flower could do under the circumstances was to head the launch straight in the direction of each attack to present a smaller target. Pieces of the launch flew off in whirling splinters while the crew and the Naval party laid flat on the deckboards. When the Stukas finally veered off, amazingly no-one was seriously hurt.

Corporal Flower slowly headed back to where Collings' boat had sunk, with the intention of picking up the survivors. He found the crew and the naval personnel apparently unscathed in the water, but they were now suffering from fumes and skin burns from petrol which was on the surface.

The senior naval officer swam to the side of the launch and ordered Flower to proceed to Dunkirk without the men from ST 243. Corporal Flower argued against this, but the SNO pointed out that with the extra weight of personnel, it was unlikely that the ST could complete the mission.

Flower's position was untenable, but eventually both the will of the SNO and the discipline of the service prevailed. After making promises to return, the conscience-stricken Corporal reluctantly turned ST 276 away from the 17 men in the sea and motored towards the shambles of Dunkirk harbour.

When the naval party had been safely set ashore, ST 276 went alongside an MTB for further orders. Flower was told to scuttle the damaged seaplane tender and take his crew home on one of the destroyers. None of the crew was particularly enthusiastic about the idea, for there were too many wrecked examples all around them. Unfamiliar with Air Force practices, the naval commander was dumb-founded at the absence of an officer aboard the RAF launch and would not let it proceed. Flower was furious; besides, he had promised to return for the men from the other seaplane tender. As a compromise, a RNVR Lieutenant was taken aboard on the understanding that Corporal Flower remained in command.

The launch left the harbour at sundown and proceeded to the position off Gravelines where ST 243 had foundered. Despite the darkness and the disabled state of their boat, Flower and his crew searched all night before reluctantly heading towards the Kent coast empty handed. At 0730 hrs on Monday 3 June, ST 276 made fast in Dover harbour. The crew discovered later that the entire naval party, Pilot Officer Collings and all except one of the crew from their sister launch had perished. Only Aircraftman Kernohan, MBC, had been picked up alive.

Corporal Les Flower received the Military Medal for his actions on that day, but he always maintained that the bravest men were the ones in the water who had waved salvation away.

Over the next two days, four more destroyers were sunk and four badly damaged. Ferries, excursion ships, cargo vessels, paddle steamers and scores of smaller craft were sunk or crippled by gunfire, air attack and E-boats. The beaches and harbour were littered with the detritus of the furious battle, but despite this 132,000 were evacuated.

By Sunday 2 June, enemy activity had forced the rescue fleet to restrict sailings to the hours of darkness, but on this day and the next, comparatively few troops were left to be picked up. Sunday and Monday saw a total of 52,000 embarked and on the last day, Tuesday 4 June, a final 26,000 were taken off before the remnants of the rearguard surrendered.

Among the last of the destroyers and rescue ships to leave was HSL 120 under the command of Pilot Officer R. G. Spencer RAFVR. HSL 120 was the penultimate boat of the 64 ft class and had only just been handed over to the RAF. The engines were stiff and had a tendency to overheat. At the briefing, Spencer was ordered to accompany MTB 102 to Dunkirk on a VIP trip. The MTB, under the command of Lieutenant C. W. S. Dreyer, RN, had run the gauntlet of the German attacks many times and was now on her eighth crossing. On Saturday 1 June, Dreyer had rescued Admiral Wake-Walker and his staff from the sinking destroyer HMS *Keith*. On Sunday, he had picked up General Alexander, successor to Lord Gort, and had returned him safely to Dover.

His task on 3 June was to ferry Admiral Wake-Walker back to Dunkirk to supervise the last of the French troops to leave. HSL 120 was to provide a back-up if the MTB should be prevented from completing its mission.

Both boats left at 1900 hrs and proceeded at high speed for the French coast. The operation went smoothly, the main hazards being the amount of flotsam and sunken wrecks in the Channel and the inner harbour at Dunkirk. During the outward journey Spencer discovered that two Wireless Operators from a Sunderland squadron at Calshot had stowed away on the launch. When HSL 120 returned to Dover, she had two more crew than she had officially departed with, and several more hours on her engines.

On the morning of 4 June, the last King's Ship, a small 40 ft experimental MTB commanded by Lieutenant J. Cameron, RNVR, left Dunkirk.

Operation Dynamo snatched 338,226 men from death or captivity. For many of the seaborne rescuers, it was their first taste of the conflicts to come.

# Chapter 8

# Saving the few

*Beneath the contrails, the rescue services waited, but when airmen started falling from the sky, the RAF sailors were too few and too widely dispersed to save but a small number of pilots.*

By mid-1940 the pressures of war were bearing heavily on the RAF sailors much as they were for all the armed forces and the civilian population. The 64 ft HSLs and 60 ft pinnaces were being delivered, albeit in small numbers, whilst the 37½ ft seaplane tender and armoured target boat contracts had almost reached completion.

All these craft, and their crews, were very much in demand as Bomber Command embarked on a concentrated training programme for hordes of aircrew recruits. The trend towards bigger aircrews meant more men to train in the skills of gunnery and bombing. Support vessels such as bomb scows, refuellers, planing and flarepath dinghies, were fully occupied whilst new designs and replacements were fed into the pipeline. The Marine Craft Section now came under the auspices of Coastal Command. The sailors at last had an identity within the Air Force command structure. With it came a marked improvement in organization.

After many years of pressurizing the Government, the Admiralty had, in 1937, finally won its battle to take over the Fleet Air Arm of the RAF, but it did not succeed in a parallel attempt to gain control of RAF Coastal Command. Co-operation between the services at functional levels was excellent, to the extent that over 40 FAA pilots served with Fighter Command during the ensuing Battle of Britain.

The original direct entry HSL Masters were granted RAFVR status and the qualification requirements for new Marine Officers were relaxed as the demand increased. Before the Battle of Britain commenced, it was recognized that the SNCO Coxswains provided an ideal source for officer trainees. The Air Ministry reversed the regulation which had excluded them from applying. At last, the MBCs had full career prospects. The sailors were also relieved of some of the more irksome shore duties and their working uniform was revised, much along the lines recommended by T. E. Shaw. Gone were the dog-collars, breeches and puttees. The cumbersome peaked cap had been replaced by the forage or side cap for everyday wear. Sea boots, submarine sweaters and foul weather gear were introduced to supplement the ubiquitous, dung-coloured denim overalls. Although the sailors' lot was showing marked improvement, things were not so good in the higher echelons of the organization.

Pre-war plans for sea rescue had been formulated as a result of requests by Bomber Command for an improved coverage of the North Sea and the Eastern Approaches. These were the main areas where aircrew were trained for offensive missions over the continent of Europe. In the event of a bomber having to ditch, the procedure was for other aircraft from the same squadron to carry out a search and inform the base of the downed aircraft's position. Coastguard, RNLI and HSL stations were alerted via the public telephone system. GPO Wireless Telegraphy Stations then made a broadcast to shipping and diverted nearby vessels to the location.

The system was probably adequate on paper, but after war was declared it was decided that the GPO W/T broadcasts could not be used as they would reveal shipping movements to the Germans. This left a substantial gap in communications when rapid response to emergencies was essential.

In March 1940, Fighter Command, whose aircraft frequently overflew the Channel, took the initiative and introduced a plan whereby the crew of an aircraft in difficulties would transmit a Mayday (M'aidez) R/T signal or an SOS via W/T on a pre-determined emergency frequency of 500 kc (kilocycles). Thereafter, before baling out, they were instructed to screw their morse keys down to enable a fix to be taken on the continuous signal. (This rarely helped, because more often than not, the transmission merely indicated the last known position of the aircraft and not necessarily the position where the crew abandoned it.) The recipients of the signal would relay the message to Fighter Command who would pass it in turn to the rescue services. When the Government eventually agreed to reintroduce GPO shipping broadcasts in the revised belief that rescuing aircrew justified the security risk, the system was appreciably better, but far from perfect.

The plan was introduced at a time when an enemy assault from the sky was expected to be limited to the odd intruder or paratroop attack. It was believed that the fighting line and the airfields behind it would remain on French soil, thus the number of ditched aircrews was likely to be small. Although Government-inspired precautions against attack from the air were well under way, by early 1940 the frantic activity had subsided into a determined and more practical quietude. Underlying this, was an understandable complacency about Britain's invulnerability to invasion. Only Air Chief Marshal Sir Hugh Dowding was out of step with general opinion. Not only did he refuse to commit more of his Fighter Command Squadrons to the BEF in defiance of the Government, but he foresaw the possibility of a defensive air fight in the skies above Britain and her offshore waters. 'Stuffy' Dowding was labelled as an eccentric and a pessimist, but thanks to his obstinacy, in July 1940 Fighter Command had some 800 aircraft in Britain, of which 400 Hurricanes and 200 Spitfires could be considered front-line.

In 10 hectic weeks, the air battle which followed the withdrawal of the last elements of the BEF from Dunkirk was to illustrate the supremacy of air power in contemporary warfare. The ensuing 'blitz' removed for ever the British belief that their islands were inviolable. On the plus side, the Battle of Britain demonstrated to the world that the Luftwaffe was not invincible and Hitler could be stopped. The battle also demonstrated in tragic manner, the shortcomings of the rescue services. Many of Dowding's young airmen were plunged into the sea and far too few others were there to help them.

Of the 537 Fighter Command aircrew lost during the battle of Britain period, between 10 July and 31 October 1940, some 215 were declared missing or killed in the North Sea and the English Channel. South-east England and the adjacent waters became known as 'Hellfire Corner' to both aircrews and boats crews alike. As the battle raged and whirled above, the casualties plummeted down. Some pilots were dead, or mortally wounded, when they hit the water, whilst others managed to escape from their twisted aircraft only to drown or die from exposure. Once in the sea, their chances of survival were slender. Less than a fifth of all the Battle of Britain fighter aircrew who ditched or baled out over water, were subsequently rescued. Of these the majority were retrieved by the contingent efforts of the Royal Navy, the RNLI, the RAF, fishing vessels and merchant ships. A few were picked up by the highly organized German rescue services. Some even swam ashore to fight again.

At the time of the Battle, fighter aircrew were equipped with inflatable Mae West life-jackets which were not regularly checked and were often swapped between pilots, or passed on when a pilot changed squadrons. There were no dinghies or survival kits. The principle of baling out over land was so prevalent that no consideration for the possibility of crash-landing into the sea had been incorporated in aircraft design. The Hurricane and Spitfire had large, scoop-like radiator intakes and a variety of other orifices which allowed rapid ingress of water. Single-seat aeroplanes invariably nosed over and sank within seconds, dragged down by their heavy engines. Furthermore, airmen received little, if any, training in ditching procedures and the few who did tended to disregard it on the basis of 'it can't happen to me'.

In accordance with the sea rescue plan, individual fighter squadrons were responsible for their own, either by pinpointing the position of their downed colleagues, or carrying out a search for them. At the height of the battle, this was a demoralizing additional burden for already exhausted pilots.

The case of Pilot Officer P. G. Dexter of 603 Squadron, illustrated the kind of frustration experienced by many of the airmen. In September 1940, Dexter was escorting Pilot Officer 'Pip' Cardell, as he nursed his damaged Spitfire towards the Kent coast after a dogfight over the Channel. Before reaching land, Cardell was forced to bale out, but his parachute failed to open and he pitched headlong into the sea. Unable to attract anyone's attention, Dexter promptly crash-landed his own aircraft on the beach at Folkestone, grabbed a boat and rowed out to his friend. Despite his desperate action, he was too late.

As the battle intensified, German air raids disrupted lines of communication. When a pilot was located, Fighter Command controllers were often unable to alert would-be rescuers promptly, and once they did make contact, the disposition of high speed launches was totally inadequate. Only 13 HSLs were deployed in the home islands and of these, just 10 covered the entire East Coast and English Channel from Aberdeen to Guernsey. Routine servicing schedules kept at least three boats non-operational at any one time, and the need to change engines after 360 hours of running became more frequent as sea time was stepped up. HSL engine changes were complicated and laborious, and the Napier Sea Lions also appeared to suffer an inordinate level of unserviceability. Hard use was fostering a sneaking disenchantment with the overall design of the '100 Class' launches.

During July and August most of the air battles took place over the sea, with heavy losses on both sides. Eleven British and 10 German aircraft crashed in the sea during the two days 20 and 21 July alone. Six of the RAF aircraft were the outclassed Boulton Paul Defiants of 141 Squadron, all of which were shot down near Dover. Of the 28 German and 12 British aircrew to ditch, only six were recovered alive. One of these, a Bf 109 pilot was rescued by the Seenotdienst, the German Rescue service.

On 11 and 12 August, in the build-up to Goering's ill-fated *Adlertag* (Eagle Day), the day on which the RAF was supposed to be annihilated, many Fighter Command pilots were lost in the sea area south of Portland and the Isle of Wight. By 19 August, although fighters from coastal bases were still engaged over the sea, losses became noticeably fewer as the battle moved inland.

Individual records show that a high proportion of pilots quite rightly considered that their chances of survival were much better over land. Battle damaged aircraft from both sides would instinctively head for the nearest friendly coastline before their crews attempted a crash-landing or bale-out. A large number of these airmen survived to fight again and many of their crashed aircraft were repaired. Of those who were obliged to ditch or parachute over water, over 80 per cent were recorded as missing. Besides the persuasive logic of making for land, the idea of pancaking a damaged Hurricane or Spitfire on the sea was then as unthinkable as parking an ailing car on a lake. This attitude changed as the war progressed and, as sea survival equipment and rescue methods improved, aircrews (particularly bomber crews) were encouraged to ditch rather than to crash on land.

The most successful day for sea rescue was 26 August, when three Spitfires were shot down, two near Dover and one off the Sussex coast, whilst two Defiants and two Hurricanes came down in the Herne Bay area. Altogether six pilots were saved, but one Spitfire pilot and the two Defiant air gunners were lost.

From 7 September onwards, when the Luftwaffe shifted its emphasis to attacking London, the 'Big Wing' theory was put to good effect. RAF losses were fewer and such ditchings and bale-outs that did occur were largely over the Thames estuary where enemy aircraft were using the river as a navigational aid.

With the confusing and imprecise nature of the available information it is impossible to define exactly how many of the forty-odd Battle of Britain aircrew saved were picked up by RAF craft, but it was only a small proportion. The too few HSL crews did everything in their power to achieve results, but the lack of accurate fixes, the problems with communications and serviceability allied to the weight of demand, simply overwhelmed them.

The profound shock of the high fatality figures at sea highlighted the shortcomings to all concerned. Even as the German invasion fleets were being dismantled, measures to resolve the problems were initiated. Life-jackets were subjected to regular inspections and inflatable dinghy packs were copied from the Luftwaffe. Designs for the next generation of fighter and bomber aircraft included escape hatches, watertight compartments and survival equipment. New training programmes were welcomed by those who had participated in the battle. But these activities were still not enough. They were all based on the premise that airmen would not only be fit and able to leave their doomed aircraft, but would thereafter be in a physical and mental condition to face the rigours of hours, perhaps days, afloat in a hostile environment. Clearly, if the flyers were to be provided with the means to help themselves, other measures were needed to locate and recover them as quickly as possible. The RAF sailors were frustrated and anguished at having been too ill-equipped to save more lives and they were left with a fierce determination to excel.

Less than six weeks after the Battle, while the night blitz raged on, the Chief of Air Staff ordered that the provisions for sea rescue be reorganized, streamlined and expanded. The lessons learned from trying to save some of 'The Few' in the desperate summer of 1940, ensured that many of their heirs were successfully snatched from the maw of the hungry sea.

# Chapter 9

# The Spitfire of the sea

*The 63 ft high speed launches designed and built by the BPBC became synonymous with the image of the Air Sea Rescue Service. To the sailors they were known as 'Whalebacks'.*

After the Battle of Britain, the weary pilots of Fighter Command were aware that they had averted a defeat but would hardly have acknowledged it as a momentous victory. The invasion may have been postponed, but no-one dared to think that the threat had diminished more than temporarily. With the enemy now firmly established 20 miles away in France and Belgium, and with Bomber, Fighter and Coastal Command aircraft engaged in a multitude of sorties by night and day, every mission demanded that RAF aircrew would be flying over the sea. Losses mounted as the autumn of 1940 drew into winter. In October alone, 260 aircrew of all Commands went missing, the majority over water.

By December, the Chief of Air Staff, Sir Cyril Newall found it necessary to chivvy his subordinates into taking action to avert further losses, and appoint a Senior Officer to co-ordinate matters on a more efficient basis. Group Captain L. G. Le B. Croke, from Coastal Command, was appointed Director of Air Sea Rescue with Captain C. L. Howe, RN as his deputy. The Directorate commenced work at Coastal Command Headquarters on 6 February 1941, the day that the RAF Air Sea Rescue Service was formed. It adopted the motto 'The Sea Shall Not Have Them'.

The staff included Air Sea Rescue liaison officers at the four area Coastal Command Group Headquarters, a Marine Craft Officer and others to liaise with Naval Area Commanders, Supply, Training, Aircraft Production and Medical Directorates. The Directorate of ASR was answerable directly to the Deputy Chief of Air Staff.

There was much for Croke's team to do. From the beginning, it was clear that sea search activities by both Fighter Command aircraft and the HSLs of Coastal Command were hopelessly inadequate and relatively non-productive. More search aircraft and a larger fleet of launches were highly desirable, but these could neither be spared nor produced in sufficient quantities to provide a short-term solution. In the interim, means of sustaining survivors throughout prolonged search periods were essential.

The Germans were already more advanced in their rescue efforts. They had a large fleet of E-boats and they operated several Heinkel He 59 floatplanes exclusively for rescue purposes. One-man dinghies were supplied for their fighter pilots and larger inflatables, with portable radio transmitters and signalling equipment, for their bomber crews. In addition, the Seenotdienst placed rescue floats at strategic locations across the North Sea and the Channel. These floats were small dumb barges that contained shelter, clothing, bedding, food, water and simple cooking facilities for up to four men. Long grab-lines were trailed to enable survivors to haul themselves aboard.

Initially, the D of ASR copied the German methods. One-man triangular 'C' type dinghy packs were incorporated in all fighter aircraft. Improved dinghies were introduced for bombers and transports, although it was to be some time before either type were fitted with radio transmitters. Industrial bungling and administrative delays eventually culminated in the adoption of an American copy of the German set in mid-1942.

British-made ASR floats, and a few captured German ones, were moored in various likely spots, but were never utilized in the manner for which they were intended. Channel markers and mooring buoys were equipped with ration kits and signalling gear. These proved useful for seamen from stricken ships although there is no evidence of aircrew ever using them.

In 1940, two Coastal Command stations made independent attempts to explore ways of prolonging the lives of ditched aircrew by means of air-dropped light survival gear. The first of these was the Thornaby Bag developed by RAF Thornaby in Yorkshire. It was a simple valise containing basic food, drink and first aid equipment and kept afloat by kapok life jackets. Meanwhile, just inland from the Wash, RAF Bircham Newton came up with the Bircham Barrel. Similar in concept, but more robust than the Thornaby Bag, the Barrel was a cylindrical container fitted with a finned tail unit to give it stability during descent. Both of these devices were adopted by other stations and had the advantage of being easily constructed from readily available parts. Either assembly could be carried under the wings of several types of single-engined aircraft. Neither system was ideal, but a much more advanced concept that followed, had its origins in the Bag and the Barrel. The highly successful Lindholme gear was another product of local initiative, this time by the Bomber Command station of RAF Lindholme near Doncaster. It comprised a string of containers which included protective clothing and a comprehensive range of survival equipment to sustain a number of survivors. The original idea had been to include automatically inflating multi-man dinghies, but these were not available until mid-1941, so at first, smaller types were substituted. The Admiralty, as sorely pressed for *matériel* as the other services, declined a request to transfer a number of Supermarine Walrus seaplanes, so Fighter Command Blenheims and Bomber Command Hampdens were adapted to drop the various types of equipment.

Other measures, such as incorporating buoyancy aids and water tight hatches in RAF aeroplanes, could not be introduced in the short term because of the necessary design alterations, but with the help of the D of ASR, the Ministry did impose guidelines that were to be effective on later types.

In parallel with these actions, a series of 'ditching procedures' were drawn up. Several posters were produced to convey to both trainees and veteran aircrew alike that practising escape drills would give them a better chance of survival. By early 1942, each Station had an ASR Officer whose job it was to keep up to date on all aspects of survival and rescue and convey this information to the aircrews. As a result, hostility towards ditching began to diminish.

Insufficient search aircraft and a shortage of rescue launches continued to be the most daunting problems for the Directorate. Fighter Command once again solved the air-search problem. Two squadrons of Westland Lysanders were seconded from Army Co-operation Command and placed at various stations around the south-east coastal region. Repeated requests for Walruses from the Royal Navy were to no avail, until in August 1941 six aircraft were transferred after a direct appeal from the AOC-in-C. By the end of September 1941, the first four Air Sea Rescue Squadrons, Nos 275, 276, 277 and 278, had been formed, operating 36 Lysanders and eight Walruses between them.

The D of ASR achieved much during 1941. It improved aircrews awareness of the essential dinghy drills, expanded air-search facilities and, with the aid of inspired individual efforts, introduced equipment to increase the chances of survival before being picked up. But the Achilles' heel was still the lack of surface craft.

As early as September 1939, Beauforte-Greenwood had recommended that the 64 ft HSLs should be replaced by a new 63 ft BPBC design fitted with twin Rolls-Royce Merlin engines. In his report, he described how the 64 ft boats were too wet in a seaway, their crew and stretcher accommodation inadequate and their freeboard too high for the recovery of casualties. Despite his criticisms of the Napier engines, it was soon apparent that Merlins could not be made available.

Arguably, the engines were not as inherently troublesome as was claimed, particularly as hundreds of them were to give sterling service throughout the war and for many years thereafter. It is significant that when the HSL fleet was created there were few fitters who were familiar with aircraft engines. Regulations called for two fitters on each crew, one of whom had to be a Senior NCO, and both had to be able to withstand the rigours of HSL life. It was impossible to find and train sufficient numbers of men of the right calibre at short notice and the eternally poor reputation of the Napiers was probably forged in those early days of inexpert engineering knowledge.

The new BPBC Type 2 HSL was adapted from George Selman's 63 ft by 16½ ft beam, Motor Anti-Submarine Boat. Although shorter than the '100 Class' boat, the layout was improved to give more accommodation, including a large sunken sickbay abaft the wheelhouse. Maximum speed was around 36 knots. The popular press dubbed the new boats 'Spitfires of the Sea', but it was the curvature of the moulded plywood sickbay deckheads, combined with the reverse sheer of the main decks, which prompted the sailors to nickname them 'Whalebacks'. The 'Whalebacks' were the first HSLs to be fitted with Armstrong-Whitworth aircraft-style gun turrets, each with a single .303 Vickers or Lewis machine-gun. Sixty-nine were built and numbered 122–149, 156–190, and 2546–2551. Twenty-one of them were delivered before October 1941, HSLs 122–133 being part of the original order for '100 Class' boats, and HSLs 141–149 being switched to the RAF from a contract for the South African Air Force.

By the end of 1941, despite the desperate circumstances, only 39 HSLs of either type were available in the UK. This was less than half the proposed establishment. Boatbuilders Thornycroft, Fairmile and Vosper were wholly engaged with supplying the Royal Navy and had no spare capacity. In fact, Vosper's Chief Executive, Commander Peter Du Cane, RN, used his popular standing with the Admiralty to monopolize the entire UK allocation of American Packard and Hall-Scott engines. Meanwhile, Scott-Paine and the RAF had to be content with the output of Lion engines from Napier.

The ambitions of the ASR Service were further thwarted at this inopportune moment, when the British Purchasing Commission suffered an attack of bloody-mindedness. Scott-Paine had set up a Canadian Power Boat Company at Montreal in late 1940 which, immune from air raids and material shortages, was able to accept bulk orders for HSLs and MTBs. BPBC 70 ft boats were being licence-built for the US Navy by the Electric Boat Company of Bayonne, New Jersey, which gave Scotty access to supplies of Packard 4M-2500 1,200 hp engines. The Admiralty and the Purchasing Commission ignored his entreaties to build for the RAF or the RN, and he was obliged to supply the RCAF, the RCN and the Royal Netherlands Navy instead. None of this was sufficient to utilize the full production capability of the factory and to stay in business, Scott-Paine eventually resorted to fabricating wooden components for Mosquito aircraft. At one stage, Scotty appealed to Churchill to intervene, but this only infuriated the Admiralty who, as a result of its own lack of foresight, was monopolizing supplies of fast boats and high-powered engines everywhere else. The RAF was barred from taking advantage of the Canadian production.

Paradoxically, while Scott-Paine was busy promoting his Montreal facilities, HSLs were being built elsewhere in Canada. Six 70 ft boats numbered 150–155, were built by Aero Marine Craft of Trenton, Ontario. They were powered by triple 500 hp Liberty Vee-12 engines which had been converted to marine application by Scott's old racing adversary, Garfield Wood. The choice of the Liberty engines proved to be a disaster. Broken crankshafts, dropped valves and seizures were frequent, although some of the problems were due to internal rust in the engines when they arrived. Inexplicably, the boats were fitted with a 32 volt electrical system which was incompatible with the standard 24 volt system common to British marine craft. HSL 151 and a shipment of spares was lost *en route* to the UK aboard a freighter sunk by enemy action. HSLs 152 and 155 were re-engined with twin Thornycroft RY12s. All five were considered unsuitable for ASR work and, after a sojourn at Calshot, they were transferred to the MCTS in Corsewall for training purposes. Even here, they were considered unsound in rough weather conditions. As the serial numbers indicate, these unsuitable craft had come right in the middle of the BPBC production of 'Whalebacks'. Scott-Paine had every right to be furious.

Before the US Congress changed the ruling preventing the United States from supplying war materials to the belligerents in Europe, there were many ways to circumvent it, judging by the frenetic efforts that were being made to secure supplies. Although obtaining high-speed boats for the RN and the RAF (notwithstanding the CPBC situation) was a big enough problem, even the purchase of motor yachts being considered, the main constraint was a lack of suitable engines. The production of Napier's Sea Lion engine was at full stretch and was dependent on the sole distribution agreement pertaining to the BPBC. Thornycroft RY12s, which had evolved from the unreliable Y12s, required further development. A proposed 900 hp high-speed diesel from Perkins had not materialized and Rolls-Royce Merlins could not be spared for marine use.

Among the American engines reviewed were Chrysler Crowns, Scripps, Graymarines, Stirling Admirals, Libertys, Hall-Scott Defenders, Kermath Sea Raiders and Packard 4M–2500s, but only the last three types were found to be acceptable for importing in quantity. The Admiralty promptly snapped up the lot and it was these that enabled Vosper and Fairmile to meet their obligations to the Royal Navy.

After some more inter-Service wrangling, the Admiralty released a number of boats which were designed and built by the Fogarty Boat Yard, which later became the Miami Shipbuilding Corporation. These 'Miamis' were originally under construction for the South African Air Force and nine of them were allocated to the RAF. 'Miamis' were used exclusively on overseas units and did not directly boost the UK complement, but they did relieve the pressure on UK resources.

Perhaps as a gesture of compensation for their intransigence, the Admiralty eventually made available 20 110 ft Fairmile 'A' type motor launches, but only in a secondary role. Manned by their naval crews, these MLs and a few requisitioned yachts could be called upon for rescue around the southern part of the British Isles. At the same time, the RN accepted responsibility for all sea rescue in the Irish Sea which at the time was not a particularly busy area, although several accidents and ditchings did occur to training aircraft.

The net result of all the efforts by the D of ASR was that the ratio of rescues to ditchings improved to 35 per cent in 1941, compared with the 17 per cent of the Battle of Britain period. Of those who were rescued, almost 40 per cent were saved by the RAF itself, in spite of its stretched resources. The success rate was encouraging, but in the first quarter of 1941, the obverse side of the statistics had shown that some 400 aircrewmen were lost at sea, ie many more than during the whole Battle of Britain. Air activity had increased rapidly. Larger numbers of fighters and new squadrons of multi-engined bombers, with up to 10 crew members, were all carrying out more frequent sorties. Besides Luftwaffe attacks on Allied aircraft, coastal shipping was being sunk close inshore by both enemy aircraft and E-boats. At times, it must have seemed that the UK coastal waters were littered with men crying out to be rescued.

The dearth of rescue launches was further compounded when the D of ASR recommended to the Deputy Chief of Air Staff that two types of craft were considered necessary. The first type would continue to operate from coastal ports in the manner of the existing '100 Class' and 'Whaleback' launches. The second type was required in anticipation of placing launches at intervals under the bomber streams, on 'rendez-vous'. These would be larger, more seaworthy boats capable of spending many hours at sea in all weather conditions, and as they would already be on station, speeds of 20–25 knots would suffice. The D of ASR estimated that 110 such craft would be needed. Once again, the RN was approached for a number of Fairmile MLs and once again, the request was rejected in deference to their own needs.

The 'Whaleback' building programme at the BPBC was not expected to be completed until the end of 1942. Estimates made in the first half of 1941 stated a need for 49 boats in addition to the 21 either in service or laid down, plus another 44 for overseas units. They were far in excess of availability. Only four '100 Class' and one 'Whaleback' HSL were stationed abroad until the 'Miamis' and a second 'Whaleback' were shipped out in the latter half of the year.

The timely arrival of a new version of the seaplane tender relieved some of the pressure. George Selman, who had now become Chief designer at the BPBC, had re-drawn the launch, increasing the loa to 41½ ft and the beam to 11¾ ft. The new 'broad beam' ST proved to be an excellent sea boat and a worthy successor to the '200 Class'. Fourteen of these entered service during 1941, serial numbers 357–366 and 436–439. Although they were originally intended for seaplane support, it was quickly realized that they were ideal for inshore rescue in moderate conditions, or in locations which could not accommodate HSLs at all states of the tide.

To reinforce offshore operations, the Directorate placed orders with other boatyards for forty 60 ft general service (GS) pinnaces, modified for ASR work. The derricks were replaced with lightweight masts to carry WT/RT aerials and the hold coamings were increased in height to provide stretcher accommodation.

Scrambling nets were attached to the decks aft. The triple Perkins-powered variants could just about manage 17 knots, but the later addition of shrapnel matting and gun turrets increased the weight and cut the speed accordingly. At first, they were re-designated special duty (SD) pinnace, but this was later changed to ASR pinnace. All of these boats were promised for delivery before the end of 1941, but material shortages and myriad other reasons were given for the non-appearance of the vessels from the yards concerned. Only one ASR pinnace was delivered before the year's end, and that had been converted from an existing GS version.

The pinnaces had been steadily entering service since 1938 and were popular with their crews, but ASR work was a different matter entirely. When the bulk of them did emerge in 1942, they were mainly deployed in areas around Scotland, where sea conditions prevented HSLs from utilizing their full speed, but it was soon discovered that the pinnaces were not able to operate in such weather either. They were seaworthy enough, but their low freeboard made hazardous work of recovery. Ultimately, the ASR pinnaces were moved south and restricted to operations in moderate sea conditions only. This was an implied redundancy ticket, for in such conditions the HSLs and ASR seaplane tenders were able to operate at high speeds anyway.

The stop-gap adaptation of the pinnaces improved the disposition of the launch network on paper, but in practice did little to improve the overall situation. Meanwhile, before the end of 1941 doubts were being expressed about the suitability of the 'Whalebacks' to operate in rough sea conditions. They were being used and abused in the quest to save lives, but this was taking its toll. Hull and machinery damage was frequent and inherent shortcomings in sea kindliness was wearisome on crews and survivors alike. 'Whalebacks' were by no means dangerous or unseaworthy boats, but they pounded violently, and were too short and too skittish for some of the conditions they encountered. Larger hulls with a 'softer' forefoot were desirable, and if this concept were to be pursued it would allow for increased range and more spacious crew accommodation.

By the late summer of 1941 the Directorate of ASR was under pressure from Bomber Command to improve performance. The Admiralty, engrossed in its own expansion of Coastal Forces had even withdrawn Captain Howe to look after the Navy's own air-sea rescue development. There were too many departments of both services working in isolated pockets to achieve what was in fact a common objective, that of aircrew safety.

To bring all the conflicting elements together required the attention of a very senior officer with the diplomatic ability to win co-operation from all RAF Commands as well as the ambivalent Admiralty. Although the post was beneath his rank, Marshal of the Royal Air Force Sir John Salmond accepted the role of Director of Aircraft and Aircrew Safety. His brief embraced aircraft homing systems, navigation and landing aids, crash survival and air-sea rescue. He took up his new post in September, 10 days after the Deputy Chief of Air Staff, Air Vice-Marshal N. H. Bottomly, held a conference to examine all aspects of the Air Sea Rescue organization and its plans for the future. One of those who attended the conference was the Assistant Chief of Naval Staff, Rear Admiral Power, RN, and with his co-operation the barriers were broken down at last, and the Navy agreed to help.

As an immediate measure, fourteen 63 ft BPBC Motor Anti-Submarine Boats and crews were seconded to the ASR Service, whilst 50 Fairmile 'B' type motor launches were promised from March 1942 for full-time rescue purposes. Entitled Rescue Motor Launches (RMLs), these would provide the low speed, heavy weather facility which the service so badly needed. Fighter Command Spitfires and Lysanders which had undertaken limited radius inshore searches were to be supplemented by two squadrons of long-range Lockheed Hudsons. At the same time, plans were made to boost the supply of launches to the RAF. Orders were placed with Thornycroft and Vosper. At the BPBC, George Selman commenced work on a new concept of HSL. This time, he was uninhibited by the attentions of Scott-Paine, who was now based permanently in Canada.

The expansion of the Air Sea Rescue Service also placed a heavy demand on manning levels. The need for trained Coxswains and MBCs could not be met overnight. The RAF embarked on an extensive national advertising campaign for Motor Boat Crew. Although some nautical knowledge was desirable, it was no longer mandatory. Men from all backgrounds were encouraged to join the service for training. This action sowed the seeds of the myth that the ASR Service was an all amateur force. It was true that all the men were volunteers, as were the pre-war regulars, but those same regulars were the professional spine of the Service and they resented the 'amateur' connotation of the legend. As the recruiting campaign continued, serving men with experience of aircraft engines were encouraged to volunteer for re-mustering to Marine Fitter. The first of a series of Fitter 2E conversion courses started in March 1941, and when these men were integrated into their new units some months later the serviceability of the HSLs noticeably improved.

Once more, the Royal Navy cast its covetous eye towards the RAF sailors. Admiral Power proposed that the shortage of manpower in both the RAF and the RN would be overcome if the entire rescue service was absorbed into the Royal Navy. The suggestion was tactfully rejected by the Air Council on the grounds that the structure of the ASR Service was now established and further major changes would only be detrimental. However, the RAF sailors came close to exchanging their grey-blue for the dark blue of the RN.

In mid-1941, the first B17C, four-engine Flying Fortress daylight bombers arrived for the RAF. The early Fortress 1s, as the RAF called them, were mechanically unreliable and unable to defend themselves when deployed in small numbers. They were quickly accorded the unfortunate nickname of 'flying coffins', but these lessons were well heeded and put to good use by the Americans. The result was the much improved B17E, F and G variants.

Germany and Italy declared war on the USA on 10 December 1941, three days after the Japanese attack on Pearl Harbor. Churchill and Roosevelt agreed that the war in Europe should take priority over the Pacific. Thus the grounds were laid for the US Eighth Air Force to place vast numbers of B17 and B24 strategic bombers and their escort fighter groups in the UK.

By the beginning of 1942, it was crystal clear to the sailors that they were about to become very busy indeed. The RAF was entering a remarkable 20 year period as the world's largest seaborne rescue service.

# Chapter 10

# Wooden ships and iron men

*The RAF sailors cheekily laid claim to an expression that had been applied to Nelson's navy. They mocked the Senior Service for being of 'Iron ships and wooden men', but the sailors modified their views when they found Naval Rescue Motor Launches and MTBs working alongside them.*

When HSL 141, the first completed 'Whaleback', entered service in February 1941, the upper works and deck were painted bright yellow. The superstructure sides were in slate grey and the hulls gloss black. The launch numbers on each cheek of the bows were also yellow, and a yellow ring encircled the RAF roundels. The launch number was repeated on the foredeck in black, for ease of identification from the air. The bright colour scheme was presumably intended to deter enemy attack, but there is no recorded reason for the choice of yellow, except perhaps for its high visibility at sea. It may well have had its origins as a simple 'keep clear' warning, for similar colours were used on certain RAF vehicles and on all training aircraft.

Whatever the background, the Germans were not deterred from attacking the HSLs whenever an opportunity was presented. It has often been said that there was a kind of chivalry between the Luftwaffe and the ASR Service at the beginning of the war, and that by unwritten agreement each side left the other's rescue service alone. Most, if not all, of the pointers were to the contrary. The survivors from the Dunkirk operation knew only too well the Germans' disregard for ships of mercy. Regardless of their own experiences, these sailors were aware that all four legitimately marked hospital ships which took part suffered heavy attacks, both from shore batteries and the Luftwaffe.

HSLs frequently operated close under enemy guns, in minefields and amid flotillas of marauding E-boats. The risk of air attack was ever present and on numerous occasions the use of the boat's radio gave away the launch's position to the enemy.

This happened in the case of HSL 108 on a July afternoon in 1941. The launch arrived safely at a 'Crash Call' position in the North Sea, but a wireless transmission gave it away to the Germans. The launch was attacked by Heinkels and severely damaged, with two men wounded. During the night the crew tried to bung the holes in the hull, but by dawn the HSL was still in a sinking condition. The Wireless Operator had died from his injuries overnight. The survivors were rescued by enemy seaplanes and became prisoners of war. Later, the launch was retrieved by the Germans. In the same year, HSL 143 was sunk by seven Messerschmitt Bf 109s and the crew was captured.

In August 1941, the D of ASR instructed that all HSLs should be equipped with two twin Browning .303 turrets for self-defence. This applied to all craft in build and, for the first time, to all existing vessels. Some measures were taken to add to HSL armament by means of Vickers 'K' type gas-operated guns on swivel mountings each side of the wheelhouse, but not until after the Dieppe Raid in 1942 did the RAF seriously act on the question of defensive armament. The continuing shortage of weapons, the priority demands of other arms of the services and, surprisingly, a reluctance on the part of some HSL skippers to install the guns, brought little change.

The skippers' attitude was understandable when seen in the light of other protective measures which were taking place. Armour plating was introduced to protect the Masters, Cox'n's and Engineers and the variously named 'flak', 'splinter' or 'shrapnel' matting was strapped to the outside of the superstructure for added protection. This matting was heavy enough when dry, but after a soaking it became a considerable additional burden. When the prototype HSLs were on trials, they were of a relatively streamlined shape. The add-ons not only increased the displacement, but were also a cause of extra aerodynamic drag at speed. Some skippers and crews were of the opinion that their best defence was their high-speed capability, and they were averse to exchanging this for protection and fire power.

In time, it was realized that the extensive use of yellow paint merely drew attention to the launches. The upperworks and decking were repainted in slate grey, leaving only a small area atop the wheelhouse in yellow. Later, when the HSLs were fitted with VHF sets, the deck numbers were replaced with a red and white chequered band with the VHF call-sign number superimposed in white. All ASR launches used the call-sign 'Seagull'.

The BPBC Naval Rescue MASBs were warships in every sense, with rescue as their secondary role. They carried depth charges and much heavier defensive armament, but from a distance it was impossible to differentiate between these and the 'Whalebacks'. A rescue MASB was attacked by Bf 109s near Dover as early as April 1941, killing the Captain. Fairmile RMLs were also indistinguishable from their more warlike ML counterparts, and such similarities served only to encourage enemy attacks on naval and Air Force rescue vessels alike.

There were inevitable exceptions when, on rare occasions, German aircraft ignored the boats and allowed them to complete their mercy missions unmolested. There was even one recorded instance of a Heinkel 111 guiding an HSL to the survivors of a ditched Wellington and then, with a waggle of its wings, flying off.

Unfortunately, it was quite common for Allied aircraft to fire on their own rescue launches mistakenly. In such circumstances, the launches would send frantic identity signals and if these were disregarded, they simply fired back!

With the formation of the co-ordinated Air Sea Rescue Service, the RAF sailors were under regional naval command. Both Navy and Air Force provided deep search facilities via Walrus and later, Catalina flying boats, and all the units concerned worked in close co-operation with Coastal Command. The new structure was sound, and remained basically unchanged until the cessation of hostilities. Air Sea Rescue Units were formed and given designation numbers accordingly. ASRUs were usually located in sheltered harbours with accommodation, slipways and workshops close by. Accommodation for the crews ranged between tumbledown shacks, temporary Nissen huts, and comfortable hotels. In 1941–2, No 28 ASRU at Newhaven and No 27 ASRU at Dover, with a detachment in Ramsgate, bore the brunt of the rescue calls around 'Hellfire Corner'.

The HSLs were highly mobile, and in 1941 boats were detached from as far away as Calshot to support the ASRUs which were overloaded by the activity around the south-east and east coast areas. The crews lived aboard their launches, indented for or scrounged their own rations and other essentials, and retained a degree of autonomy outside the immediate demands of their duties.

Living aboard the early '100 Class' boats and the 'Whalebacks' was no sinecure. Eight or more men and their kit were crammed into the equivalent of a modern single garage. Headroom was limited throughout the vessel and a 6 ft crewman could not stand erect anywhere, other than in the wheelhouse. The galley, with its paraffin stove, was just big enough for one man to work in and each of the two heads (toilets) required a great deal of contortional dexterity both to use and operate. Crews' quarters were only lit by yellowish tungsten bulbs, even in daytime, for there were no portholes. The ship's generator had to be running at all hours to provide power for the lights, the radio and the starting batteries.

Everything was permanently dank. Clothes wetted by the sea, rain, or mist, remained wet or were dried in front of the diminutive foc'sle radiant heater. Any absorbent item, no matter how carefully stowed, soon became soaked by the condensation which streamed down the insides of the hull in defiance of the ventilators. One of the consolations of putting to sea was that the hatches could be opened and clear salty air force-drafted through the launch.

The camaraderie of the sailors was similar to that of bomber crews, but much more profound. Bomber crews did not spend as many hours in the air as launch crews spent at sea, nor did they live together on their aeroplanes between times. When a bomber returned from an operation, cleaning, repairs and maintenance became the responsibility of a ground crew. Not so with the boats. The Cox'ns, deckhands, fitters and wireless operators maintained their own craft between ops. Even the tradesmen engaged ashore on major servicing alternated with seagoing crewmen.

Marine Craft personnel were arguably the most unique and special-ized of all RAF non-flying trade groups, and were certainly second only to aircrew in the operational nature of their calling. Strangely, there never was a time when *all* the sailors could be distinguished from 'ordinary' RAF tradesmen. Only those engaged on ASR during the latter part of the war displayed any identifying insignia, and even this had to be removed on posting to an MCS. In contrast, aircrew had always sported their full and half wing brévets, even if they no longer flew. Medics wore the traditional insignia on their lapels, musicians had their lyre, and all air or ground wireless operators bore a 'sparking fist' badge on their right sleeve. The men of the RAF Regiment had their own distinctive shoulder badges from inception in 1942 to the present day.

The crews of 27 ASRU were the first to adopt an outward display of élitism and pride in the maritime service. In 1941, personnel at Dover designed an Air Sea Rescue badge comprising RAF wings surmounting a lifebelt inscribed 'ASR'. It was made by Falconers of Dover at a cost of half-a-crown (12½ p). The badge was worn on the left breast pocket of the jacket. But aircrew personnel objected to the use of the coveted wings by non-flyers, and the badge was soon withdrawn as unauthor-ized. However, an official ASR badge was authorized shortly afterwards, a silhouetted 'Whaleback' worn on the upper right sleeve. It was only issued to ASR crews and did not extend to the many sailors who manned the flying boat bases and maritime training establishments. This seemed an unfair distinction, because the MCS men had an arduous job dealing with accidents and fires on flying boats and they were involved in many rescues. (The highest award won by an RAF sailor was for rescuing two men from a burning Sunderland which was likely to blow up. Coxswain Peter Anderson won the George Medal in 1950 after putting his 24 ft tender alongside the aircraft amid a sea of flaming petrol.)

The definitive pride of achievement for the boats' crews was, how-ever, nothing to do with regalia. It was successful location and rescue. Many veterans can recall specific events where success lingers satis-factorily in their memories, others remember the humorous occasions. Most knew the bitterness of failure and some can recount tales of death or injury to their own colleagues. All ex-sailors remember the boredom and discomfiture of hours of steaming, lolling at 'rendezvous' or tediously square searching and finding nothing. All can recount tales of storm-torn seas, freezing fogs, minefields, and the constant fear of air or

E-boat attacks. Unlike aircrew, the sailors did not carry out a pre-determined number of operations to complete a 'tour' before being rested. The only extended rest periods were dictated by the routine need to slip the launches for servicing and maintenance.

The 'rendezvous' system was introduced to cover bomber sorties, fighter sweeps and the 'circus' operations, in which a few bombers were used as decoys to draw the Luftwaffe into the air. The crews who drew the 'shortest straws' were briefed to maintain the positions which were furthest from base. This invariably meant they could expect to face many hours at sea regardless of weather conditions. Often, the 'rendezvous' position would be close to the enemy shore, thereby putting these crews at greatest risk.

The string of launches departed for their stations three or four hours before the squadrons set out. Those nearest to the friendly shore sailed at the same time to stand-by while the formations assembled above them. This was a particularly lengthy and often hazardous operation for the bombers and their escorts. When the USAAF daylight raids began, the first 'Crash Calls' of the day were frequently the result of collisions between formating aircraft.

Once the 'rendezvous' points had been reached, the boats stayed roughly in place throughout the duration of the raid. This was the most uncomfortable time for the sailors because of the HSL's propensity to turn beam-on to the scend and roll sickeningly or snatch violently at their anchor cables.

Depending on the target distance, many hours might elapse before the aircraft returned. Those which were damaged or low on fuel, and thus more likely to ditch, were the ones which the sailors watched most anxiously. The launches remained on station until all had been accounted for. The only event which induced them to leave their 'rendez-vous' positions was a 'Crash Call'. Boats which carried VHF sets tuned to the airband and listened to the chatter between the flyers and their bases. Sometimes this eavesdropping gave the sailors an early warning of aircraft in trouble. Frequently, enemy fighters still picked at the Allied aeroplanes as they crossed the sea and sometimes these fighters turned their attention to the launches. The slower RMLs were usually allocated a mid-position from which they could provide flexible rescue coverage and bring defensive fire power to bear in support of the lightly armed HSLs.

When the returning aircraft had landed and all hope for any missing ones had expired, the crewmen would wait attentively for the most welcome of all morse signals — 'RTB', Return To Base.

When air operations were suspended because of adverse weather, it did not necessarily bring respite for the sailors. Searches might continue for several days after a 'Mayday' had been intercepted.

An example of this occurred in mid-1941, when a Hampden bomber, on its way to attack industrial targets in the Ruhr valley, suffered engine trouble and ditched in the North Sea 60 miles from Great Yarmouth.

Although the aircrew carried out their ditching drill to the letter, they were unable to send a position report before the aircraft struck. All four crewmen clambered into their dinghy, but found that there were no paddles. Unable to control their drift, they were not discoverd until nine days later, close to the Dutch coast minefields. Lindholme gear was dropped and they were recovered, weak but alive, by an HSL from Gorleston. Search activities were thus often related to long-forgotten air operations.

Sometimes an apparently straightforward rescue mission would become prolonged for other reasons.

A 'Whaleback' crew from Dover were on 'rendezvous' near the Dutch island of Texel when they were directed to search for the crew of one of the new Lancaster bombers which had relayed its position before splashing down. The aircrew made a perfect exit to their dinghy before the aircraft sank, but were still undiscovered when a dawn mist began to shroud the sea. The HSL searched for several hours in freezing fog, until the skipper decided to cut the engines and drift until the fog cleared, reasoning that their position relative to the dinghy would remain more or less constant. A few minutes later, the sense of total isolation which fog-bound seafarers know well was disrupted by the sound of loud voices close by. The surprised sailors called out and received welcome replies from the seven men in the dinghy. It had been a lucky fluke.

Soon the survivors were aboard, dry and warm, but getting wetter on the inside as copious tots of rum were shared with the crew. Before the celebrations were over and the launch engines restarted, one of the deckhands heard more unseen voices and the sound of diesel engines. This time the language was German. The HSL was in the midst of a flotilla of E-boats. For several hours the sailors played a cat and mouse game with the enemy. The HSL would run for a few minutes, then stop engines and listen, then repeat the process again and again, all the time edging in the direction of the English coast. Once, they came under fire, tracer appearing from the fog and passing over their heads.

Eventually they were able to make a dash for it, and after some time spent lying alongside an anchored freighter, the fog lifted and they finally entered Lowestoft harbour having spent some 40 stressful, and not entirely sober, hours at sea.

Early in the war, many RAF aircraft carried homing pigeons as an alternative means of relaying information when radio emissions might be detected by the enemy. On one occasion a pigeon was able to lead to the rescue of the crew of a Bristol Beaufort. Eighteen Group in Scotland were aware that the aircraft had ditched off the north-east coast, but a subsequent search by a Catalina aircraft near the last known position had not produced any result. Then 'Winkie' arrived. When the bedraggled pigeon made landfall there was no message attached, but an expert from the RAF Pigeon Service was able to deduce from the wind speed and direction, the elapsed time and the bird's general condition, that the true location of the Beaufort was some 50 miles from the given position. It was a kind of pigeon fanciers' forensic analysis.

A full-scale search involving 15 aircraft was initiated until the survivors were spotted by a Hudson of 320 Squadron which dropped a Thornaby bag. An HSL from Blyth in Northumberland brought them home and 'Winkie' was awarded the pigeon VC.

Sadly, the sailors' tenacity and dedication to saving lives did not always pay off. Sometimes bad luck played a tragic part. In February 1942 over 100 lives were lost in one operation, despite the fact that the rescue services were virtually on the spot in strength. Eight RMLs and five HSLs had been given 'rendezvous' positions to cover an allied fighter operation when the German battleships *Scharnhost* and *Gneisenau* with the largest cruiser of the Kriegsmarine, *Prinz Eugen,* made a daring but unexpected dash from Brest through the Straits of Dover. The RAF and the Royal Navy mounted a massive but hasty campaign to try and intercept them. Two flotillas of MTBs and two MGBs were deployed, but the fastest group with the best chance of an intercept ran aground in the Thames estuary. Smaller, Napier Lion-powered MTBs at Dover were called into action, but they were only capable of 24 knots. The flotilla commander, Lieutenant Commander Pumphrey aboard MTB 221, led the boats at full emergency speed, but engine trouble slowed first one boat, then another. The escorting E-boats resisted the temptation to engage the MTBs and merely tightened the protective shield. The MTBs came under attack from enemy aircraft and one of the escorting destroyers, and were forced to fire their torpedoes at extreme range. They were only able to claim one hit, under the bridge of *Prinz Eugen.*

Swordfish pilots of the FAA made many low level attacks, while Bomber Command flew over 200 sorties. Coastal Command aircraft attacked 41 times and Fighter Command flew more than 300 escort missions. The air operations mounted by the RAF resulted in the loss of 15 bombers, 17 fighters and five aircraft from Coastal Command. Six FAA Swordfish, led by Lieutenant Commander E. Esmonde in a number of suicidal attacks, were all destroyed. Esmonde was awarded a posthumous VC. With their destroyer and E-boat screen intact, the ships cleared the Channel at an invincible 27 knots.

Air and sea searches for survivors were mounted for the remainder of the day and resumed again at dawn on the following morning. Bad sea conditions, poor visibility and enemy air activity hampered the rescue attempts. Of the 120 missing men, only five were recovered, all of whom were from Esmonde's group of 18 naval aviators. Three were retrieved by MASBs and two by MTB 45. An RML recovered two bodies, but of the other 113 naval and RAF aircrew there was no trace. When *Scharnhorst* was eventually sunk by the battleship HMS *Duke of York* at the end of 1943, the 'Channel dash' of 12 February 1941 was remembered by one British newspaper which headlined the victory, 'The Scharnhorst Doesn't Look So Gneisenau'.

Besides the losses sustained in pursuit of the battleships, a further 192 airmen engaged on other operations came down in the sea during February, of whom only 33 were located and rescued. Rescue percentages were at an all-time low. When so many flyers and sailors were making superhuman efforts to save lives, such failures were demoralizing in the extreme.

Sometimes circumstances arose where the cost to the rescue services in terms of aircraft, marine craft and personnel did not appear to justify the endeavour. In the summer of 1942 this was illustrated firstly by the attempt to locate and save Wing Commander Paddy Finucane, and secondly, by the rescue of the crew of a Coastal Command Wellington downed in the Bay of Biscay. In the former case there were fatalities among the HSL and RML crews, and in the latter more aircrew lives were lost then saved.

Wing Commander Brendan (Paddy) Finucane, DSO, DFC, had been one of the leading lights of No 65 (Spitfire) Squadron during the Battle of Britain. By July 1941 he had scored 32 confirmed kills, and in any other air force would have been accorded the title of 'Ace'. On 15 July 1942, Finucane was leading a fighter sweep over the Pas de Calais.

At approximately 1000 hrs, HSLs 138 and 140 from Dover, with RMLs 139 and 141, had proceeded to 'rendezvous' points close to the Bullock Bank in mid-Channel. The four boats then separated to take up individual positions. HSL 140 was lying to westward of the others when a message was received that a Spitfire had ditched off Le Touquet and a square search was to commence. The pilot was Paddy Finucane.

Only a few minutes into the search pattern, HSL 140 came under a surprise attack from 10 Focke-Wulf Fw 190s. The enemy aircraft approached at low level in three waves from port, starboard and astern. The launch took evasive action and the gunners returned the enemy fire whilst the Wireless Operator, Leading Aircraftman Motyer, radioed for support. The aft gunner claimed one enemy aircraft shot down before the attackers flew off towards the French coast. HSL 140 had miraculously escaped unscathed. Shortly afterwards HSL 138 and the two RMLs arrived in response to the call for help and the captains held a megaphone conference. The skipper of HSL 140, Flying Officer Shakeri, was ordered to continue the search for Finucane, but was hardly underway when the Focke-Wulfs returned. Their first pass raked the launch from stem to stern. The aft gunner was killed in his turret and several of the crew were wounded, one seriously. Nursing Orderly, Leading Aircraftman Arthur Scarrat, found his services heavily in demand.

The German fighters then turned their attention to HSL 138. In the first attack the forward gunner was hit, but continued firing. The skipper, Flying Officer W. E. Walters, was wounded and fell from the wheelhouse into the foc'sle just as a bomb hit the HSL amidships. By this time, every member of the crew had been injured and the boat was burning fiercely.

Down in the sickbay, the 'Doc', Leading Aircraftman Bill Morgan, continued to tend the casualties despite multiple leg wounds and having his forearm severed. A few minutes later, Morgan was killed by cannon shells. The launch was full of smoke and fumes and seemed to be in imminent danger of blowing up. The rest of the crew began to abandon ship, but Walters and a wounded deckhand, Aircraftman Pring, dragged the injured gunner from his turret and on to the side deck where all three men promptly collapsed. Pring was the first to recover his senses and he pushed the other two overboard before jumping clear.

The next boat to receive the attention of the German fighters was RML 139. Five passes were made, each one inflicting damage, but the naval gunners scored hits in return. A fire started in the tankspace and another in the aft compartment. Armed with pyrenes, Chief Mechanic L. Adams and Able Seaman G. Sandford squeezed themselves into the tankspace and doused the flames. The fuel tank held over 1,000 gallons of petrol, which could have exploded at any moment. The Captain, Lieutenant A. Hodgson, RNVR, later maintained that the two men saved the boat and its crew by their courageous action. As soon as the attack was over and the enemy aircraft had flown away, Hodgson's RML went to the assistance of the burning HSL 138 and picked up three survivors.

Meanwhile, further attacks had continued against HSL 140. Flying Officer Shakeri conned the launch from the port side-deck where, although dangerously vulnerable, he could see the aircraft approaching and shout the appropriate helm orders to the coxswain. In this manner he was able to save the launch. Although the attacks were pursued until she was close to the English coast, HSL 140 made it back to Dover that night.

RML 141 had stood close by throughout the battle, firing continuously at the enemy aircraft, but had not come under attack. An escort of Spitfires from 402 (Canadian) Squadron arrived to provide air cover for the crippled RML 139, whilst Lieutenant P. Williams and the crew of RML 141 retrieved the remaining men of HSL 138 from their Carley float before sinking the burning hulk. As RML 141 turned for home in the wake of the others, six Fw 190s returned and strafed it. One officer was killed and three ratings seriously wounded.

When the three boats returned to Dover, they were greeted by Commanding Officer Squadron Leader Coates and a team of naval medical officers. Bodies were extricated, the wounded taken to the hospital and those who were fit were sent on 72 hours survival leave. HSL 140 was slipped for repairs. On the following day, a Spitfire of 402 Squadron dropped a wreath on the spot where HSL 138 had sunk.

All the carnage and loss of lives had been to no avail. Paddy Finucane was not rescued. Some time afterwards it was discovered that he was already dead when the search had started. In a further cruel twist of fate, Flying Officer Walters, Master of HSL 138, was killed in an air raid whilst he was in London on sick leave following the action. The cost to the

Luftwaffe was one fighter destroyed and one damaged.

Just over a month later, more lives were lost during a rescue operation, this time in more distant waters.

Wellingtons of 172 Squadron, Coastal Command, specialized in 'Leigh light' operations by night over the Bay of Biscay. The 'Leigh light', invented by Squadron Leader H. de V. Leigh, was a searchlight linked to air-to-surface radar and used to good effect against enemy submarines. By the end of the war the Squadron achieved 27 U-boat kills, with a further 23 damaged.

On 12 August 1942, one of the Squadron's 'Wimpys' suffered engine failure and was forced to ditch in the notoriously fickle waters of the Bay. The seven-man crew took to their dinghy in steep, breaking seas. In the course of the next few hours they saw several searching aircraft and fired all of their flares without being spotted. Eventually, the crew of a Whitley saw fluorescent green dye from the dinghy's emergency pack and dropped another dinghy and a Thornaby Bag. The Wellington crew were unable to reach the dinghy, but they did succeed in grabbing the bag and its welcome contents.

The Whitley relayed the position of the survivors and a Sunderland flying boat was dispatched, escorted by fighters. On the way, the Sunderland came under attack from a single Fw 200 Kondor and had to take avoiding action, but the enemy aircraft was eventually chased off by the escort. As the Sunderland was resuming its course for Biscay, yet another Whitley spotted the dinghy. It signalled that the sea was 'slight'. This was a common mistake, as it is impossible to judge the height and movement of waves from directly above. The Sunderland pilot decided to alight near the survivors, but the deceptive sea turned out to be too rough and the big flying boat spun in, caught fire and sank.

The flying boat's inflatable burst in the impact. One courageous crew member swam through the heavy swell to try and retrieve the dinghy which had been dropped by the first Whitley. He made it, but was unable to get it back to his struggling crewmates. One by one, they drowned.

On the second day, two more Whitleys located the drifting dinghies, but before they could take any action they were attacked by enemy aircraft and one of them was shot down.

For the next two days, bad weather prevented further activity. The survivors of the Wellington, who had witnessed the series of disasters which befell their erstwhile rescuers, managed to rig a jury sail in an attempt to save themselves. Meanwhile, more help was on the way in the shape of a Royal Navy destroyer, HMS *Tynesdale*, but she was unable to locate the dinghies in the appalling weather conditions.

On the fourth day the weather abated a little and a Hudson was able to drop Lindholme gear. After retrieving it, the Wellington crew linked up with the sole survivor from the Sunderland.

At dawn on the fifth morning HSLs, RMLs and MASBs from Newlyn raced towards the search area while several attacks by Fw 190s were beaten off by Beaufighters. Finally, after six days, the survivors were picked up by two RMLs, one of which was damaged by an enemy fighter.

Seven aircrew had been saved and one Ju88 destroyed. On the debit side, one Sunderland and one Whitley had been lost in addition to the Wellington. Two other aircraft were damaged and 17 aircrew were killed. Several sailors aboard the damaged RML were wounded.

Statistically, neither this operation nor the search for Paddy Finucane had been worth the sacrifice, but in human terms, no-one questioned their justification, including all those who took part.

Two days after the Bay of Biscay disaster, the Air Sea Rescue Service met with tragedy again during the abortive Commando raid on Dieppe. The events of Operation Jubilee finally ensured that the sailors would receive heavier armament with which to defend their boats, their rescued charges, and themselves.

*Chapter 11*

# Valuable services rendered

---

*Three words extracted from the official citation for the award of the British Empire Medal (Military Division), to LAC Albert Dargue, Nursing Orderly aboard HSL 122, for his courage during the Dieppe Raid of 19 August 1942.*

The débâcle of the Dieppe Raid, Operation Jubilee, began in April 1942 with the plan for Operation Rutter. It was to be an attack in strength to determine German resistance, study the logistics of a larger assault, and establish a beachhead on the French coast. Both Stalin and Roosevelt were pressurizing Churchill to open a second front in Europe. Always willing to strike at the enemy, the Premier was none the less sceptical about Rutter. 'It will not advance the Russian or Allied cause if we embark on some operation which ends in disaster,' he said.

To alleviate his misgivings, Churchill appointed one of his protégés, Lord Louis Mountbatten, as Chairman of the Combined Operations Executive, the organization set up to co-ordinate Allied invasion plans. Mountbatten favoured the Cherbourg peninsular for the assault, but his naval adviser, Captain John Hughes-Hallet, who had devised the triumphant St Nazaire attack in March, suggested that the invasion should take the old peacetime ferry route, Newhaven to Dieppe.

Mountbatten was unable to secure a heavy bombardment from seaward to cover the assault. The First Sea Lord, Sir Dudley Pound, still smarting from the recent loss of HMS *Prince of Wales* and HMS *Repulse* to Japanese air attacks, said, 'Battleships by daylight off the French coast? You must be mad, Dickie.' Aerial bombing to soften up the defences before the ground troops landed was also written out of the plan. It was agreed instead that ground attack aircraft would be deployed at dawn, along with a large fighter cover to keep the Luftwaffe contained. Proposed bombing operations were limited to an attack on the airfield at Abbéville. The Allied Command was committed to a frontal assault with un-tried Canadian troops, on a thirteen mile front, against a heavily fortified target.

On 12 June, a practice landing was carried out near Bridport in

Dorset. It was a shambles. A second rehearsal went a little better and Mountbatten decided that, given the right conditions of weather, moonlight and tides, Operation Rutter could go ahead on 4 July. Troops were embarked on 2 July and the landing ships were assembled south of the Isle of Wight. RAF commanders were given their targets and operational orders and the RN Coastal Forces were briefed. The ASR Service and Coastguards were advised of probable intensive air activity over the Channel.

On the evening of 4 July, high winds and inclement weather took a decisive hand. Wind conditions were unsuitable for the paratroops who were to secure the flanks of the landing area and Operation Rutter was cancelled. No secret was made of the intended destination and the British press reported fairly freely in the aftermath.

Despite the doubts Churchill had expressed about Rutter, he continued to urge for a second front before the end of the year. The COE convened again, and during the discussion it became clear that there was insufficient time before autumn to start all over again with a fresh plan. Mountbatten proposed that Rutter should be reinstated. The suggestion was greeted with disbelief, but Mountbatten argued that the Germans would never believe the Allies could be crazy enough to go for Dieppe again, now that the secret of Rutter was out!

Across the Channel, Hitler's High Command had been aware of the build up of Allied invasion forces. Now, even the advantage of surprise was lost to the Allies.

In Britain, the revised Operation Rutter was renamed Operation Jubilee.

For the first time, Americans were to take part in the ground war in Europe. A token detachment of 50 US Rangers joined the assault forces. In the air, the Spitfire pilots of the 31st Fighter Group USAAF were briefed for their first self-contained offensive operation without supervision by battle-hardened RAF pilots. The new Bomber Wings were also included. After their first historic daylight raid two days before, 24 B 17s of the 97th Heavy Bombardment Group USAAF were briefed to attack the airfield at Abbéville.

British Commando veterans, Lieutenant Colonel Lord Lovat and Lieutenant John Durnford-Slater, were to lead their men in the opening assault. Lovat was unimpressed by the Canadian ground commander, General Roberts, observing that he was a 'nice fellow, but..thick..bovine and solid'. Although the plan was analysed in meticulous detail, no changes were made on the questions of seaborne or aerial bombardment.

Before dawn on 19 August, the infamous Dieppe Raid was underway.

When rendezvous positions were allocated to the ASR crews in the early hours, they were already aware that 'something big' was on because of the intense aerial activity and the sound of gunfire from across the Channel, but they had no idea that an assault on such a scale was in progress. Once at sea, they were incredulous to learn that the target was Dieppe again. 'Tin hat job,' somebody said. 'God help the pongo's.'

In all, 14 HSLs and 17 RMLs set sail for positions off the beachhead, among them HSLs 122, 123, 147 and 186, all 'Whalebacks' from Dover; HSLs 104, 106, 116 and 117 of the '100 Class', and a 'Whaleback' No 177 from Newhaven. Four boats from the Dover detachment at Ramsgate, including 120 and 127 also took part. Once again, the sailors from 'Hellfire Corner' were to go into action.

The air campaign proved to be the most successful event of the operation. Two units of ground attack Typhoons, four of Hurribombers, three of Bostons and two Blenheim squadrons undertook the tactical support role against the enemy positions. Four squadrons of Tactical Reconnaissance Mustang 1s from 39 Wing patrolled far inland to warn of any major enemy movements. Fighter cover was provided by 56 squadrons of Spitfires and six of Hurricanes. Some 3,000 sorties were flown and RAF losses were high. One hundred and six aircraft were lost, including ten of the Mustangs and eight of the bombers.

Four Flying Fortress squadrons of the US 97th BG bombed with effective accuracy and the Spitfires of the US 31st FG flew 123 sorties on 11 separate missions. Only three of the bombers suffered damage, but the inexperience of the American Spitfire pilots was underlined when eight of their 13 aircraft were shot down. (The veteran American pilots of the three Eagle Squadrons were still part of the RAF.) Luftwaffe losses amounted to just 48 destroyed and 24 severely damaged, but the Allied air forces succeeded in their prime objective of preventing the bulk of axis aircraft from attacking the surface and ground forces.

The rescue flotillas had left in the pre-dawn on a slight sea and beneath clear skies. The boats converged in mid-Channel and proceeded in a loose, widely spaced formation, to patrol a line between Dungeness and Dieppe. Thereafter, they operated independently or in pairs as the 'Mayday' calls came in.

The German bombers were late in entering the affray, not appearing until after 0900 hrs. Some of them, finding the Allied fighter screen impenetrable, sought out the unprotected surface craft farther offshore. Bombs rained down, and many of the HSLs and MTBs experienced near-misses. One launch, HSL 106, was so wracked by shock waves from an enemy bomb that it began to take on water at an alarming rate, and was obliged to head for base.

By late morning, the ground forces in Dieppe were pinned down and hopelessly overwhelmed. The invasion plan had failed and a rout was inevitable. At 1100 hrs, the order to abandon the campaign was issued. All efforts were then focused on evacuating the troops.

Beneath the aerial mêlée, amidst the confusing smokescreens and among the milling fleets of assault craft, the rescue launches and Coastal Forces' boats tried desperately to cope with the numbers of parachutes and aircraft which were raining into the sea around them. One of the launches, the original 'Whaleback' HSL 122, became the centrepiece of a drama that was to dominate the sailors' stories of the raid.

Just after 1300 hrs, HSL 122 was in a holding position in company with HSL 123, when the Wireless Operator received a signal that survivors had been spotted due south of Dungeness. Together, the HSLs hunted without success, eventually returning to their former positions. Another call was received at about 1600 hrs, when both boats were directed to look for two pilots near the French shore. The launches made for the positions at high speed, zig-zagging to avoid falling bombs. HSL 122, under the command of Flying Officer J. R. Hill, took the inshore leg, while Pilot Officer S. S. Bates aboard HSL 123 steamed a parallel course farther out. Again they were unlucky, not a trace of the pilots was found.

As HSL 122 headed back from the coast, she passed near to an outward bound convoy which was desperately fighting off an attack by up to a dozen enemy fighters. On seeing the easier target of the rescue launch, the fighters wheeled in echelon and raked the boat with gun and cannon fire. The skipper died in the first attack and the Cox'n, Sergeant F. Osborne was seriously wounded. All the crew were injured in some degree. After each pass, the enemy aircraft re-formed and swooped down again and again until their ammunition was expended. As one group of fighters left to refuel and re-arm, more took their place. The attacks lasted for an interminable one and a half hours.

To the surviving crewmen, it seemed they were the only target that the Luftwaffe could find. One after another, the boat's systems were put out of action. The guns stopped firing, the tanks were holed and the launch burst into flames. The electrics failed and the radio was shot to pieces.

During the onslaught, the wounded Cox'n died, along with the 2nd Cox'n Corporal Appleby and two MBCs, Leading Aircraftman Dennis and Leading Aircraftman Good. The two engineers, Corporals Noy and Greenhalgh, were so shocked when they dragged themselves on deck and surveyed the carnage that they decided then and there to abandon ship. They were destined to survive as POWs.

Down below in the sickbay and foc'sle, the heat from the fires was intense. The mutilated crewmen lay in their own gore or staggered mutely about, crouching, hopelessly trying to evade the flying bullets. Leading Aircraftman Albert Dargue, the 'Doc', although badly wounded himself, did what he could to tend the other crew members. Finally, the launch was bombed by Heinkel 111s and Dargue realized that there was no alternative but to abandon the burning wreck. There were only four men left alive. Painfully, Dargue dragged the other three survivors on deck and to his utmost relief, saw HSL 123 pulling alongside, despite the threat from the raging fires.

HSL 123 had been having her own problems. Shortly after she had begun to search for the downed pilots, she had come under attack from a pair of Focke-Wulf 190s and a shore battery. Two deckhands had been wounded. A few minutes later, four more Fw 190s made further strafing runs. This time the launch took evasive action and there were no casualties, but damage was inflicted on the hull and superstructure. When the German aircraft departed the Skipper, Pilot Officer Bates called for a damage assessment, and while waiting for this saw HSL 122 on the horizon, burning fiercely and still under attack. Without hesitation, he called for maximum emergency rpm and raced to the spot.

As HSL 123 approached the stricken launch, the crew could see Albert Dargue struggling with the survivors. Bates quickly circled to windward of the flames and eased his vessel alongside. Just as Dargue began to transfer the wounded across, six Fw 190s bore down from the port side and poured lethal bursts of machine-gun bullets and cannon shells into both boats.

HSL 123 caught fire, adding to the conflagration. In the radio cabin the Wireless Operator frantically summoned help. Two men were killed instantly, Leading Aircraftman Wilkins, MBC, and Leading Aircraftman Kraft, a Wireless Operator. Five others were wounded, two of them seriously.

At 1720 hrs, Bates gave the order to abandon ship. Dargue, still aboard the hulk of HSL122, made sure that his crewmates' Mae Wests were inflated, then pushed them overboard.

The enemy aircraft continued to strafe the area around the flaming HSLs for another half hour. During this time, 2nd Class Cox'n Corporal Stanley Banks swam among the exhausted survivors, comforting the injured and ensuring that their Mae Wests stayed inflated. By this time Albert Dargue was semi-comatose and weak from his wounds. All told, there were 14 men, including the badly wounded, who were left floating in their lifejackets as the launches burned out and sank.

Meanwhile, the Master of HSL 177, Flying Officer Frank Conway, had had a busy day. He and his crew had already saved one airman. For several hours, a Canadian Spitfire pilot, Pilot Officer Don Morrison, had been sharing experiences with the crew of the HSL. Earlier that morning he had shot down a Fw 190 but oil from the damaged aircraft had spread all over his windscreen and pieces of debris had caused the Spitfire's engine to stop. Morrison had baled out and, after spending only a few minutes in the water, had been picked up. The pilot was none the worse for his dip, and had remained aboard the launch while it responded to several more 'Crash Calls'. Morrison was still aboard when, after summoning nearby RML 513, Conway ordered his Cox'n to make all speed for the smoke pall of the two Dover boats.

As HSL 177 raced to the rescue she was attacked five times by enemy aircraft. Undeterred, the crew hove-to near the bobbing heads of the survivors. Fortunately, the attacking aircraft left at that moment. The deckhands lowered the scrambling net and proceeded to bring the shipwrecked sailors gently aboard.

Meanwhile, the unconscious Albert Dargue had drifted away from the other survivors. Don Morrison saw this, and without hesitation, dived overboard. The fighter pilot swam to the medic and brought him alongside the launch, where he was soon hoisted to the deck. Nine of the 14 men rescued were injured, seven of them seriously. When they had been taken below, HSL 177 made for Newhaven at full speed. One of the survivors from HSL 122, Leading Aircraftman Moss, died of his wounds the next day.

RML 513 and HSL 177 were not the only boats that went to the assistance of their comrades. Another Newhaven boat, HSL 117, also made an attempt to join in the rescue. As she approached the spot, she too came under fire from Fw 190s. Splinters flew off the hull and the launch was holed in several places, but the gunners returned the fire and no-one was hurt. At one stage, an Fw 190 made a diving pass over the launch and promptly flew straight into the sea. The crew of 117 had no time either to check the ditched enemy fighter or to help HSL 177. A 'Crash Call' was received and they were obliged to veer away from the scene and go to the aid of another pilot.

In another sector of operations, two more of the Dover boats were kept busy. HSLs 186 and 147 were heading south of Dungeness when Pilot Officer Lang aboard HSL 186 was given the position of a baled out pilot. She too was subjected to heavy fire from enemy fighters, but although two of the deckhands were wounded, the launch rescued the Canadian flyer before making for base.

When HSL 147 had separated from HSL 186, she had moved close inshore, suffering multiple air attacks and shelling from shore batteries. The Master, Flying Officer J. R. Broad, the Cox'n, Sergeant Stephens, deckhand F. Curtiss and Nursing Orderly A. Sutton on his first trip were killed outright. Two more MBCs, R. Stephenson and E. Bainbridge, succumbed in the water after the HSL sank, and five of the crew were taken prisoner. Of the two remaining crew members, there was no trace.

Farther away, Les Flower, the hero of Dunkirk, was now a Flying Officer and Master of HSL 127 from Ramsgate. The orders he had received were somewhat sketchy and he found himself outside the main theatre of activity. He was directed to a ditched aircraft, but after hours of square searching found only the body of an American airman. Meanwhile, one Spitfire pilot from the US 31st FG had the distinction of being the first USAAF flyer to be saved from the sea. He was retrieved by an RML.

On 20 August, RAF Fighter Command, the US Eighth Air Force and the ASR Service carried out extensive searches for further survivors, but none was found.

The cost of the Dieppe raid to the ASR Service was high. Three HSLs were destroyed with several more HSLs and RMLs damaged. Of the RAF and RN crews, 15 were killed, seven missing, seven captured and eight seriously wounded. The number of RAF launches lost or damaged represented over 20 per cent of those deployed and the casualties over 23 per cent. These figures were more than double the 'acceptable' attrition rate for Bomber Command aircraft.

On the positive side, 16 aircrew were rescued, although two died afterwards. The majority of them were picked up by naval craft, including Coastal Forces boats which were not part of the rescue services.

The Royal Naval assault forces lost one destroyer and 34 landing craft, while the Army left 29 battle tanks, many firearms, and a number of vehicles on the enemy shore. Only 2,078 troops returned from an embarked number of 4,963. Almost 900 were killed, the remainder being either wounded, taken prisoner, or both.

In the post-raid analysis, many aircrew complained bitterly of surface-to-air gunfire from the very fleet they were meant to be protecting. Despite the yellow banding (the 'keep clear' colour again) which was applied to the rear fuselage of all Allied aircraft, many surface ships fired at them in the confusion. Peter Scott, captain of Steam Gun Boat SGB 9, admitted that at least once during the Dieppe evacuation his gunners had fired at British aircraft. Five Allied aircraft were known to have been shot down by 'friendly' guns. Subsequently, an intensive aircraft recognition programme was introduced by the Royal Navy.

The faults were not all one-sided. Some of the RN Coastal Forces craft claimed to have been shot at by Allied planes, even after recognition signals had been transmitted. Mistakes were also made at sea. At one point Peter Scott had lined up his ship to attack what he thought were two approaching E-boats, but he was warned away by a destroyer. The two boats in his gunsights were RAF HSLs.

Many painful lessons were learned from the Dieppe raid. Earl Mountbatten was to observe in 1944, that if '...the battle of Waterloo was won on the playing fields of Eton, I say that the battle of Normandy was won on the beaches of Dieppe.'

After Dieppe, HSL armaments were extended to include the much discussed twin Vickers guns on swivel mountings. Engine room deckheads were reinforced to carry 20 mm Oerlikon cannon. Not surprisingly, among the first to adopt the new weaponry were the boats stationed around 'Hellfire Corner'.

After the raid, the RAF sailors received their share of the many decorations. Flying Officer F. Conway of HSL 177 was awarded the MBE, and crew members Corporal Felloch and Leading Aircraftman Hermitage were Mentioned in Dispatches.

Among the British Empire Medals awarded for gallantry, was one to Albert Dargue whose citation reads as follows:

## BRITISH EMPIRE MEDAL
### 1331108 Leading Aircraftman Albert Dargue
Leading Aircraftman Dargue was Nursing Orderly on a High Speed

Launch during the combined operations on 19 August 1942. In spite of his wounds, he endeavoured to carry out first aid to the wounded until he was picked up in a seriously weakened condition. The courage and valuable services rendered by Leading Aircraftman Dargue are typical of the high qualities displayed by the nursing orderlies, who have carried out hazardous operations in High Speed Launches which play an essential part in air-sea rescue.

On the 25th anniversary of Operation Jubilee, a new generation of RAF sailors took HMAFV 2760 (a descendant of the HSLs) to lay a wreath at sea off Dieppe. On board the launch were members of the Air Sea Rescue/Marine Craft Section Club and veterans of the raid. Whilst they were alongside the harbour wall, an elderly French woman hailed them and handed over a sea-boot stocking. It was clearly marked 'HSL 123'.

# The Webfoot Brigade in action

**Top** *Concrete Lighter RAF 109 built at Whitby in 1919.*

**Above** *Ex-Naval Brooke seaplane tender 153 at Basra, Iraq, 1928.*

**Right** *16 ft planing dinghy. The MBC is wearing the early version of the uniform.*

**Top** *Pinnace P4 with Brooke Motor Boat 159 and Blackburn Iris seaplane at RAF Cattewater. Note steering position of P4 abaft the funnel.*

**Above** *Pinnace 17 with forward helm position. Later pinnaces had wheelhouses.*

**Left** *37½ ft seaplane tender 201. This launch was completed before a fire destroyed the BPBC factory.*

**Top** *The ill-fated 62 ft Thornycroft HSL 151 in 1931.*

**Above** *Supermarine S6B floatplanes of the High Speed Flight at Calshot in 1931.*

**Right** *CMB on loan from the Royal Navy for the Schneider Trophy races.*

**Above** *Lawrence as T.E. Shaw on his Brough Superior.* Photo courtesy of the Bodleian Library

**Left** *Lt Col T.E. Lawrence of Arabia.* Photo courtesy of the Bodleian Library

**Below** *Shaw with Mrs Sydney Smith aboard Biscuit in Plymouth Sound.* Photo courtesy of the Bodleian Library

**Above** *ST 200 at speed, Shaw at the controls.*
Photo courtesy of R.J. Manson.

**Right** *Trials of prototype armoured target boat in the Solent.*

**Below** *50 ft seaplane refueller on trials.*

**Above left** *The first triple-engined 60 ft pinnace.*

**Above** *63 ft 'Whaleback' HSL 142 at speed off Dover.*

**Left** *64 ft HSL 116 in an early composite photograph for a recruiting poster.*

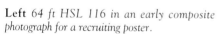

**Right** *The cramped wheelhouse of a 'Whaleback'.*

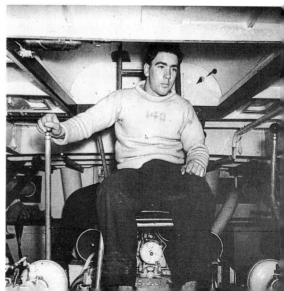

**Left** *HSL 108 in Holland after capture by the Kriegsmarine. The Germans have arrowed the gun turrets.*

**Right** *The engineers' position on 'Whaleback' HSL 140.*

**Left** *HSL 120 on a rescue operation in 1941. Note the open 'dustbin' type of gun mountings.*

**Below** *ASR Walrus amphibian rescuing a pilot.*

**Bottom** *ASR 10 rescue float being moored in the North Sea by RN Masby and HSL.*

**Right** *41½ ft seaplane tender 363. An improvement on the '200 Class', broad-beam STs were used for ASR.* Photo courtesy John Blagg

**Below** *Pinnace P 1241 converted to ASR specification.*

**Bottom** *'Miami' Class HSL 2541 in the Mediterranean.*

**Above left** *67 ft Thornycroft HSL 193 operating from Exmouth in late 1942. Photo courtesy of H.J. Field*

**Left** *63 ft HSL 142 pounding through a slight sea.*

**Below left** *Gunners manning two twin machine-guns on pedestal mountings. The turret seems to have been abandoned.*

**Above** *The end of HSL 138.*

**Right** *Survivors of HSL 138 being picked up by a Royal Navy launch.*

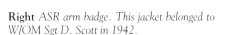

**Right** *ASR arm badge. This jacket belonged to W/OM Sgt D. Scott in 1942.*

**Left** *HSL 130 picking up a ditched Halifax crew on 9 June 1942. At this time the launch was painted with all-yellow decks.*

**Below** *ASR Pinnace P 1288.*

**Bottom** *67 ft Thornycroft HSL and seagull. 'Seagull' was the universal R/T call-sign for all RAF rescue launches.*

**Above** *The first 73 ft Vosper, HSL 2564.*

**Right** *HSL 2679 rescuing the crew of 96 BG Flying Fortress near Aldeburgh on 23 March 1944.*

**Below** *Vickers Warwick ASR1 of 275 Squadron with airborne lifeboat. The photograph dates from late 1944 and shows 'D-Day stripes'.*

**Left** *Survivors paddling towards an ABL.*

**Right** *HSLs of 33 MASRU tucked away in the German U-boat pens at Ostend.*

**Left** *HSL 2706 on fire after an erroneous attack by USAAF, 3 March 1944. The crew were rescued by HSL 2679.*

**Right** *D-type Fairmile LRRC 017 of 101 ASRMCU bound for Burma under the command of Flt Lt Saville in 1945.*

**Below right** *Sunderland of 228 Squadron, Malta, being towed ashore after attack by Messerschmitt Bf 109s in April 1941.*

**Below** *The crew of HSL 156 at 28 ASRU Newhaven.*

**Left** *Malta veterans aboard HSL 128. F Sgt George Head, Cox'n; WO Gage, SWO; F/O Joe Houghton, Master; F Sgt Nobby Clark, Fitter.*

**Left** *The scoreboard of HSL 128 painted on the inside of the sickbay hatch. Each lifebelt depicts a pick-up, the encircled dots representing the numbers of survivors.*

**Below** *HSLs 176, 175 and 182 in Algiers 1943. HSL 175 was used for covert operations.*

**Above** *Series 3 'Miami'.*

**Right** *Series 1 'Miami' of the SAAF.*

**Below** *Crew of HSL 2543 sitting on a 'Hants and Dorset'. Eric Parham is back row, second left, Jack Rogers is front row, third from left, and Jack Hill is front row, far right. Photo courtesy of A.J. Hill*

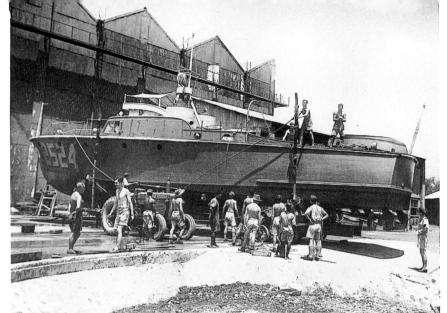

**Above** *HSL 2524 slipped at Jui near Freetown in 1944. F/O Tom Carroll is standing with hands on hips.* Photo courtesy of T.M. Carroll

**Left** *HSL 2524 approaching Sunderland 'K204'.* Photo courtesy of T.M. Carroll

**Below** *70 ft Canadian Power Boat Company HSL in India, 1944. The Selman ancestry is obvious.*

**Above** *HSL 2557 was converted to RTTL after the war.*

**Right** *Remote Control Target-Towing Launch 2688.*

**Below** *40 ft 'Narrow Beam' seaplane tender in post-war overseas colours.* Photo courtesy of J. Blagg

**Left** *23 ft wireless servicing tender.*

**Right** *41¹/₂ ft Seaplane Tender 357 from Bridlington in 1952. Cox'n F Sgt Banks recovering a girl swimmer in heavy seas on a lee shore.*

**Below** *The casualty was carried ashore, but died later. Note the clearly marked Crash Kit in the cockpit stern.*

**Above** *24 ft Marine Tenders, refuellers and GS pinnace at RAF North Front, Gibraltar in 1950. The Sunderland is from 202 Sqn.*

**Right** *60 ft GS pinnace in post-war finish at Aden.*

**Top** *RSL 1593 (previously ST 1593) at 1105 MCU Porthcawl in 1956.*

**Above** *Inshore Rescue Craft 3000 on trial in Gibraltar.*

**Left** *Wessex helicopter with a survivor in a single strop.*

**Right** *Winchman with a survivor in a Robinson stretcher.* Photo courtesy of C.J. Allen

**Right** *RTTL 2555 after the fire.*

**Below** *The first Mk IA RTTL with three Napier Sea Lions. After conversion to Griffons the engine room deckhead was raised.*

**Left** *RTTL 2753 from 1110 MCU Immingham in 1956 before conversion to Griffons. Note the flat-sided superstructure.*

**Below** *Ali-top RTTL 2751 after Griffons were fitted, hence the raised engine room.*

**Bottom** *RTTL 2760 off Plymouth Hoe.*

**Above** *An interesting comparison between RTTLs Mk II, 2758 and Mk I, 2631. The picture shows how closely Vospers followed the 'Hants and Dorset' design.*

**Right** *All aluminium prototype RTTL 2762E.*

**Below** *RTTL 2772E after the number change and the deletion of the 'E' when the hull had been re-skinned with mahogany planking.*

**Above** *Thornycroft 43 ft RSL Mk II. RSL 1657 operating from Porthcawl.* Photo KMB

**Below** *The elegant D-boats of Sylt, 1956.*

**Bottom** HMS Bridlington *Offshore Minesweeper J 65.* Photo courtesy of J. Blagg

**Above** *HMAFV* Bridlington *in Malta,* *October 1955.* Photo courtesy of J. Blagg

**Right** *LCM 7083 at Hittadu, Addu Atoll* *1959.* Photo KMB

**Below** *RAF Tug 'Tanac 25' with dumb barges* *at Gan quay. RTTLs 2747 and 2748 are in* *the background.* Photo KMB

**Left** *Flt Lt Duncan Gibbons and F Sgt Peter Munnion on the bridge of RTTL 2767, Khormaksar, Aden, in 1964.* Photo KMB.

**Below** *The recovery of Argosy 413 at the MCS slipway, Aden.* Photo KMB

**Bottom** *Z12 alongside the quay at Masirah, 1964.* Photo KMB

**Right** *RTTL 2761 from Bahrain.* Photo
courtesy of R. Symons

**Above** *Pinnace P 1378 towing MV Podromos
after HMAFV 2769 had rescued the crew.*

**Right** *The 'wardroom' at Limassol after the
bombing.* Photo courtesy of R.J. Manson

**Above** *Two Hunters of No 1 Fighter Squadron and HMAFV 2753 escort RMS Queen Mary in 1967 as she leaves Gibraltar for the last time.* Photo courtesy of R. J. Manson

**Left** *The view of HMAFV 2754 from HMS Keppel.*

**Below** *Interim Recovery Vessel HMAFV 5010 abeam of HMS Dolphin in 1969. This IRV was previously HMS Bottisham and IRV 5000.*

Top HMAFV Seal, *the first of the LRRSCs.*
Above HMAFV Seagull. *She was plagued by cylinder head problems and smoked profusely.*
Below *The first Mk III RTTL,* HMAFV Spitfire.

**Top** HMAFV Spitfire *with modified bow and cutaway gunwhales.*

**Above** HMAFV Sunderland. *The second of the Mk III RTTLs, built after the design problems had been resolved.*

**Left** *Sgt (later S Ldr) R F Moore, BEM.* Photo courtesy of R. F. Moore

# Chapter 12

# You can see more from the top of a Hants and Dorset

*A slogan which applied equally to the BPBC 68 ft HSL and the vehicles of the local bus company from which the new double-decker launch took its nickname.*

The arrival of the USAAF and the revised plans for the rescue services meant that the establishment for HSLs needed to be upgraded urgently. The numbers which had been authorized at the end of 1941, ie 76 in service, plus a reserve of 20, were stepped up by a further 20, bringing the target figure to 116. The actual number of HSLs available by August 1942 was a mere 56 in the home islands and nine overseas. The conversion and new-build pinnaces to ASR configuration had proceeded very slowly. Only 22 craft had entered service, whereas 80 were required. In the autumn, it was decided that a further 136 HSLs would also be required abroad as part of the world-wide expansion.

New 'Whalebacks' were still coming off the line at the Power Boat Company's works at Hythe and Poole and 'Miamis' were filtering through from the US for overseas stations, but obviously more resources were necessary.

The BPBC were at full capacity, because in addition to building HSLs, they were still struggling to keep up with other RAF orders. Alongside Admiralty orders for MASBs and MGBs, 41½ ft seaplane tenders, new 24 ft marine tenders, planing dinghies and bomb dinghies were all being built. The Admiralty and the Purchasing Commission continued to ignore the potential of Scott-Paine's Canadian factory.

The Marine Craft Policy Committee had been both active and intuitive. Boatbuilders who had been approached previously, were again invited to submit HSL prototypes early in 1942. Among them were the two ultimately successful firms, John I. Thornycroft and the Vosper Company, both of whom produced designs which were based on hulls already in production for the Royal Navy.

The below deck layouts and the superstructure arrangements of the new boats were very similar to the pattern established by the 'Whalebacks'. The reverse sheer of the deck and the 'hump' were not in evidence, but a family likeness was clearly discernible.

Both Vosper and Thornycroft diverged from the 'Whaleback' concept in one major area. Experience had taught the RAF sailors that a high top speed was less desirable than the ability to maintain a moderate speed in a seaway without undue hardship on hull or crew. Both types attained this objective and were generally located in the rougher northern waters and the notorious Western Approaches.

The Thornycroft HSL was 67 ft long with a straight sheer and a beam of 15 ft. The beam was some 18 in less than the 'Whaleback' and was part of an endeavour to present a more slender and sea-kindly hull shape. Gun turrets were deck-mounted either side of the wheelhouse with a third turret aft. Of the 104 boats built to the Thornycroft design, half were powered by the usual trio of Napier Sea Lions and half by a pair of Thornycroft RY12 petrol engines of 650 hp. Maximum speed of this latter type was about 25 knots, but the Napier version had a marginally higher top speed. Although modifications and improvements to the RY12s had been introduced, they continued to be plagued by troubles. More 67 ft Thornycroft HSLs were used by the RAF than any other type, but they did not stir the imagination as the 'Whalebacks' did. With the latter referred to as the 'Spitfire of the Sea', the Thornycroft boat was at least entitled to the tag of 'Hurricane'.

Thornycrofts were built during the four year period of 1942 to 1945 and were numbered in batches, 191–9, 2500–514, a single 2563, 2583–92, 2632–41, 2651–76 and the last batch, 2717–37.

Vosper's launch appeared almost identical to the Thornycroft, and incorporated a similar 'squared off' version of the 'Whaleback' super-structure, but differed in the sheer line. The Vosper deck curved in a more conventional concave style. The gun turrets were deck mounted in cylindrical 'dustbins' similar to the Thornycroft arrangement.

Vosper HSLs were 73 ft long with a 16 ft beam and were based on the 'compromise hard chine' form of the Fairmile MTB. This was a combination of hard chine for speed and round bilge for sea-keeping, but they had a poor reputation for handling in a following sea. These craft could achieve a maximum speed of 27 knots with their two RY12 main engines. They were also fitted with two 65 hp Vosper/Ford V8 cruising engines, which together gave a creditable 10 knots. The cruising engines proved useful in extending the range of the launches when on passage or prolonged square searches. Some of the crews referred to them as 'spares' in view of the troublesome main engines.

Due to the builders' heavy commitments to the Royal Navy, only 15 73 ft HSLs entered RAF sevice. The number group being HSL 2564–78.

While Thornycroft and Vosper concentrated on their tried and tested hull designs, George Selman at the BPBC was able to adopt a more expansive approach. In late 1941 and early 1942, with the factory already producing the current HSLs and with 'Scotty' on the far side of the Atlantic, Selman was free to exploit his own creativity. His close working relationship with the MCPC enabled him to conceive an original design close to the sailors' ideal.

The resulting 'Hants and Dorset' was a big and beamy boat by comparison with all other HSLs. Sixty-eight ft long and just over 17 ft at the broadest point of the beam, the interior seemed palatial after the confined space of other types. This spaciousness was further enhanced by Selman's concept of placing a full height deckhouse above the main deck instead of the customary half-height, recessed deckhouse. It contained a large wheelhouse and chart area, a full conning bridge, wireless cabin and gun alley, all within a single modular unit. Two forward gun turrets were incorporated with only their plexiglass cupolas projecting above the deckhouse.

At the after end of the superstructure, wide foldable double doors provided access to a companionway which led down to a large sickbay and Master's cabin. Farther forward, access to the galley and crews quarters was via a watertight bulkhead door. Another watertight door opened to the crew head and forepeak stowage.

With the exception of the engine room, which was separated from the forward sections by the tank space, all working and accommodation areas of the vessel were interconnected. The sailors were able to move from any part of the deckhouse, via a hatch and ladder to any part of the lower deck without venturing outside. In severe weather it was only the engineers and the rear gunner who were obliged to cross the open deck to and from their action stations.

A rear gun turret and, latterly, a 20 mm Oerlikon cannon were surface-mounted on the engine room deckhead. This in turn provided for a more spacious engine room with greater headroom. The propulsive power was a triple Napier Sea Lion installation with the wing engines on direct drive to the outboard propellers and the centre engine transmitting via a Vee-drive to the centre shaft as in the 'Whaleback'. The fitter had a padded and armoured seat over the centre engine gearbox, from whence he could easily reach the throttle trimmers and the gear levers. The throttles were controlled from the wheelhouse, leaving fine tuning and synchronization to the engineers. A telegraph indicator was mounted on the forward engine room bulkhead. The cox'n 'rang' for 'ahead', 'neutral', and 'astern' on any of the three engines as necessary.

The Power gearboxes fitted to the Napier engines were described as having a positive 'ahead' gear and a manual 'astern'. When each 3 ft gear lever was placed in the 'ahead' position, it stayed there until it was pulled out again. The manual reverse, however, was a different matter. Considerable strength was needed to hold it in engagement. A call for three 'asterns' would only be made in dire emergency, or more commonly when the skipper had made a misjudgement! To hold all three levers in astern required an application of body weight involving both hands and a buttock! This was no mean feat in a heavy seaway and the engineer would invariably become as heated as the engine room and hurl obscenities at the man on the bridge. Fortunately, engine noise prevented these from reaching their target — most of the time. Traditionally, the skipper would buy pints for the engine room crew at the first opportunity afterwards. The tradition prevailed until the last 'Hants and Dorset' was taken off charge in 1962.

George Selman's hull was advanced for its day. The chines were lifted at the forward end to create a deep vee forefoot and a soft wave entry, twisting to an almost flat planing section aft. The 68-footers did pound, and if they left the water they slammed down very hard indeed, but compared to the 'Whalebacks' the ride was much less uncomfortable.

The new boats were heavier than the 'Whalebacks' and absorbed more of the available power to maintain a planing condition. At 28 knots, their top speed was lower by almost 10 knots, but they could hold that speed in rough seas. The 'Whalebacks' higher speed had been achieved by a combination of a shallow vee hull shape and low weight. The bone-breaking slamming of the earlier boat was partially attributable to the fact that the crews tended to 'over drive' them, especially when responding to 'Crash Calls'. If prudence dictated that speed should be kept 'off the plane' in bad weather, the sailors ignored it and pressed on in great discomfort. This meant that to maintain even 20–25 knots, the physical stresses on crews, hulls and, significantly, survivors could be extreme.

When the sailors experienced the relative comfort of the new launch at similar speeds in like conditions, they were highly impressed and immediately thought that the 'Hants and Dorsets' should have more power to go faster! (Perhaps their perception was right. See later chapters 17 and 18 about Mk II RTTLs.)

HSL 2552, the first of the 'Hants and Dorsets' arrived at Calshot in October 1942 and was greeted with murmurs of discontent among the sailors. The boat looked top heavy and ungainly. Gone were the low, rakish and friendly lines of the familiar 'Whalebacks' and Thornycrofts. One webfooted wag commented that the new boat made a bigger target. Another observed dryly that with so much top hamper, you could always sail it home if the engines failed. The last comment proved to have some basis in truth, for the high superstructure made the boat windborne and care had to be taken when manoeuvring in strong cross winds. Navigators had to allow for an element of leeway due to the 'sail' effect.

Despite their initial misgivings, the sailors soon adapted to this new concept. The spaciousness and comfort were appreciated, the sea-worthiness and apparent indestructibility respected, and even the height of the deckhouse was found to have some virtue. As one deckhand put it after his first spell as lookout on the bridge, 'D'you know Skip — from up there you can see for bloody miles.'

None the less, the new boats did not endow the crews with the ability to see in the dark. Thornycroft HSL 2609 was the first launch to be fitted with radar, but it was not original equipment on the 'Hants and

Dorset' class. This was illustrated rather graphically by the prototype, HSL 2552, shortly after it had entered service. The launch went aground outside Aberdeen harbour whilst steaming at 15 knots in pitch darkness. All the engines stopped and it careered over on to one chine. Fortunately, the grounding had happened at low tide, but as the flood came the HSL started making water before righting. When the tide had risen enough, the two wing engines could be run but the propellers had been damaged and one had penetrated the hull. Despite the problems, the crew nursed the boat to its quay whereupon it was towed to a local yard and lifted out. The damage to the projecting underwater gear was serious, but the hull had stood up well to the collision and proved the inherent strength of the new HSL quite convincingly.

Selman's 'Hants and Dorset' made the Mobile Rescue Units of the Mediterranean and post D-Day era possible. It was the only one of the 10 different wartime HSL types to be retained by the RAF in the big sell-off after VJ Day. Many 'Hants and Dorsets' continued to give excellent service into the late 1950s and even the very fast Rolls-Royce Griffon-powered launches which replaced them were a direct and recognizable derivation of the Selman original.

A total of 90 'Hants and Dorsets' were built at Hythe and Poole in the years 1942–6. Serial numbers were, 2552–62, 2579–83, 2593–2606, 2619–31, 2677–2716, 2739–46.

An incredible 69 boats were produced in 1943 alone, with the balance of all but seven completed during 1944. Of these seven, the last two were delivered in March 1946. A re-assessment of requirements made in November 1944 led to the cancellation of an order for a further 32 boats, Nos 2747–78. Most of these numbers were eventually allocated to MKs IA and Mk II RTTLs over 10 years later. *

---

*By the time HSL 2552 entered service, the RAF had reorganized the system for the numbering of various types of marine craft. With so many boats allocated, including the increased numbers of pinnaces, scores of new seaplane tenders, marine tenders, wireless tenders, GS dinghies, refuellers, bomb scows, ferry boats, etc, the simple three-digit series was leading to confusion and duplication.

Soon after the first batch of nine Thornycrofts were taken on charge in July 1942, it was decided that each category of boat would be allocated a numbering series that would identify it. Thus all new HSLs were given four-digit numbers commencing at No 2500. Pinnaces commenced with No 1100 and seaplane tenders with No 1500. The system for all other craft was also revised.

The outcome of the revision meant that the last three-digit 'Whaleback' was No 190 which was followed by Thornycrofts Nos 191–9. Thereafter, the next HSLs were from Thornycroft batch, Nos 2500–514. These were followed by a delivery of 'Miamis' to overseas stations, Nos 2515–45. The last group of 'Whalebacks' before the factories rejigged for 'Hants and Dorset' production were numbered 2546–51.

*Chapter 13*

# The wide blue
# yonder

*The USAAF flyers soon discovered that the heroic words of their song bore little
relationship to the miserable reality of air fighting in the ETO. The American
crews found themselves in a hornets nest of flak and fighters.*

With the establishment of the US 8th Army Air Force in 1942,
the US Commanders and the DGAS met to discuss air-sea
rescue for American aircrews. The meeting took place on 8
September, just two days after the USAAF had sustained its first bomber
losses over Europe, an event which must have added poignancy to the
talks. Two B 17s had been shot down whilst returning from a raid over
Meaulte. One of these, piloted by Leigh E. Stewart of the 92nd BG, was
seen heading for the British coast with five enemy fighters in pursuit.
Although HSLs were quickly scrambled and searched for several hours,
no trace of the aircraft or its crew were found.

The meeting covered all aspects of ditching procedures, survival
training, survival equipment and search and rescue. It was agreed that
the existing RAF and RN services would be extended and that at some
future date, the US would provide additional deep search air support.
This agreement was vindicated a month later on 9 October, when the
first successful pick up of a US bomber crew was achieved.

The 8th Air Force lost four aircraft from the 105 that set out on its first
large-scale strategic daylight raid of the war. The targets were the steel
and locomotive factories in Lille. After an inaccurate attack, the home-
bound bombers met with heavy fighter opposition and two of them
were brought down over the Channel. The first of these was another
aircraft from the 92nd BG which, despite an extensive search by Spitfires,
was not located. The second B 17, from the 301st BG, failed to shake off
an Fw 190 which scored several hits, causing the bomber to lose power.
The aircraft was shedding height rapidly when the pilot, 1st Lieutenant
Donald Swenson, unable to use the intercom, went to each crew
member in turn and told them to prepare themselves for ditching. There

was a 10–15 ft swell running and Swenson was obliged to slam the aeroplane down between crests and hope for the best.

Although the radio operator transmitted a 'Mayday' it is not clear whether the message was received. Various stories pertained that the crash was observed by a patrolling Spitfire or by the crew of an HSL, but whatever the facts, a launch from 27 ASRU was dispatched.

Aboard the doomed bomber there were problems. The impact when the aircraft hit the sea injured two of the crew, but as the aircraft settled, all 10 scrambled out through the gun hatch in the radio cabin or via the cockpit windows. Only one of the two liferafts inflated properly, the other having been damaged by shells from the enemy fighter. The bomber disappeared beneath the waves in the alarmingly short time of 1½ minutes.

Once in the water, the flyers discovered that their Mae Wests would not keep them afloat in their heavy, waterlogged sheepskin clothing, and they spent several minutes helping each other to wriggle out of their flying jackets. Only three men were able to sit in the serviceable rubber raft; the others remained in the sea clinging on. Potentially, the chances of survival were slim. The sea temperature was very low and the crew had no time to gather any of their vital survival equipment before they vacated the sinking bomber. However, the HSL was with them in 15 minutes. The heavy sea conditions complicated the pick-up, but the first rescue of a US bomber crew was completed to everyone's satisfaction.

This event highlighted both the inadequacy of American aircrew training on ditching procedures and the fact that US aircraft were not as well provided for as their RAF equivalents.

On 3 January 1943 85 B 17s and B 24s set out to bomb the submarine pens at St Nazaire. Seventeen aircraft aborted for one reason or another, but the bombing proved to be fairly accurate with some scattering due to cloud cover over the target. Seven aircraft were shot down by flak or fighters, one of them ditching after four of the crew had baled out over the sea. They were never found. Another B 17, *Sons of Fury* from the 306th BG, was observed to sink rapidly with the mid-upper guns still firing as the water closed around the red hot barrels. The gunner, Technical Sergeant Arizona Harris, and all the crew perished. A further 47 bombers were damaged with a total of two crewmen killed and seven wounded. Two formations became lost on their return journey and had to attempt landings at various emergency fields. Two of the disorientated bombers ran out of fuel and crash landed with casualties. It was known as the 'Notorious St Nazaire Raid'.

American attacks on U-boat bases at St Nazaire, Lorient, La Pallice and Bordeaux had commenced in the previous November and were part of an ongoing campaign to reduce losses of Allied shipping in the Atlantic convoys. The US bomber crews dubbed St Nazaire 'Flak City'.

At this time the US Army Air Force had not yet been sent over

Germany. They were using the so-called 'soft' targets of occupied France and, later, German harbours, to try out their formation tactics and test their armaments. In all respects they had much to learn and no US aircrew had then achieved an American 'tour' of 25 missions. 'Soft' target seemed an unfair description, particularly as nine aircraft and over 75 men were lost on that one day, but by comparison RAF Bomber Command had been in action for over three years and had already lost 20,000 men, either dead, maimed or captured. The RAF had first bombed Berlin almost two and a half years earlier and had maintained constant night attacks against heavily defended German targets ever since. The first 'Thousand Bomber Raid' against Cologne had taken place 10 months before, with a loss of 51 aircraft. Many Bomber Command crews were already on their second or third voluntary 'tour' of 30 operations. Shortly before a US bomber crew completed its first 'tour' of 'soft' targets, Wing Commander Guy Gibson's legendary 617 Squadron had breached the Mohne and Sorpe dams on the famous raid of 16 May 1943.

The first US aircraft to complete 25 missions was the *Memphis Belle* which did so in a blaze of publicity in late May 1943. The *Belle's* penultimate mission was filmed in colour by William Wyler and this was the inspiration for the totally fictitious 1990 cinema epic. An HSL from Gorleston saved nine men from B 17 *Mersa Lass* during this operation.

The publicity surrounding American air activities in late 1942 and early 1943 was essential to win over US public opinion. The US air crews may have been novices but their courage was beyond doubt, and with RAF help they learned quickly. Before long, the USAAF was suffering more losses than all other Allies combined and it became one of the biggest customers of the ASR Service.

The rising numbers of aircraft lost through lack of training and non-adherence to emergency procedures became a serious matter for the Eighth Air Force command. Both the B 17D and E Fortresses and the B 24 Liberator were death traps in a ditching situation compared with RAF bombers. The later B 17F and G models were better in this respect, but little could be done to modify the B 24, owing to its high wing and its semi-exposed bomb bay. On-board survival equipment was improved once it was accepted that a ditched crew could expect to spend at least several hours in their dinghy before being picked up. At the same time, the ASR establishment for Walrus and Catalina amphibians was increased and the airborne lifeboat was introduced.

The original concept for an airborne lifeboat had come from George Selman in 1939. He had designed a boat to be carried by, of all things, Heinkel He 59 floatplanes (of the Swedish Air Force). The idea was resurrected by Group Captain Waring, the officer behind the Lindholme gear. Waring and a Naval Lieutenant Boatbuilder, Lieutenant Robb, designed a lightweight wooden boat of 30 ft which was both aerodynamic in shape to be carried by an aircraft and hydrodynamically stable to perform well at sea. Early ABLs were fitted with an Austin engine, and later alloy-hulled versions with Vincent motor cycle engines.

Masts, sails, food, water, clothing and radio location gear were stowed aboard. The ABLs were dropped by a cluster of parachutes with an ingenious combination of automatic devices to eject the parachutes when the lifeboat hit the surface, stream drogues to prevent drift and fire lifelines for survivors to grab.

The first ABLs were built by the yachtsman and naval architect Uffa Fox, and after the war a large number of them were modified to become a very successful class of fast sailing dinghy.

To help with the training of American airmen, the RAF set up a sea survival school in Blackpool. The school opened in May 1943 and operated in conjunction with the HSLs of 52 ASRU from Fleetwood. Besides lectures and practice emergency drills, the aircrews were instructed in inflating and climbing into their liferafts and systematically working all the aids and equipment stowed therein.

After several 'dry' runs, the airmen would be taken out to sea by an HSL and dumped overboard to practise their new-found knowledge in the real environment. Once it had been established that the flyers were safely aboard their life-rafts, the attendant launch would steam away over the horizon just long enough for the airmen to feel the loneliness and isolation which they would experience in reality. 'Wet Dinghy Drill' was a wretched, if invaluable, part of the training schedule. Quite often, the flyers would be seasick long before they were in the water. Every RAF sailor who has been involved in wet drills has heard pale-faced aircrew say, 'I wouldn't have your job for anything!' After the airmen were picked up they were invariably given a tot from the skipper's rum barrel.

On 26 July 1943, one B 17 crew had either not yet received their training or they chose to ignore it when they ditched after a raid on the synthetic rubber plants in Hannover. Altogether, three aircraft crash landed in the sea that afternoon, two of them close to Sheringham and Overstrand, which kept the ASRUs at Gorleston and Lowestoft busy until all 20 men were rescued.

The third B 17, from the 94th BG, ditched near the Dutch coast 125 miles from Cromer. Although there was plenty of time, the aircrew completely disregarded their ditching instructions. An HSL from Gorleston was dispatched and due to the mirror-like sea conditions, was able to reach the aircraft in about three and a half hours. When the launch arrived, the sailors found the entire bomber crew sitting astride the still floating wreck, swigging brandy and whooping with joy at the sight of their rescuers.

The Cox'n of the HSL, Harry Field, skilfully placed the bows of the boat between the wing and the fuselage of the aircraft whereupon the grateful airmen stepped aboard the launch without even getting their feet wet! Within five minutes, the B 17's nose dipped and it slipped beneath the waves.

Shortly after the HSL had left the scene and the rum barrel had been drained, the launch was hailed by an RN minesweeper, the crew of which passed bottles of Scotch and cartons of cigarettes to the 10 Americans. Suitably re-stocked with goodies, the party warmed up as the launch sped for its base. The bomber crew decided that they wanted to act like 'real' survivors. They gave their leather flying jackets to the sailors and promptly donned all the white sweaters, grey trousers and other survival clothing that was aboard. As the HSL neared the harbour entrance, the inebriated airmen dragged out all the boat's signal flags and proceeded to rig them around the launch in their own interpretation of 'dressing overall'.

While the HSL was returning to base, the Vice-Admiral, Commander-in-Chief Nore heard the news of all three successful rescues. He was already on an inspection tour with his retinue of senior brass and decided that he would greet the incoming HSL and its passengers as a 'hands across the sea' gesture. When the launch pulled alongside, looking for all the world like a tripping boat on a bank holiday, the Americans scrambled ashore, singing, dancing and generally creating havoc among the dignitaries. The Captain of the B17 grabbed the Vice-Admiral and, to the delight of the onlookers, proceeded to jig around the quay.

Next day, when the furore had died down, Harry Field received a very curt letter informing him that spirits should be issued with more moderation. By then, he also had in his possession a one hundred Franc note from the B17s 'escape money'. The pilot had written his name and address on it and recorded, 'Rescued 7.45 pm. 7/26/43'. The name of the bomber was also inscribed: 'Destiny Tot'!

Sometimes, unlike the crew above, ditched airmen did not have time to indulge in their survival skills.

Cox'n Eric Blackman recalls a pick up where 'Hants and Dorset' HSL 2690 was outward bound from Lowestoft on a North Sea 'rendezvous' when the launch was suddenly straddled by bomb blasts. The crew had no idea where they came from, but did gather their wits in time to see a B17 dive into the sea about half a mile away. As they veered towards the spot, one of the sailors saw someone in the water. Scrambling nets were lowered and an American Sergeant was pulled aboard. He was both amazed and gratified at the speed of the pick up. After he had gathered his breath, he told the launch crew that nine men had been on board the aircraft and after dumping their bomb load, at least six had parachuted to safety. The skipper of the HSL requested search assistance from HSL 2563 and square searches led to the recovery of seven survivors. HSL 2690 received a recall, but although two other HSLs continued searching for a further five hours the ninth airman was not found.

There were other, more tragic, circumstances when aircrews had no chance to put their training to good effect.

On 29 July 1943, 139 B17s bombed Kiel whilst another 54 attacked the Heinkel aircraft factory at Warnemunde. Having already saved the crew of a 385 BG Fortress which aborted before the mission, the Gorleston HSLs were once again off the Cromer coast near Sea Palling, to cover the bomber streams on their return. As the smaller group headed home, the sailors noted with relief that there were no 'holes' in the formation; all had returned safely. Then, right above them Harry Field's crew saw a 96th BG aircraft collide with a 388th BG plane. There was a massive explosion followed by a hail of debris splashing into the sea. The HSL dashed about looking for survivors, but there was no trace of the aircraft or of the 20 men who had manned them, except one torso in a leather jacket. The remains of the airman were taken aboard the launch.

All that could be found in the man's pockets was a note of his mother's address and £90 in sterling. Harry returned these to the US liaison office and in due course received a letter of thanks from the mother, who was at least comforted to know that her son had been looked after.

In September, when 388 B 17s took off to bomb an instrument bearings factory in Stuttgart, bad weather and cloud cover forced the formations to seek alternative targets of opportunity. Four bombers landed in Switzerland and one crashed into a lake. The shorter range aircraft of the 1st Bomb Division ran out of fuel on the homeward leg, eight of them crash-landing in southern England and 12 crashing into the sea. All 118 men were picked up by the RAF sailors. It was an outstanding achievement.

During the period August 1942–8th May 1945 (VE day), 1,547 bomber crewmen of the US 8th Air Force were saved, mostly from B17s. Proportionally fewer B24 Liberators ditched, their pilots clearly preferring to belly down on land, for of the B24s that did go down in the sea the majority had the notation 'Crew lost' on record. In virtually every case where a rescue was effected, only a part of the crew was saved. American fighter pilots also seemed to avoid ditching or baling out into the water, but of those that did a high proportion were rescued, several of them from near the enemy coast.

In May 1944 the Americans kept their promises and lent practical support to the rescue services. The 65th Fighter Wing Detachment, generally known as the Air Sea Rescue Squadron, was formed at Boxted in Essex. The unit was equipped with 25 war-weary P47D Thunderbolts which were fitted with two 108 gallon wing tanks, a container for two RAF 'M' type dinghies and four smoke marker bombs. At a later date this configuration was changed, as it was found to have an adverse affect on the aeroplanes' stability. In January 1945 the unit was moved to Halesworth in Suffolk and re-designated No 5 Emergency Rescue Squadron. Thirteen Catalina amphibians (OA–10A) were added to the strength, and in March an ex-457 BG Fortress was introduced to carry airborne lifeboats. The deep search units flew a total of 3,616 sorties, of which no less than 3,520 were effective, against the loss of one P47 and two OA–10As. The Squadron was disbanded in May 1945.

With all the resources the US forces had at their disposal and their customary proclivity for being self-supporting, it was considered a compliment that the Americans so unquestioningly relied upon the British Air Sea Rescue Service. Other than meeting their deep search obligation, it did not even occur to the US High Command to set up an independent system.

# Chapter 14

# Second front

*With the Atlantic campaign won and the bomber offensive intensifying, the 2nd Tactical Air Force was created to support the Normandy invasion. Meanwhile, scores of RAF marine craft were directed to the south coast of England for this largest seaborne assault in history. Operation Overlord: D–Day.*

T he available figures for all allied aircrew rescued at sea in the year ending December 1943 showed 524 from a total of 1,346. It was a respectable achievement of about 40 per cent, but this could be interpreted to mean that the rescue services were *unsuccessful* in 60 per cent of their efforts. This was patently not true, for within this larger balance were all those aircrew who disappeared without trace, were picked up dead or in pieces, or died shortly after being rescued and were buried at sea.

One of the most disturbing aspects of the task of air-sea rescue was the frequency with which the sailors were obliged to recover bodies, many of which were burnt or mutilated. Not all were aircrew, for there were many victims of the sea war.

After a few days in the sea, bodies became bloated and the faces and exposed flesh often ravaged by fish, sea creatures and birds. Such corpses were always difficult to handle and yet they had to be brought aboard, identified where possible and either buried at sea or returned to base. Occasionally, the decomposition or mutilation was so severe that there was nothing recognisable left to recover.

Although a smattering of effective rescues helped to sustain the sailors through the tedious or the more macabre aspects of their job, competition also played a part. There was always a healthy rivalry between adjacent ASR units and between boats on the same unit. Pick-ups, sea time and top speeds were the main points of contention, but all the sailors were united in their derision for the RAF and RN airmen who flew the rescue Walruses. So often, one of these diminutive amphibians would alight on the water and scoop up survivors just as an HSL approached, perhaps after hours of steaming. The consolation for the launch crew was that the airmen had been saved, but all too frequently the Walrus pilots over-estimated their own capabilities and the aircraft were damaged by rough seas or unable to take off with the extra weight of survivors.

The ASR pilots took many risks to save lives, but sometimes the keenness of the flyers put other lives in jeopardy. This happened to the crew of HSL 2564, the first 73 ft Vosper boat, based in Scotland. Bad weather always played a part in thwarting efforts to maintain success rates during the winter months, but in these northern waters adverse conditions could almost be guaranteed for 99 per cent of the year.

Flight Lieutenant Alec Hugget and his crew (which included deckhand Alistair MacLean) had collected the brand new HSL from Calshot and sailed her up to their base at Port Ellen on the Isle of Islay, where they familiarized themselves with the boat and the local geography. Twenty miles to the south was Rathlin Island on the north eastern tip of Northern Ireland, and to the west the grey Atlantic. The FAA base at Machrihanish on Kintyre was to the east and it was from here, in November 1943, that an aircraft was reported missing.

With another boat in support, HSL 2564 searched in the area of the aircraft's last known position. The air temperature was near freezing, visibility was poor and a high sea was running in a strengthening wind. Both launches were forced to return soon after dusk, without success.

Next day, with the wind blowing half a gale and amid frequently violent squalls, Hugget searched in a different area and succeeded in locating the three FAA men who had taken to their dinghy. They were cold and weak and had great difficulty catching a heaving line which was thrown. In the steep waves, the dinghy was above the deck level at one moment and way below it the next. One of the survivors managed to grab the line, but the dinghy dipped to a wave and the man was pulled overboard and carried away. While the launch crew were attempting to get another line across, a Navy Walrus appeared, and to everyone's horror promptly landed in the impossible conditions. The flying boat was immediately swept away by the wind and disappeared into the spray and rain.

After bringing the two remaining FAA survivors aboard, the HSL crew set off in search of the Walrus. Miraculously, after many uncertain moments, Hugget located it and with consummate skill and timing, succeeded in taking off one of the crew as the bow of the HSL pitched past him. The operation was repeated for the second man, but the next wave dropped the bows of the launch on top of the aircraft with a mighty crash. The HSL was badly holed below the waterline and started making water fast.

The Wireless Operator immediately sent out a 'Mayday' call and stayed by his transmitter until his wireless cabin was awash. An RN destroyer which was on passage to Londonderry picked up the launch crew and the four naval aviators, all of whom were found clinging to the almost submerged HSL. The launch was later washed ashore, a write-off. The whole affair was a costly operation, for the value of one rescue launch was equivalent to five Spitfires. Flight Lieutenant Hugget and his Wireless Operator were Mentioned in Dispatches for their actions.

Royal Navy ships were also guilty of beating the ASR launches occasionally, although this rarely caused any added risk for the RAF sailors.

In one such case, the broadcaster Richard Dimbleby was sent by the BBC to make an outside broadcast about the busy ASR Unit at Grimsby. Murphy's Law prevailed, and for several days the Grimsby HSLs kept their 'rendezvous' without receiving a single 'Crash Call'. Just as the project was about to be abandoned, a call came in to pick up the crew of a Beaufighter which had ditched in the mouth of the Humber river. Complete with the BBC men, the HSL raced to the position through vicious seas, only to find that an RN minesweeper had beaten them to it and had retrieved two injured airmen. However, the intrepid (and queasy) Dimbleby did get a story after all.

There were no medical facilities aboard the minesweeper and the Doc from the HSL, Leading Aircraftman Spencer Capper, made an extremely perilous leap from one violently pitching deck to the other. Capper stayed with the injured airmen aboard the RN ship until they were safely ashore in Grimsby. This alone was enough death-defying material for the BBC. Unfortunately, Capper never did get to hear the broadcast when it was transmitted a few days later. He was back at sea searching for a B17 which had ditched on the Dogger Bank.

Many decorations were won by RAF sailors, but there was some confusion as to which medals were appropriate for this unusual branch of the Air Force. The standard decorations which applied to the RAF were concerned mainly with flying duties. The DFC and AFC for officers and DFM and AFM for other ranks could no more be issued to sailors than to ground crew. Les Flower had received the Military Medal, an army decoration, for his actions at Dunkirk, and Leading Aircraftman Albert Dargue had been awarded a military division BEM after the Dieppe Raid; yet both men had displayed exceptional valour whilst at sea.

Certain decorations could only apply when the action took place 'in the face of the enemy' and more often than not, the RAF sailors did not qualify. Later in the war, a commendably large number of marine officers were awarded the DSC (Distinguished Service Cross) and crewmen the DSM (Distinguished Service Medal), decorations which hitherto had applied to the Royal Navy. With all such honours, the basis for qualification was action 'beyond the call of duty'. In the case of most RAF sailors, normal duty demanded a great deal of courage and resourcefulness anyway. To receive a decoration for extending themselves beyond this implied the highest forms of bravery.

There was an outstanding example of bravery in 1944 when an RCAF

Catalina crew flying 'in the face of the enemy' and an HSL crew defying the cruel sea came together on the very edge of the Arctic Circle.

The peaceful Orkney and Shetland islanders, descendants of the Norsemen, fished and farmed quietly, and with a watchful eye on the elements played out their long lives in normally tranquil isolation, but the war changed it all. The giant natural harbour at Scapa Flow brought a larger Service population than that of the islanders themselves. Disused airfields were re-opened and new ones built from scratch. Troops were moved in. Norwegians arrived to run the clandestine activities of the Shetland Bus from Lunna Voe, while the RAF set up seaplane bases in Lerwick and Sullom Voe as part of the northern chain of flying boat stations stretching from Shetland to Iceland via the Faroes.

Bitterly cold dark winters were succeeded by cold light summers where dawn followed dusk within minutes. From here, the seaplanes spent long hours over the ocean protecting the Arctic Convoys from enemy U-boats. Beneath them, the HSLs stood by. The launches were Thornycroft and Vosper types which were more suited to the rough sea conditions. Because of the vast distances covered they carried reserve petrol in drums on the afterdeck, a highly dangerous but unaviodable practice. In order to place some launches as far north as possible, HSLs were detached to Baltasound in the island of Unst from the ASRUs at Lerwick and Aberdeen.

On 25 June 1944, Flight Lieutenant David E. Hornell and his seven-man crew of a 162 Squadron RCAF Catalina were dispatched from Iceland on a routine U-boat patrol. Just south of the Arctic Circle, they caught an enemy submarine on the surface. Hornell pressed home an attack quickly, expecting the U-boat to dive, but instead he saw the German sailors run out on to the casing and man the guns. Their fire was accurate, scoring several hits. With all but one gun out of action, the control surfaces damaged and the starboard engine ablaze, Hornell kept the big amphibian on course. Depth charges were dropped on target and the U-boat sank as the crippled aircraft wheeled away.

By this time the engine fire had spread and the Catalina's wing was severely weakened. There was no alternative but to ditch. As Hornell approached for a crash landing, the burning engine fell off into the sea. Shortly afterwards a wing collapsed, but the crew survived the landing and the aircraft stayed afloat long enough for them to escape.

Only one waterlogged liferaft was serviceable, which meant that two men had to remain in the sea until the raft could be lightened. All the survival gear except the flare kit was thrown overboard to reduce the load. Hornell had his crew bailing the water out, setting an example by using his flying boots for the purpose. Eventually the two men who had clung to the side were dragged aboard, but the tossing boat threatened to capsize with every wave. The wind was bitingly cold and spindrift sluiced off the tops of the breaking waves. After three hours of fighting to stay afloat, they were found by a Catalina from a Norwegian squadron of the RAF which dropped markers and called for assistance before continuing to circle the spot until its fuel ran low.

The 'Crash Call' was received by Thornycroft HSL 2507 in Baltasound shortly before midnight. Although it was still daylight, the wind was rising and as the launch left the sound and headed north, it was punching a heavy sea in poor visibility. The skipper, Flying Officer W. Garret, drove the protesting HSL at all possible speed, but after only an hour of this punishment one of the RY 12 engines expired. The Fitter reported that nothing could be done, there was no oil pressure.

Garret had to make a decision. On one engine, the HSL would have to steam through heavy seas for 15 to 20 hours before it could commence a square search. What were the odds on the remaining engine packing up? Should he put his boat and crew at risk on the very slim chance of finding the dinghy in such conditions? Could the airmen from the Catalina survive the intense cold for that length of time, even if they were found?

Garret decided to press on. The boat rolled and pitched sickeningly in the steep seas. With all the thrust coming from one propeller, steering was back-breaking work and many a fatal broach was narrowly averted. Even the hardiest members of the crew felt seasick. Seventeen hours later, HSL 2507 passed the last known position of the aircraft and commenced a square search. An ASR Warwick aircraft located the drifting dinghy and tried to drop an airborne lifeboat, but the men in the rubber boat were too weak to reach it in the storm tossed waves.

When the HSL came within visual range, the Warwick pilot headed towards it, signalling frantically with an Aldis lamp, but the movement of the launch was so violent that the crew were unable to read the morse code. Garret decided to break radio silence and speak directly to the aircraft. The Warwick gave Garret a new heading and they were soon cresting the ever steepening waves towards the dinghy. Now came the tricky part of completing the pick up without crushing the survivors under the launch, but the combined seamanship of Garret and the superb boat handling of Cox'n Sergeant Low ensured that the dinghy was finally pulled safely alongside. Only six men were alive. Two of the airmen had died, their bodies having been heaved overboard to aid the chances for their crewmates. The men had been adrift for 21 hours and were suffering from acute exposure and exhaustion. Flight Lieutenant David Hornell had slipped into a coma.

HSL 2507 turned southwards for the long voyage back to Shetland. The Catalina crew gradually began to revive in the sickbay, but their skipper did not emerge from his coma. Despite the efforts of deckhand Charles Deverell who applied his own body heat, the pilot died in his arms five hours after the rescue.

Still the HSL fought its way south, but after sighting the tip of the Shetlands at Muckle Flugga, fuel was dangerously low. Garret put into a sheltering bay and radioed for petrol which was floated out to the launch in 50 gallon drums. Finally, HSL 2507 steamed triumphantly into Lerwick harbour, the crew exhausted by two days at sea and two nights without sleep, but with the survivors safe. The one engine had not missed a beat.

A month later, Flight Lieutenant David Hornell was awarded a posthumous VC. Garret received a severe reprimand for breaking radio silence. One year later, he received the MBE.

Sometimes awards and decorations were won for valour on a cumulative basis. The London Gazette of 20 February 1945 listed three DSCs which were awarded to HSL Masters for sustained effort, as opposed to a single outstanding act.

Squadron Leader Esmond Haines was the CO of Dover ASRU for over two years and was decorated for his personal example in keeping the unit operational despite recurring damage from the constant enemy shelling of the harbour. Whilst under his command 27 ASRU made an impressive contribution to the Normandy and Arnhem campaigns. Flight Lieutenant E. R. Watson's DSC was awarded for high courage, fortitude and devotion to duty resulting in the saving of many lives. From July 1943 Watson had commanded detachments in North Africa and Italy and had personally led several rescue operations whilst his launch was under fire.

A third officer to be honoured at the same time was Flight Lieutenant Geoffrey Lockwood. Lockwood arrived at 28 ASRU Newhaven, towards the end of 1942 and was appointed Master of HSL 156. His ensuing adventures were many and various. On one occasion he had gone to the rescue of a Whitley crew who had ditched close inshore at Cooden bay. Four of the airmen were clinging onto the wing while the fifth, who was wounded, was in a partially inflated dinghy attached to the aircraft. Heavy breaking rollers made the rescue extremely hazardous and Lockwood displayed a great deal of skill in keeping the launch away from rocks whilst successfully picking up all the aircrew. At another time, in equally adverse weather, Lockwood and his crew located and rescued two B 17 crews on the same day, 19 men in all. Twice he retrieved USAAF fighter pilots who had baled out, one of these from the middle of a minefield near the French coast.

HSL 156 and most of the Newhaven, Dover, Ramsgate and Felixstowe boats stayed on station during the build up to Operation Overlord, but other HSLs were drawn from all quarters to supplement the south coast ASRUs for the duration of the D–Day landings. During May 1944, many officers and men from Marine Craft Sections and ASRUs found themselves en route to the Channel ports to provide the extra manpower for this concentration of resources. Behind them at their units they left shorthanded crews aboard Pinnaces and STs to continue the work of the seconded HSLs.

Among the massive numbers of ships gathered for the assault were 90 HSLs, 40 RMLs and six seaplane tenders. These were supplemented by

60 rescue cutters of the US Coastguards, 15 lifeboats of the RNLI and 14 MASBs in reserve.

In addition to the eastern units, HSLs were concentrated in Newlyn, Mount Batten, Torquay, Poole, Weymouth and the Isle of Wight, with the STs standing by at Sheerness and Lyme Regis. At Lyme Regis, the unit was under the command of the eccentric Flight Lieutenant Sir Algernon Guinness. The RMLs were formed into five flotillas spread between Newhaven, Dartmouth, Devonport and Falmouth.

Four of the HSLs were relatively new to the service, having been brought on charge just five weeks before. These were Packard-powered ex-US Navy MTBs, built to a George Selman/Scott-Paine 70 ft design and produced in America by the Elco Naval Division of the Electric Boat Company. Originally designated PTs 1–12, these craft were supplied to the Royal Navy under lend-lease in 1941, and had since served variously as MGBs and MTBs, numbered 82–93. The four which were temporarily handed over to the RAF, became HSL 82, 83, 88 and 89. The launches were very fast indeed at 45 knots laden and 52 knots light. However, they were returned to the Navy one at a time from August 1944.

For the D-Day operations, all HSLs were grouped according to type in relation to local prevailing sea conditions. The 'Whalebacks' continued to operate from the south-east where they had proved their ability to ride the short, steep chop of the Channel, while in the West Country and Irish Sea, where Atlantic swells could be expected, the Thornycrofts and Vospers were stationed. The 'Hants and Dorsets', with their all-weather capability, tended to be spread at various points. A new mobile ASRU commenced operations with 14 'Hants and Dorsets' based at Calshot. Their long-term purpose was to set up self-sufficient ASRUs on the French coast.

All the RAF launches had white stars painted on their foredecks for identification, much as all Allied aircraft bore black and white 'invasion' stripes.

Eighty search and rescue aircraft of the newly formed Air Defence of Great Britain group were deployed for ASR duties in the immediate invasion area, whilst the USAAF 5th ERS was responsible for the outer fringes of the main assault.

In the early hours of 6 June, HSLs of 32 MASRU were among the first allied surface ships to approach the beach head. Three pairs were attached to three Fighter Direction Tenders whose task it was to co-ordinate tactical air strikes and initiate rescue operations in each sector.

Over 5,000 vessels, ranging from heavy cruisers to small LCAs, formed the assault force. In the first wave alone 60,000 troops were landed. Among them were the veterans of the Canadian divisions who had been so badly mauled at Dieppe.

The skies belonged to the Allies. Thousands of sorties were flown with virtually no Luftwaffe opposition. Of flak there was plenty and in the overall mêlée there were the inevitable collisions and confusions. An HSL from 40 ASRU in Weymouth was attacked by RAF Beaufighters, but fortunately, was undamaged when the aircrew realized their mistake. The same launch picked up an American air gunner who had baled out of what appeared to be a perfectly serviceable, homeward bound B 17. The aircraft was unmanned but was flying onward like an airborne *Marie Celeste.* It transpired that the rest of the crew had abandoned the bomber without telling the gunner.

Two other Weymouth boats rescued 115 men from HMS *Blackwood,* which had struck a mine. A Dover boat picked up 45 survivors from a merchant ship. Five soldiers were saved from a sinking pontoon and even the crew of a sunken U-boat were lifted from their life-rafts by an RAF launch.

During the first 10 days of Overlord, the ASR Services saved 163 airmen, 58 soldiers or seamen and two Germans. A total of 355 men directly involved with the operation were rescued by the Service during the month of June.

Towards the end of the month, as the battle moved inland and air bases were set up in the re-conquered territories, the mobile ASRU was split into two units, 32 and 33 MASRUs, to provide rescue cover from the French mainland. HSLs were stationed from Cherbourg to Le Havre and, ironically, in Dieppe harbour. With the capture of former Luftwaffe bases in France and the Low Countries, there was a marked reduction in the number of aircraft operating over the Channel and the bulk of the routine ASR work befell the MASRUs who eventually set up a permanent base in the U-boat pens at Ostend.

Three months later, massed rescue services were in action again during the daring but abortive attempt to secure the bridge at Arnhem in Holland. Operation Market Garden was launched on 16 September 1944. Before dawn, some 1,400 allied aircraft attacked German troop concentrations in the target area. At 9.45 am, the first of over 2,000 troop-carrying aircraft, tugs and gliders took off to assemble over March in Cambridgeshire and Hatfield in Hertfordshire, to begin the biggest air armada in history. Stirlings, Dakotas, Halifaxes and Albemarles lumbered into the air, towing Hamilcar, Horsa and Waco gliders. Above and around them, Spitfires, Mustangs, Typhoons, Tempests, Thunderbolts and Mosquitoes flew escort and ground attack missions.

Beneath the formations, the HSLs occupied their 'rendezvous' positions. One glider pilot commented, 'There wasn't much navigating to do, the launches below us were set out like stepping stones across the Channel.' Eight gliders ditched from the first wave, but within minutes virtually all the aircrews and troops were saved by the HSLs and RMLs. During the four days of the campaign, 102 men were saved by the rescue services.

In Holland 17,000 British, American and Polish troops were killed, missing or wounded with a further 10,000 Dutch civilian casualties. The military losses were higher than those of the D-Day landings, yet the Arnhem bridge remained in enemy hands.

In the period between Overlord and Market Garden, some of the launch crews were seconded to a new task force. A requirement for larger, Long Range Rescue Craft (LRRC) had been anticipated by the MCPC early in 1944. Such craft were needed for the Far East theatre, where the struggle against Japan was expected to be long and costly in men and materials. Tenders were invited and design proposals were submitted by the BPBC, Thornycroft, Vosper, Aldous Successors, J. Samuel White, Morgan Giles and Camper & Nicholson. A variety of power units were offered, ranging from three to six engines driving fixed or variable pitch propellers, either Packard 4Ms, Rolls-Royce Griffons or Napier Sabres. The Bristol Aeroplane Co submitted an all-metal hull design with four Bristol Hercules air-cooled radial engines. For once, Napier Sea Lions were not in the frame.

By November 1944, the Policy Committee were considering the proposals, but with the war in Europe drawing to a close, it was clear that new boats would not be available in time for the redirection of forces to the Far East. Of the designs which were submitted to the MCPC, only the privately constructed Bristol boat was completed in a near-specification 'yacht' form. The 111 ft BPBC/George Selman design had offered the sailors a comfortable conformity of lines similar to the 'Whaleback' and a streamlined superstructure with 'Hants and Dorset' overtones. The hull was built, but never completed and the last air-sea rescue launch from the company which had produced so many was sold ignominiously as a houseboat at one-tenth of its build cost.

The problem was resolved by the Royal Navy finally keeping its 1942 commitment by allocating 40 MTBs to the RAF, which were made ready between November 1944 and August 1945. The boats were sleek, fast and able to stay at sea for long periods. They were also bigger than any other HSLs in service.

The Fairmile 'D' types were 115 ft loa by 21 ft 6 in beam. Naval torpedo and depth charge gear was removed, but the distinctive torpedo cutaway each side of the bows was part of the hull structure and therefore remained. Two single Oerlikon cannon were retained on the foredeck, with twin Oerlikons aft and twin Vickers machine-guns on each wing of the bridge. Fitted with four Packard 4M-2500 engines of 1,250 hp each, the performance was impressive. Maximum speed was 33 knots with a continuous cruising speed of 28 knots, and a range of 1500 nautical miles with auxiliary deck tanks. The range could be increased further by running on two engines at 15 knots. The crew was twice that of previous HSLs, varying between 18 and 22 men and providing for a full three-watch system.

Twenty-one of the Fairmiles had already served in Allied navies and these were the first to be converted to RAF specification at various boatyards around the country. The other 19 were in build as MTBs, but were completed as LRRCs. The number sequences were LRRC 001 to 040.

The boats assembled at Calshot for final equipping and fitting out and were divided into five flotillas of eight boats each, forming Nos 101–105 ASR/MCUs (Air Sea Rescue/Marine Craft Units).

The LRRCs did not spend long enough in RAF service to make a reputation for themselves. Only two of the flotillas had sailed by the time of the Japanese surrender. One was in Malta on its way to Burma, while the other reached Gibraltar. The flotilla commanders were instructed to stay in the Mediterranean and await further orders while the rest of the fleet remained at Calshot.

The LRRCs in the Med were divided between several ASRUs to relieve boats which had been on station during the war. Some of the sailors found themselves in war ravaged but pleasant locations such as Malta, Marseilles and St Tropez, while others were sent to the Canal Zone to help sort out the massive quantities of surplus war materials which had accumulated there. Six of the launches were stripped and converted to Officers Married Quarters at Fanara in Egypt. Fanara was the assembly point for troops, marine craft and aircrews who were *en route* for 'Blighty'. Others were sold locally wherever they were based, in some cases to characters who saw their potential for use in a post-war smuggling boom.

The LRRCs at Calshot were returned to the Royal Navy or sold by Admiralty tender. Many of these also became houseboats. They were the only HSLs which due to their size, were dependent on Royal Navy dockyard facilities. Many years were to pass before front line launches of the RAF exceeded 68 ft in length again.

*Chapter 15*

# Roll on the Rodney

*For many years, RAF trooping was carried out by the notorious troop ships. In peacetime these were painted white with a blue band around the hull reminiscent of RAF kitbags. In the 1930s, the TS Somersetshire gave rise to the words of a song which was sung with gusto by the sailors everywhere until the branch was disbanded in 1986. Most of the latter-day MBCs probably had no idea of its origins in pre-war Iraq.*

*We're leaving Khartoum by the light of the moon,*
*We're sailing by night and by day.*
*We've just passed Kasfret and we've nothing to eat,*
*For we've thrown all our rations away.*

*Shire, Shire, Somersetshire,*
*The skipper looks on it with pride*
*He'd have a blue fit*
*If he saw all the shit*
*On the side of the Somersetshire.*

In 1942 another chorus was added.

*This is my story, this is my song,*
*I've been in the Air Force too bloody long.*
*So roll on the Rodney, Repulse and Renown,*
*We're stuck with this ship 'till the bastard goes down.*
*Chocks away, chocks away,*
*We'll screw all the SPs who come down our way.*

Or words to that effect.

By the time of the outbreak of war, the RAF sailors were accustomed to spending a few years overseas. They cheerfully went about their work in often quite primitive conditions. Most of them were going abroad for the first time when their overseas postings were promulgated, yet like their Victorian forbears, they took to the changes in culture and climate very well. Wherever they were, the RAF sailors counted the days, the hours and the minutes to the time they would be 'tour-ex' and 'on the boat' to Blighty.

When war was declared, flying boat bases were already well established in Singapore, India, Aden, Egypt, Iraq and Malta, but wartime expansion meant accepting primitive conditions in numerous remote places. Where no shoreside facilities existed, the squadrons took their own depot ships. Converted merchant ships such as the SS *Dumana* and SS *Manela,* manned by a mixture of civilian and Air Force crews, provided quarters for the airmen in addition to workshops and marine craft support units.

Whilst the number of flying boat bases was rapidly extending, along with their essential support craft, little could be done to expand the overseas ASR Service. Only four HSLs were stationed overseas in September 1939. HSL 105 was at Seletar, Singapore; HSL 107 in Kalafrana, Malta; HSL 109 in Aden; and HSL 110 in Basra, Iraq. Although the Air Ministry had requested more boats abroad, two HSLs which were destined for Penang and Ceylon were retained in the UK. Three years were to pass before the number of overseas rescue launches was anywhere near adequate, but in the meantime the sailors did the best they could with what they had. Nowhere was this illustrated better than at Malta, the tiny island which held the key to control of the entire Mediterranean.

When Mussolini declared war on Britain on 10 June 1940, the Middle East Command of the RAF encompassed Egypt, the Sudan, Jordan, Palestine, Somaliland, East Africa, Iraq, Aden, the Persian Gulf and the Balkans; an area bigger than the USA. With the exception of two newly equipped Sunderland Squadrons, there was a miscellany of only 300 obsolescent Blenheim bombers and Gloster Gladiator biplane fighters to cover the entire area. The situation was aggravated by a French/Italian treaty of 24 June which left Britain alone against the Germans and Italians in all theatres. The supply route to North Africa and the Far East via Suez was under threat from the Italian navy, while Italian forces in Abyssinia and Eritrea were poised to cut off the alternative route via Cape Town and the Gulf of Aden.

HSL 107 went to Malta in 1939 under the command of one of the original group of RAFOs, Flying Officer E. Hardie. When the first Regia Aeronautica air attacks on Malta began in June 1940, the defensive air arm comprised only four FAA Gladiators. Three of these were the legendary *Faith, Hope* and *Charity.* During this period HSL 107 had a couple of near misses. On one occasion it set off an accoustic mine, but escaped serious damage due to its sheer speed. On another, it was hit by an incendiary bomb. Each time, repairs were made and the launch was returned to active duty.

Fighter reinforcements trickled in, but by July there were just 10 aircraft fighting odds of 10 to one against the daily raids. On 12 August, a dozen Hurricanes, the nucleus of 261 Squadron, flew from the flight deck of HMS *Argus* to join the beleaguered forces. During this operation, the HSL steamed to a rendezvous point to cover their arrival, but came under machine-gun attack from an Italian SIAI-Marchetti torpedo bomber. The HSL returned to base intact, but the Italians claimed one British MTB sunk.

With the co-operation of the South African Air Force, the RAF succeeded in keeping the alternative Cape supply route open, but when the Italians advanced through North Africa towards Egypt and then attacked Greece in October, the RAF and the FAA were sorely extended.

On 11 November, Swordfish aircraft from Admiral Cunningham's Mediterranean Fleet, attacked the Italian fleet in its main port of Taranto. It was a copybook action. Half the Italian fleet was destroyed for the loss of two Swordfish. In December, Wellington and Maryland bombers and Beaufort torpedo bombers arrived in Malta with Sunderlands of 228 and 230 Squadrons. The island was beginning to gather the weapons to fight back.

In North Africa, with the help of the expanding air arm in Malta, Wavell's forces pushed the Italians back from Sidi Barrani, and in a series of outstanding manoeuvres, killed 3,000 of the enemy, captured 400 tanks and took 168,000 prisoners, at a cost of 500 men.

The situation began to look more promising for the British, but the Germans joined their Italian allies in the Greek campaign of February 1941 and added a much more formidable dimension to the battle. Hurricanes, Blenheims and Gladiators were seconded to the defence of Greece from throughout the Command, but they were outnumbered 20 to one and the Luftwaffe gained complete control of the skies. By April the British had lost the campaign, and with it many highly skilled pilots. The final defeat came a month later with the fall of Crete.

Throughout the actions, HSL 107 with Flying Officer Hardie, and later Flying Officer Waring, was able to provide a rescue service which was much more efficient than the contemporary UK network. Shorter lines of communication, aided by a quick response, ensured that many pilots were saved who would have otherwise perished.

While the British were evacuating Greece, General Erwin Rommel arrived in Tripoli with his Afrika Korps. His sea and air supply routes from Italy and Sicily passed close to Malta, and from here the RAF continued to disrupt the vital flow of fuel and provisions for the burgeoning German Army in the desert.

In June 1941, 48 Hurricanes were flown off the carriers *Ark Royal* and *Victorious*, but they had a long oversea flight and the majority of them missed the tiny island. Only five landed safely. Once more, HSL 107 was on the spot, but the Hurricane pilots had missed by miles.

While the Luftwaffe and the Regia blasted the RAF airfields at Luqa, Ta'Qali, Hal Far and Safi, the Royal Navy was desperately trying to ensure that the Maltese supply convoys survived the gauntlet of enemy air and submarine attacks. By the second week of January 1942, only

Luqa airfield was operational and the island fighter force had been reduced to 30 serviceable Hurricanes. In March the first Spitfires arrived, ferried by HMS *Eagle* at great risk. On 15 April, King George VI bestowed the George Cross on the island. It was the greatest honour that a sovereign could award to a nation.

On 20 April, 47 more Spitfires of 601 (County of London) and 603 (City of Edinburgh) Squadrons, reached the island from the aircraft carrier USS *Wasp*, but they arrived during an intensive raid and were immediately thrown into the fray. By the end of the day, a mere 18 were airworthy. Three weeks later, both *Eagle* and *Wasp* returned to deliver a further batch of 64 Spitfires. On 21 April, the Malta fighters deterred an attempt by the Luftwaffe to sink the fast minelayer, HMS *Welshman* in Grand Harbour, Valetta. One hundred and twenty-four sorties were flown for the loss of three Spitfires. HSL 107 saved two of the pilots.

HMS *Eagle* succeeded in delivering a total of 182 aircraft, before she was sunk by a U-boat on 11 July, but HMS *Furious* kept up the pressure, flying off over 60 fighters during the remainder of the summer.

Reinforcements for the sorely pressed ASR Service had arrived in September 1941 when 'Whaleback' HSL 128 was safely delivered. In its very first action, it came under enemy fire and the Master, Flying Officer McIntosh, was wounded. The boat was hurriedly repaired and put back into service with a new skipper, Pilot Officer Crockett. HSL 148 was lost on the merchantman SS *Imperial Star* which was torpedoed on the voyage from the UK. In early 1942 HSL 129 arrived after beating the blockade, but on 26 April it was destroyed by Messerschmitt Bf 109s. Four of the crew were killed and the skipper, Flying Officer Nicholls, was wounded.

Meanwhile, the veteran HSL 107 continued to lead a charmed life. An unusual story concerning the launch emerged recently from Denis Winstone of Barton-on-Sea and ex-crew member Ralph Ashton of London. In July 1942 the HSL was moored in St Paul's Bay and received a call to investigate an Italian Cant 506B floatplane which had alighted just off the coast after being intercepted by Spitfires of 603 Squadron. The HSL approached the seaplane with understandable caution, but the boat's crew were amazed to see a group of men perched on top of the seaplane waving white shirts and shouting in English.

Altogether 10 men were taken aboard and the aircraft was put under tow. Three of the men were members of the RAF, one was from the SAAF and the remainder were Italian. It was a difficult tow, with the Cant yawing badly astern of the launch. Running at slow speed caused the boat's engines to overheat, so with only a short distance left to go the tow was transferred to another RAF boat. This was an old Brooke motor boat, which at the time was suffering from a gearbox problem. The Cox'n of the Brooke, Corporal Walter Bramhall, accidently holed one of the aircraft's floats as he brought the ailing motor boat alongside. To prevent the wing from dipping into the water, he manoeuvred until it was propped on the cabin top. He eventually edged the seaplane into the slipway at the RAF base at Kalafrana.

On board HSL 107, the full story of the Cant was recanted.

The three RAF men and their Captain, Lieutenant Strever of the SAAF, had set out the previous day in a Beaufort torpedo bomber to attack targets near Greece. The aircraft was hit by flak and Strever had no alternative but to ditch in the sea. All four crew members were subsequently picked up by an Italian boat and taken to Corfu. The Italians then decided to transfer the prisoners to the Italian mainland by means of the floatplane. Placed under an armed guard, the Beaufort crew were crammed into the Cant with its crew of five Italians.

Shortly after take-off, the prisoners overpowered the armed guard, and using him as a hostage, persuaded the pilot to surrender. They had no precise idea of their location nor did they have any charts. Strever instructed the pilot to head south-west for Malta, but was uncertain of the fuel state of the aircraft.

Eventually, Sicily was sighted to starboard and the airmen were able to identify Malta in the distance. After the brush with the Spitfires, the Cant touched down just as the engines stopped. The tanks were completely dry.

The hi-jacked seaplane was ultimately repaired and repainted in RAF colours for use on ASR duties. The victorious Beaufort crew were all awarded the DFC. Corporal Bramhall was banned from taking any boat near an aircraft again, and the crew of HSL 107 carried on with their valuable work as usual.

The struggle to maintain the rescue services continued throughout the air raids of 1942, during which time Malta received the same tonnage of bombs as London was to suffer in the entire war. The men of the ASR unit, fearful that they could not continue with only two boats, secured the temporary loan of an Army launch. The boat was a BPBC 56 ft hard chine planing craft, similar in appearance to HSL 107. It was even complete with the familiar trio of Napiers. In the hands of the Royal Army Service Corps, the boat had been called *Clive*. The sailors soon changed that and she became HSL 100 in honour of the first HSL, which had been written off in the UK in March of 1942. More help came when 'Whaleback' HSL 166, was detached from Alexandria.

HSL 128 achieved the distinction of rescuing the RAF's highest scoring Middle East 'ace' during the air fighting. Canadian Pilot Officer George Beurling of 249 Squadron was wounded and shot down whilst trying to save one of his colleagues from a similar fate. Beurling baled out of his shattered Spitfire from only 500 ft and plunged into the sea. He was rescued after only 20 minutes. George Beurling, known as 'Buzz' or 'Screwball', was repatriated to the UK shortly afterwards. With him, he took a score of over 40 enemy aircraft destroyed or damaged, and a DSO, DFC, DFM and Bar to proclaim it.

The air raids on Malta diminished after the battle of El Alamein and

Rommel's subsequent retreat. In December, elements of the Luftwaffe began to withdraw to other fronts, leaving Malta GC to relax a little.

During 1943 roles were reversed. Instead of being a siege island under constant attack, Malta became a launching pad for the Allied assault on Sicily and the Italian mainland. Five days after Montgomery's victory at El Alamein, a powerful Anglo-American force under the command of General Dwight Eisenhower landed in French North Africa. This was Operation Torch and the date was 8 November 1942. The tide had turned at last and the long road to victory had begun.

Three days later, the Allies captured Casablanca, Algiers and Oran. By 11 November, they had advanced eastward to Bougie. The following day, British paratroops took Bone.

Meanwhile, Montgomery's 8th Army was pushing westward on the heels of the retreating Germans. In January 1943, the 8th Army captured Tripoli and then squeezed the axis forces into a pocket around Tunis during February and March. By early May, the German/Italian escape route from the seaports of Bizerta and Tunis had been severed. The enemy surrendered on 13 May, leaving almost a quarter of a million prisoners.

As the Allies advanced by land and in the air, the RAF sailors matched them to seaward. The first ASR launches to arrive in North Africa were based in Algiers at 252 ASRU and as the advance progressed, boats were detached to Bougie, Phillipeville, Bone and Oran. Before the end of 1942, ASR coverage extended all the way from Casablanca on the Atlantic coast to the Mediterranean port of Bone in Morocco.

In the new year, some HSLs were moved further eastward in parallel with the land forces and set up bases in Bizerta, Sousse and Sfax. HSLs from Alexandria spread westward as far as Tripoli to complete the chain.

One of the launches in the forefront of the North African advance was HSL 175. During its stay in Algiers, it was commandeered by the Royal Navy for covert, 'cloak and dagger' operations. The launch was repainted in black and grey camouflage and re-numbered as 'Fishery Protection Vessel No 9'. (This had been a standard colour scheme for overseas HSLs until it was changed to all grey with black numbers and a smaller roundel.) The exhaust system was converted to deflect the gases underwater for quieter running. It set off with the sickbay full of weaponry and a mixed RAF and naval crew. After several weeks of clandestine activities in the forward area, the HSL reverted to its former status.

During the aftermath of Torch, the RAF sailors found themselves engaged in all sorts of work. Some of the boats acted as communications launches, while others collected and delivered VIPs. Generally, they put in many running hours and suffered the inevitable results of unservice-ability through heavy usage, shortage of slipping facilities and lack of spares. Eventually, a servicing unit was established at Bone and the situation improved.

Gradually, 'Hants and Dorsets' and 'Miamis' began to arrive in the

Mediterranean theatre and the ex '100 Class' and 'Whaleback' crews learned to appreciate both their spaciousness and their seakeeping qualities.

With the invasion of Sicily, Operation Husky, on 10 July 1943, the rescue services were back at full stretch and once more engaged in their primary task.

During the air offensive which was a prelude to the landings, the Malta HSLs were joined by a further eight, plus four ASR pinnaces and half a dozen seaplane tenders. Air activity over the sea was frenetic. The rescue services were receiving 'Crash Calls' almost every hour. During the first few days of the air assault, 45 aircrew were saved from a total of 75 downed at sea. Early in the operation, a Walrus went to the aid of a ditched Beaufighter crew and performed the all too common trick of being unable to take off again. After taxiing for several hours, it ran out of fuel and had to be towed in by an HSL from Bizerta.

Whilst Patton's 7th Army moved clockwise from its landing beaches near Licata, Montgomery's 8th Army advanced anti-clockwise from Syracuse. General Omar Bradley's two divisions struck due north through the centre of the island. The pincer movement was completed on 17 August. The campaign cost the allies almost 400 aircraft, but the axis air forces lost an irreplaceable 1,850.

Another incident involving a Beaufighter and an amphibian occurred after the invasion, in August. This time the rescue aircraft, a Catalina, was unable to take off because of damage to a propeller caused by a big wave. The aircraft recovered the Beaufighter crew from their dinghy, but after trying to taxi away on one engine came under fire from shore batteries on the Sardinian coast. Enemy fighters attacked the Catalina, but were beaten off by P 38 Lightnings of the USAAF.

The captain of the crippled flying boat ordered both his own men and the rescued Beaufighter crew into the dinghies. These had been damaged by the attacking fighters and the survivors had to bail furiously to keep themselves afloat. By this time a series of dog fights had developed above them. At the crucial moment an HSL arrived and, ignoring the shells falling around them and the heavy seas, the crew went about rescuing the men in the dinghy. All were recovered safely and the HSL returned to its base in North Africa. The Master, Flight Lieutenant J. Lang, was awarded the DSC and the Cox'n, Flight Sergeant J. Edwards, BEM, the DSM.

On 18 August, HSL 2599 and 2699 from Bone were called to a Catalina which had recovered the crew of an American B 17 which had ditched close to Sardinia. The Catalina had damaged a float on landing. HSL 2599, after taking most of the survivors aboard, headed for Bone at high speed, leaving HSL 2699 to tow the flying boat back to base. The tow was a difficult one, which took many hours of slow steaming and involved putting a man on the wing of the aircraft to counter-balance the missing float.

157

Two weeks after the Sicily landings, Mussolini was deposed and arrested. On 3 September, as Anglo-American forces crossed the Straits of Messina and landed at Reggio on the toe of Italy, the Italians secretly surrendered to the Allies.

The Allied forces now faced the Germans on the Italian mainland and as the advance spread northwards and through the outlying islands, elements of the rescue services went with it. HSL bases were set up in Crotone, Taranto, Brindisi, Bari, Manfredonia and Ancona on the Adriatic coast. Two units were established on the Yugoslavian side, one on the island of Vis and the other at Zara on the mainland. After further Allied landings at Salerno and Anzio on the Tyrrhenian coast, launches moved north westward and were based between Ischia, off Naples, up to Bastia in Corsica. The 16 launches dispersed throughout the area were from 253 ASRU, under the command of Squadron Leader Geoffrey Lund-Lack. From the close of 1943 to VE day, the men of 253 ASRU saved over 700 lives at sea.

A unique 1945 colour film of 'Miami' class HSLs at Vis has found its way into the archives of the RAF Museum. The film is of a very high quality, but besides its technical interest and rarity, it shows the sailors in khaki battledress, which was common at the time, but tends to be forgotten when looking at black and white photographs. It helps to underline the incongruity of men dressed in army uniforms with RAF badges, who went to sea for their living!

One of these khaki-clad sailors, Jack Hill, was a 19-year-old Wireless Operator with HSL 2543 based in Bastia. HSL 2543 was among the earliest 'Miami' class launches to reach the Mediterranean. The crew was newly formed and the men were getting to know each other as well as their new boat when a Spitfire crashed into the sea near enemy occupied Elba.

A steep sea was running and white water was breaking over the foredeck as the skipper, Flying Officer Jack Rogers, drove her hard at over 30 knots. A Walrus beat the launch to the pick-up, but before taking off it was badly damaged by enemy gunfire. The Spitfire pilot found himself back in the drink and clambering into a dinghy with his rescuers.

The HSL pressed on towards the life-raft while a few ranging shots fell around it. The Italian gunnery was accurate and Rogers had to keep the launch weaving at high speed to avoid being hit. The man on the wheel, Corporal Eric Parham, handled the boat skilfully, bringing it to a surging halt alongside the dinghy. Scrambling nets were lowered and the survivors were hastily dragged aboard and shovelled into the sickbay. The firing from the shore batteries continued unabated, but the launch escaped as fountains of spray from the shells tumbled over the decks. Thus, on his very first 'Crash Call', Jack Hill received a commendation, as did the rest of the crew, while Jack Rogers was awarded the DSC and Eric Parham the DSM.

HSL 187 was not so lucky when it was sent to a position off the mouth of the river Tiber to investigate a dinghy which was seen drifting inshore. Before the HSL reached the spot, it was attacked by two Me Bf 109s using heavy calibre machine-guns. The throttles became jammed in the closed position preventing the boat from accelerating away. One by one the engines stopped and the launch slewed to a halt. Two of the petrol tanks caught fire and the Oerlikon on the after deck was blasted overboard. The boat was making water through several bullet holes in the hull.

During the attacks, the deckhand on the for'ard gun had been severely wounded in the head and arm. Corporal 'Doc' Roberts was hit in the hand and twice in the leg, but tended the injured deckhand first. Meanwhile the rest of the crew were fully occupied dousing the fires and stemming the leaks in the hull.

Just as the skipper decided to destroy all the ship's papers and abandon the launch, the fitter managed to start the port engine. Slowly, the HSL trolled towards Anzio through heavy, breaking seas. When only 10 miles away, the engine room flooded and the electrical power failed. The Carley float had been washed overboard and there was no question of the wounded man being able to swim.

As the boat drifted inshore the crew fired flares and attracted the attention of a US Naval launch which took them off their stricken craft and put them ashore. What was left of HSL 187 was later recovered from the beach and towed to Ischia before being repaired. Corporal Roberts was awarded the BEM.

The network of HSLs grew as bases were set up in the south of France and the Ligurian Sea to the east. Throughout the Greek campaigns increasing numbers of HSLs were engaged in the Dodecanese islands of the Aegean Sea to the westward.

A taste for clandestine activities was succoured again when HSLs 2516 and 2539 were disguised as Greek caiques to run agents to and from Alexandria and drop raiding parties wherever the need dictated. From October 1943 until VE day, they operated in and around the Aegean, close to enemy-held islands and the Turkish mainland. The launches were re-named MY *Bairam* and MY *Fouad*. During their 'cloak and dagger' period, they were variously commanded by Flying Officer Farnsworth, Flight Lieutenant Legge, Flying Officer Hawkins, Flight Lieutenant Power, Flight Lieutenant Evans and Pilot Officer Richards. Whenever they were called upon to use their hidden speed potential, there were some startled expressions on the faces of the observers!

The Mediterranean sea brought its challenges, its triumphs and its occasional despairs to the RAF sailors, but as they pressed on regardless, others of their brethren were facing similar hazards on more distant oceans.

*Chapter 16*

# Bwanas and Sahibs

*The RAF sailors found themselves helping other Dominion and Commonwealth countries to establish their own rescue services. Australian, Canadian, New Zealand and South African Air Forces all followed the RAF pattern, but the RAF was directly responsible for seaplane support and ASR in West Africa, the Indian Ocean, the Gulf and the South China Sea.*

While the ASR Service was desperately trying to secure more boats from the Admiralty in 1940 and 1941, the South African Government succeeded in ordering 17 boats from the Miami Shipbuilding Company. Before they arrived, the first launch to serve with the South African Marine Craft Flight was a one-off '100 Class' boat which had been fitted with twin Merlins. This launch was numbered 'R0' and given the name of *Malmok*. The first eight 'Miamis' were delivered to South Africa in May and July of 1941, but the balance of nine boats was diverted to the RAF. SAAF launches were given the prefix 'R' for Rescue, and serial Nos 1–8. These were designated Series 1 'Miami' and were fitted with two pairs of Kermath 500 hp engines. The RAF Series 2 versions had twin Hall-Scott Defenders of 650 hp mounted aft and driving through Vee-drives.

The next batch, Series 3, differed yet again, with the engines installed further forward, driving direct to the propeller shafts. Outwardly there was little difference, except that the later boats had an open well-deck aft and a two-island superstructure.

These 63 ft mostly plywood boats, were very popular with the sailors. Spacious and well suited to rough seas, they were capable of 33 knots. Compared with the boats in the UK they were lightly armed, with single .303 machine-guns or two twin Brownings of the same calibre on each wing of the bridge. The 'Miamis' were not as well finished or as well furnished as British-built HSLs, but they were extremely tough and seaworthy.

Altogether, some 40 boats from the Florida yard were operated by the

RAF and 19 by the SAAF. The RAF Numbers were 2515–45 and 2642–50.

One of the first 'Miamis' to reach the Middle East was HSL 2517. In 1943 this vessel proved the seaworthiness of the type when in January it successfully saved the seven-man crew of a USAAF B25 Mitchell bomber. The survivors had been adrift in their dinghy for 24 hours when they were picked up by the launch, but a severe storm was brewing and the HSL crew repeatedly had to reduce speed as the seas became more vicious. Eventually, the launch hove-to in sight of Tobruk harbour, unable to proceed.

Solid water cascaded over the entire boat as the hull lurched and rolled in 18 ft breakers. The radio failed, putting the launch out of contact with its base. Both crew and survivors were seasick as they battened themselves down below and prepared to ride out the storm. During the night, the storm worsened and oil bags were lowered from the weather bow while cupfuls of spare engine oil were poured into the sea toilets and pumped overboard at regular intervals, literally pouring oil on troubled waters.

HSL 2517 drifted eastward for another two nights and days until the storm eased. On her fourth day at sea and the third without radio contact, she was able to start engines and steam slowly into Bardia. Here the grateful US airmen were put ashore, the launch was refuelled, and by mid-afternoon was heading back to Tobruk. The Master, Flying Officer Bottoms, was awarded the OBE and Flight Sergeant Cox'n McLaughlin the BEM for cool-headedness and outstanding seamanship.

'Miamis' were first deployed in the Mediterranean, but as the Cape and North African supply routes were resorted to during the North African campaign, the SAAF Marine Craft Flights were hard pressed to provide adequate ASR coverage on both their Atlantic and Indian Ocean seaboards. The RAF sailors were brought in to supplement the SAAF units and operate HSLs from the flying boat bases already peopled by MCS personnel.

Among the RAF crews who worked with the SAAF was MBC John Harris. He gained the unique distinction of being promoted to Corporal whilst still a deckhand. Later, he was sent back to the UK in time to serve in the English Channel during the D-Day and Arnhem operations. It was from West Africa that he drew his material for the book *A Funny Place to Hold a War*, and from his Channel experiences *The Sea Shall Not Have Them*.

ASRUs were established at Jui, near Freetown, Sierra Leone and Bathurst in the Gambia. Sunderland aircraft flew from Freetown on anti-submarine and anti-surface raider patrols to protect the Cape route convoys.

One of the many operations carried out on the west coast was the successful recovery of Sunderland 'K' of 204 Squadron. The aircraft developed engine trouble and was forced to alight on the sea some 70 nautical miles from Freetown. The wireless had failed, thus the crew was unable to transmit a position report. Several marine craft and aircraft soon became involved in the search for the flying boat and its 13-man crew.

Pinnace P 1304 commenced the search and was later joined by HSL 2545 of 202 ASRU, Bathurst, which was on passage to Dakar. Meanwhile, P 1311 was put on standby along with HSL 2524 from 201 ASRU at Freetown. The aircraft was found by a Sunderland of 95 Squadron on the second day. HSL 2545 soon located the drifting flying boat, took the crew off safely, and commenced towing. The tow was difficult in the choppy sea and had to be abandoned. After calling for back-up, the HSL set off for Freetown with the aircrew.

In the meantime, HSL 2524 which had been carrying out a square search under the command of Pilot Officer Tom Carroll was diverted to take over the tow. After a short while, strong winds and heavy seas forced a reduction in towing speed from approximately 10 knots to less than four, but despite the difficulties Carroll and his crew succeeded in getting the aircraft to Freetown.

Towards the end of the voyage, Carroll had expected to have to abort the tow again as his launch was running low on fuel, but HSL 2724 escorted Carroll for the last few miles and stood by to take the line. Carroll made it, with barely 15 minutes of fuel left.

Altogether, three pinnaces, three HSLs and several aircraft were involved with this rescue over the two-day period of 9 and 10 April 1944. It was a classic example of a rescue operation which was 100 per cent successful. The crews who served on both 'Miamis' and 'Whalebacks' preferred the former, but today little remains as a reminder of these fine boats except a few photographs.

The fall of Singapore on 15 February 1942 cost the RAF sailors dearly. The rapidity of the Japanese advance on all fronts (they had attacked the US Fleet in Pearl Harbor, sunk *Repulse* and *Prince of Wales*, captured Guam, Wake Island, Hong Kong and Rangoon, all between 7 December 1941 and 9 February 1942) had still not given the British any reason to doubt the impregnability of 'Fortress Singapore', but the defenders were not prepared for an invasion from the landward side.

When it did come, Flight Lieutenant Robert Moore, who was Officer i/c ASR, received orders to proceed to sea with all seaworthy marine craft and head south for Palembang in Sumatra. Just as they were about to leave, the order was rescinded. The Royal Navy advised that Palembang had already fallen. The small flotilla changed its destination to Batavia (Djakarta) in the Dutch East Indies and planned to steam through the Flores and Timor Seas to Darwin in Australia.

Refueller 1186 from Seletar was loaded with diesel fuel and aviation spirit and ordered to rendezvous with the launches at an island *en route*. The main flotilla consisted of pinnaces 53, 54 and 36. These were all 60 ft boats of the triple diesel engine type. HSL 105 was instructed to stay in

Singapore in preparation to embark the GOC, AOC and other Senior Officers and their Staff. The Senior Commanders elected to stay until the end, thus the HSL, with only the HQ staff aboard and with an escort of two seaplane tenders, Nos 225 and 262, was given her sailing orders on the eve of the capture of Singapore City.

The next day, P 54 refuelled from R 1186 at the rendezvous and the refueller crew were told to scuttle their boat and join the pinnace. Travelling only by night, they crept along the coast of Sumatra keeping as close inshore as the depth of water allowed. The voyage was slow and dangerous. The 16 men aboard could find no escape from the heat and humidity. They seemed to be alone, catching only one brief, distant, glimpse of HSL 105.

The pinnace cautiously entered the narrow Straits between Sumatra and the island of Bangka. When only two miles from the tip of Bangka's Muntok Point, it was seen by a Japanese destroyer. The first hit was devastating. A shell landed immediately abaft the winch and blew the helmsman Aircraftman Smeed and one of the officers, Flying Officer Armstrong, overboard. Armstrong had both legs severed beneath the knees. Several others were killed or wounded, and those who could jumped over the side. The Japanese destroyer continued to fire on the men in the water before steaming through wreckage and swimmers alike to destroy both with its propellers.

Smeed stayed with Armstrong despite the wounded man's entreaties to be left to fend for himself. Somehow, the two men survived until the next day. Shortly after dawn Smeed saw the two seaplane tenders which had been escorting HSL 105. He waved and the crews waved back, but they were Japanese. The boats had been captured the day before. The two men were dragged out of the water and made prisoner aboard one of their own launches.

Whilst aboard the ST, Armstrong died and Smeed quietly slipped over the stern and swam away. Once ashore on Sumatra, he was soon recaptured and interned at Palembang. Of the 16 men who had been aboard P 54 three were killed, four were missing, one (Armstrong) died shortly after capture, two were wounded and six became POWs, of whom two died in captivity. Gurney Smeed survived.

Not far away from P 54, the other two pinnaces were also captured, leaving HSL 105 as the only surviving launch of the Singapore MCS. The HSL came under air attack from Japanese fighters and fought them off as well as she could with her light armament. Several of the crew were badly wounded and the launch was damaged. Just before capitulating, her Cox'n, Flight Sergeant Alec Kinnaird, tried to ram a Japanese vessel. All the crewmen were captured, but few survived the POW camps.

Alec 'Lofty' Kinnaird survived, and was awarded the MM at the end of the war. In later years, as a Warrant Officer, he was to become the popular and individualistic CO of 1105 MCU in Porthcawl, South Wales. The unit was known as 'The Kinnairdian Air Force'. At the time, the scars of his torture in Japanese hands were still visible.

After the collapse of Singapore it was a long time before any HSLs were able to return to the Far Eastern theatre, and in the interim the rescue services relied primarily on seaplanes, particularly Catalina PBY 5 amphibians. The crews of the 'Cats' took enormous risks and were very effective. In all, over 300 aircrew and more than 1,300 other lives were saved by them.

In 1944, with more boats becoming available and the Allied thrust through Burma gaining momentum, ASRUs were established to cover the air supply routes to the east. Units sprang up in Mombasa, Masirah, Korangi near Karachi, Trombay near Bombay, Cochin, Colombo and China Bay in Ceylon, Khulna near Calcutta in the Sundarbans, Chittagong, Akyab in Burma, Cocos Island in the Indian Ocean and, eventually, back on the Malayan peninsular at Port Swettenham and Penang, then at Singapore once more and across the South China Sea to Hong Kong.

In the Sundarbans area ASR pinnaces proved ideally suited to the location. Aircraft had to overfly the vast tracts of the Bay of Bengal, and any who crashed around the coastal fringes found the terrain was mostly swamp and mud. The pinnaces had the ability to cruise for many hours on one engine and then, when required, steam at a reasonable 16 or 17 knots. With the inflatable rafts they carried, pinnace crews were able to paddle into mangrove swamps and shallow waters in their search for survivors.

Most of the far eastern ASRUs operated HSLs and here 10 Canadian Power Boat Company boats supplemented the more common types. These were from a delivery of 12 70 x 20 ft launches originally supplied as MTBs to the Royal Canadian Navy. Later they were handed over to the RN who wrote one off in the Caribbean before the CPBC adapted the rest for the RAF. HSL 339 went to the Bahamas while the remainder were deployed in Trombay, Cochin and Karachi. The reverse sheer of their decks betrayed their 'Whaleback' ancestry and they were considered to be very good in a seaway. The boats were powered by twin supercharged Packard W3 engines of 1,250 hp and were capable of speeds up to 45 knots with a range of over 600 nautical miles. What an asset they would have been when the ASR Service was desperate! The boats retained their MTB numbers as HSLs 332–7 and 339–43.

In all these areas, the health hazards for the sailors were similar to those of other land and sea forces. There were foul diseases such as malaria, swamp fever, cholera and yellow fever. Drinking water was contaminated and diarrhoea and dysentry were common. Various skin ailments such as tinea and coral sores added to the effects of the sun and the humidity. Beneath the sea there were other dangers. Sharks, sea snakes, morays, stringrays and a multitude of poisonous fish and shellfish abounded, whilst on land there were scorpions and snakes, leeches, skin-boring worms and mosquitoes. Even the most minor scratches festered and took weeks to heal.

The sailors saw the job through, despite the conditions and the apparently interminable duration of their stay in the Far East. There were no 'tours' as such, merely an assumption of 'about four years', and they had no definite repatriation date to look forward to. Everyone fully expected that the campaign would grind on until the Japanese home islands became a battlefield and the Emperor's army had been wiped out one by one. Like the troops in the jungles and the navies on the high seas, none of the RAF men knew of the atomic bombs.

Suddenly, on 14 August 1945, Japan surrendered and the bulk of the fighting was over. The RAF sailors were left with only one more major job before they could leave. They had to stay on station to provide rescue cover until all the Allied servicemen and prisoners of war had been safely flown home.

# Chapter 17

# The working class...

*...may kiss my arse, I'm on the demob list at last.*
*By the end of the world war, the Air Sea Rescue Service had saved 13,269 lives.*
*In home waters alone, 5,658 priceless aircrew and hundreds of other non-aircrew*
*had been plucked from peril on the sea. Now it was a time for change, but there*
*were many delays in releasing Service personnel, despite the promises of the new*
*Labour Government. Not all the sailors wanted to leave, but at first, there were*
*few incentives to stay.*

The rot had started in 1944. Thousands of RAF personnel were deemed surplus to requirements as the years of expansion had suddenly turned into months of contraction. Without any respect for individual preference, these airmen were transferred to the seriously depleted Army and Navy. It was an unsettling action. Some young aircrew were forcibly re-mustered to MBC, and found the environment alien to them. For the most part, the hardened sailors were not impressed with this influx of 'winged wonders'.

By the autumn of 1945 the conscripted men of the armed services were anxious to be re-united with their families and get on with the much publicized 'jobs for the boys'. Airmen and troops, still lingering in far eastern zones in 1946, went on strike over the delays in shipping them home. The word 'mutiny' was carefully avoided in official documents, but feelings ran high. The heroes of 1945 had become the burden of 1946.

The offensive aircraft of the previous year became troop carriers. Stirlings, Lancasters, Halifaxes, Sunderlands, Liberators and Fortresses were fitted with rudimentary seating. They flew back and forth in long aerial convoys *to be seen* to bring home all the men they could. The truth was that the government could not allow the British presence to vanish overnight from all the territories regained until law and order had been established.

The sailors did not participate in the mutinous uproar. They were anxious to return, but a large proportion of them were regulars and all were volunteers. Those who were 'hostilities only' had already served for a longer period than some peacetime regular engagements would have demanded.

Their troubles really began after their return to the UK, but first there were flight corridors to protect, flying boat stations and staging posts to man until the trooping had finished. Over 300 HSLs and thousands of other, smaller craft had to be shipped to the UK or sold off locally. It was a daunting and often sad task which lasted many months.

At the Air Ministry there were conflicting views about what should happen to this large, world-wide seafaring service. War had stimulated its progression to a deep sea, individualistic force with exceptional qualities of improvization and self-sufficiency. The special skills of navigation, seamanship, aircraft handling and life-saving combined were unequalled by any other arm of the services. Open sea voyages were now limited only by the vessels' range, not the sailors' abilities. Pinnace 96 held the long-distance record of the time, having sailed 919 miles non-stop from Colombo in Ceylon to northern Sumatra, at an average speed of just under 10 knots.

It was assumed that Marine Craft would continue to provide target towing, range safety, torpedo recovery and survival training in support of aircrew. Meanwhile, the remaining flying boats would still need MCS facilities and there was always air-sea rescue — or was there?

At all levels the sailors believed in a future, but in the corridors of power uncertainty prevailed. Sights were set on building an Air Force for peace. The new RAF would phase out the heavy bombers, the flying boats, the piston engine fighters. The first jets were already in service. Missiles would follow.

When the sailors did come back from their overseas units, they found that only some of the 'Hants and Dorset' HSLs were to be retained. All other HSLs, with the exception of a few which were converted to Remote Control Target Towing Launches, were to be written-off or sold. The remaining '100 Class' boats had been transferred to the Navy in 1944 for Special Operations use and most of the surviving 'Whalebacks', Vospers, Thornycrofts, 'Miamis' and Fairmiles were worn out. The plans for bigger and better HSLs had been hurriedly scrapped and the prototypes cancelled.

ASR pinnaces were up for disposal, leaving only the 60 ft GP version in service. All the 37½ ft seaplane tenders were to go, with only a few 40 footers and most of the 41½ ft boats remaining. Some of these were to be fitted out as fire floats. Refuellers, 24 ft marine tenders, 23 ft W/T tenders, ferry boats, bomb scows, GS planing dinghies and whalers were all to be drastically reduced.

Cox'ns, MBCs, Fitters, Mechanics and Wireless Operators were 'demobbed' in droves. Others who were unable to find a regular place in the MCS re-mustered to other trades. The Nursing Orderlies, who had served so courageously, were no longer required and many of those who stayed in the Air Force found themselves treating colds and minor ailments in various sick quarters of the 'proper' RAF. To add to the general disincentives, the coveted ASR shoulder flash was withdrawn and rescue crews were once again indistinguishable from other airmen.

The plethora of Marine Officers who had so recently commanded the HSLs and pinnaces was far greater then the much reduced Marine Craft Section could absorb. The Officers were subjected to an oblique insult when they were advised that some of them would be invited to apply for transfer to other branches of the RAF. The Branches on offer were Administration, Equipment, Provost and Catering. Not surprisingly, hardly any HSL Masters even considered the suggestion. The majority of those officers who were unable to stay with the MCS opted for Civvy Street. Once more, the NCOs were blocked from applying for commissions.

By the late 1940s, when the Air Ministry eventually woke up to the fact that there would be other, more limited conflicts and that marine craft would still be required, the mass exodus had gone out of control. The RAF started recruiting Direct Entry Marine Officers over the heads of the NCOs once again.

For the same reason, the regular sailors were left seriously short-handed. On various overseas units, local labour was recruited, mainly in the capacity of deckhand. In the UK, airmen from other trades were invited to re-muster to Marine. Unfortunately, there was little career incentive to attract them.

This general lack of direction was typical throughout the RAF. In some branches, the recruiting figures and the rate at which serving men were extending their engagements had fallen to an unacceptable low. The manpower shortage was even more pronounced in the Army and Navy. Concern expressed in Government led to the introduction of National Service in 1947. Because of the all-regular nature of the MCS, the 'call-up' did nothing to boost its level of recruitment, but indirectly two other events did bring encouragement to potential recruits and to the sailors themselves.

The first was the granting of full Branch status on 11 December 1947. The Marine Branch was given responsibility for its own planning and for co-ordinating much of the work which had been under other Commands. This included Marine Craft training, RAF depot ships, recovery ships (HMAFVs *Bridport* and *Bridlington,* of which more later), the new role of the HSLs, range safety, flying boat support units and the Moorings Branch. (Moorings Branch operated 12 moorings 'drifters' and was responsible for the laying and servicing of all RAF moorings throughout the world. The work was mostly contracted by Air Ministry, but the civilian officers of the branch welcomed marine RAF officers looking after their affairs.)

Encouraging as it was, there were some drawbacks. There was much internal wrangling in the Air Ministry before the only Marine Officer of the new Directorate, Wing Commander H. L. Rudd, was able to convince his seniors that Branch affairs at top level should be managed specifically by Marine Officers under a Marine Group Captain. For some obscure reason, even when this had been achieved the Deputy Directorate of Marine Craft remained under a combined Directorate of Mechanical Transport and Marine Craft which even absorbed Balloon Command in 1951! One of the less exciting results of this was the odd circumstance of Marine Officers regularly serving with MT Sections or barrage balloon units. Most of the sailors were philosophical about it, took it in their stride and sometimes actually enjoyed the break. In later years, when the opportunity to apply for commissions was restored to SNCO Coxswains and Technicians, this was a deterrent. The NCOs worked out for themselves that commissions might oblige them to leave the Branch in which they wished to continue serving.

The second morale boost for the sailors came in 1948. On 25 June, His Majesty King George VI approved the use of the designation 'His Majesty's Air Force Vessel' for all operational RAF craft of 68 ft and over, commanded by RAF Officers and manned by RAF personnel in uniform. This entitled HMAFVs to fly the Union flag from the fore jackstaff between dawn and dusk when not underway. In all British history, the RAF Marine Branch was the only organization which shared this distinctive honour with the Royal Navy. Not only was this singular event in recognition of the sailors' contribution to lifesaving during the war, it was also an acknowledgement of the professionalism of the King's youngest seafaring service.

While the Deputy Directorate of Marine Craft wrestled with the format for management of the Branch, the Marine Craft Policy Committee were faced with the difficult task of pre-determining the types of marine craft that would be required in peacetime. Only when the role of the Marine Branch had been settled and the types of craft to fulfil that role defined could attention be turned to recruitment, training and manning levels.

Thirty-eight 'Hants and Dorset' HSLs were retained and converted to the new post-war designation of Rescue/Target-Towing Launch (RTTL). The armoured plating and guns were removed and the turret mountings blanked off by flat discs over-painted with roundels. All UK-based boats were repainted with the new standard black hulls and a lighter grey superstructure. The serial numbers on the bows were changed to white and the yellow rings removed from the roundels. Overseas boats reverted to peacetime white with large black numbers each side of the bows. Tiller compartments aft of the engine room were opened up to receive Ford driven power winches for target-towing and raised cuddies were built to protect the operators. Steel rollers were fitted in the transom to guide wire hawsers.

Four of the 'Hants and Dorsets' (and strangely one 'Whaleback', HSL

168) were considerably altered to be employed as Launch/Target-Towing Remote Control. The boats were fitted with extra armoured protection and extensive radio control equipment, but were unsuccessful. The four 68 footers reverted to manned RTTLs and the 63 footer was sold.

A new designation was also applied to seaplane tenders, many of which had been employed in a purely air-sea rescue role during the war. Units such as 37 ASRU, Lyme Regis, 46 ASRU, Porthcawl, and 29 ASRU, Littlehampton had operated them successfully from tidal harbours and in shoaling waters. After the war, the job of the STs was mainly directed at policing practice ranges, as relatively few were now engaged in attending to the depleted number of flying boat squadrons. The STs became known as Range Safety Launches (RSL).

The sailors were slow to adopt the new names, with the result that RTTLs and RSLs were still referred to colloquially as HSLs and STs for many years. Not until a new generation of launches, and to some extent a new generation of sailors, was firmly established in the 1960s did the old descriptions disappear from the jargon.

Marine bases were also retitled to suit their post-war roles. The term 'Marine Craft Section', which had been jointly applied to both the forerunner of the Marine Branch and the seaplane support units, now applied to any unit where marine craft afloat were in support of flying boats or other activities.

In the shuffling of responsibilities within the post-war Air Force, the old Marine Craft Repair Units became Maintenance Units, incredibly under Maintenance Command. At Marine Craft Maintenance Units, the sailors who were employed 'on the Section' operated the pinnaces and tenders used for handling craft before or after repair. They were responsible for all the MUs' slipping and launching, and for the security of all boats afloat.

Similarly, numbers of craft were allocated to Marine Craft Training Schools. These were operated not by instructors but by the sailors of the school's MCS. (The schools stayed mostly within the Marine Branch, but did wander into Training Command for a while, as one might have expected!) To add to the confusion, the MCSs in their support capacity at these stations remained part of Coastal Command.

At one stage, the MCS at RAF Calshot provided waterborne support to three Commands: resident and visiting seaplane squadrons, the Maintenance Unit, and the MCTS, all of which were located there at the same time. (A large contingent of sailors performed a like task at RAF Seletar in Singapore, but within the Far East Air Force.)

Anomalies and complications in day to day procedures were rife. Eventually, the last Maintenance Unit, 238 MU at Calshot, was disbanded. It was moved to Mount Batten in 1961 and, with the MCTS, returned to the direct control of the Marine Branch once again.

All MCSs provided a rescue facility in addition to their main activities. Other marine craft bases, where the primary task was range patrolling or target-towing and where sea rescue featured highly, became Marine Craft Units. These MCUs were invariably self contained, small outfits that were strategically placed within a few miles of the flying stations or ranges they served. Most of the old ASRUs remained in place as MCUs, but everything was scaled down. There were fewer aircraft in the RAF carrying out fewer sorties, and in the UK at least no-one was shooting them down. Whereas ASRUs had operated a dozen HSLs or more, the MCUs rarely controlled more than three RTTLs or RSLs and perhaps a couple of MTs or GS dinghies. Some MCUs were pinnace orientated, while others operated this type of craft in a multiple role alongside the faster boats.

In the early 1950s, recruiting finally balanced with demand. The Marine Branch became the 'closed shop' it had been before the war. Few joined; few departed; all were signed on for a substantial stretch.

There was one useful exception. The rules surrounding National Service dictated that Merchant Seamen were exempt if they stayed in the Merchant Navy until the age of 35. Many, particularly those with families, did not relish the prospect of staying deep-sea for so long, neither did they take kindly to the idea of spending a wasted two years or 18 months in the Army. The RAF provided a seafaring alternative in exchange for a commitment to a three-year regular engagement as MBC.

Soon there were to be new boats, new conditions of service, new pay levels and new uniforms ashore and afloat. As the twilight of the 1940s turned to the dawn of the '50s, the sailors felt assured of their future. Flying boats may have been fading from fashion and aircraft crashes rare, but there would always be people in peril at sea. The beaches that had so recently been spiked to repel invaders were now cleared to attract an invasion of a different nature.

Coaches, trains and private cars had shed their wartime dust and drab and were now bringing hordes of carefree and sometimes careless holiday-makers to the fringes of the oceans. Yachts, motor boats and sailing dinghies became brilliantly coloured dots on seas which had been populated by dull grey smudges for so long. The sailors could see for themselves that there would be much to do. Depleted it may have been, but the RAF Marine Branch was still the biggest lifeboat service in the world.

It did not occur to them that ideas pioneered before the war by a Spanish engineer in England and a Russian émigré in the USA would gradually oust them from their exalted position.

The pioneers were Juan de la Cierva and Igor Sikorsky. Ere long, names such as 'Dragonfly,' 'Sycamore,' 'Whirlwind' and 'Wessex' would enter the sailors' vocabulary. Already, the RAF had combined air-sea, jungle, desert, arctic and mountain rescue under the all-embracing title of Search and Rescue. It was all in anticipation of the coming of the ubiquitous helicopter.

# Chapter 18

# What d'you think you're on — Daddy's yacht?

*An oft-repeated expression used by NCOs to chide idle crews. The new boats with their Rolls-Royce engines were certainly more yacht-like than any of their predecessors, but it wasn't all plain sailing.*

In the mid-1950s, the Government was concerned about the unpopular and inefficient National Service scheme. The Korean war created a surge of volunteers, as all wars seem to do, but as the conflict dissolved into an unsatisfactory peace, the rate of recruitment was far from achieving the desired all-regular, high technology force. Drastic measures were required to make service life more attractive, and with unseemly haste a series of Armed Forces' Bills were passed through parliament. Social changes swept through all three armed services.

The RAF, which in a few years had risen from a position of junior Service to that of senior Service in all but name, was in the forefront of the social revolution. The most publicized event was a pay revision which for the first time ever put service pay on a par with civilians. A new Technician career ladder offered guaranteed promotion and higher wages for specialist tradesmen. Marriage allowances were increased, and the approved age for marriage was lowered from 26 to 21. 'Living out' allowances were paid to those without Married Quarters and 'Disturbance' allowances were introduced to compensate for disruption of families. Weekly Pay Parades became obsolete; monthly salaries were paid into bank accounts instead.

On a more personal level, most of the irritating duties such as fire picquet, guard, kit inspection and routine parades were either eliminated or reduced in number. Kitbags were replaced by holdalls and the webbing packs and straps which had been issued since the 1920s were finally discarded. Gas cape groundsheets and greatcoats were replaced by stylish raglan raincoats. Number One Home Dress or 'Best Blue' uniforms were no longer cut from uncomfortable serge. The individually tailored T63 'Smoothie Blue' barathea uniforms were similar in quality and finish to the officers'. To the sailors' delight, brass buttons and buckles were replaced by anodized ones.

Working rig for the sailors underwent some changes. Aircrew shirts with collars attached were issued in place of the collar and stud type. The white submariner's sweater was replaced by a navy blue guernsey, and, most sensible of all, the wind-prone forage cap gave way to the beret.

A new payment known as 'Hard Lying Money' could be claimed for every night spent aboard a marine craft on passage. It was a useful bonus which especially boosted the income of the sailors of Ferry Pool. Ferry Pool was a high-seatime unit which was set up at Calshot to collect and deliver marine craft between manufacturers, MUs and marine bases in similar manner to the Ferry Pilots who delivered aircraft.

The sailors reaped the benefits of all the changes, although the Marine Branch had no need to attract recruits; it was almost impossible to gain entry when, as the 1960s approached, many of the UK MCUs were closing down. Air-sea rescue was no longer the main occupation, although launches were held at immediate readiness for emergencies. Most of those in distress in peacetime were civilians who found themselves in difficulties around the coast. Quite often, marine tenders and GS dinghies were deployed for inshore work of this type, as they were more suitable and could present a rapid response. The sailors later adopted the '3000 Class' rigid inflatables for such rescues, an idea that the RNLI had developed with their inshore rescue boats, and which had proved effective with the RAF in Gibraltar.

Whether it was for a merchant ship or a trawler in trouble, a capsized pleasure boat, a swimmer, a child on a 'Li-Lo' or a walker stranded by the tide, the sailors still put to sea. Whatever the emergency, it was always known as a 'Crash Call'.

The majority of the sailors' time was devoted to the training of the new jet-age aircrews. Anti-submarine exercises were introduced where a launch played the part of a submarine while searching aircraft dropped a pattern of sonar detectors to provide its position. After locating it, the aircraft would carry out a mock attack. The launch skipper would report the accuracy to the pilot via R/T, and at the end of the exercise the boat would retrieve the sonobuoys.

Target-towing, torpedo recovery and gunnery range patrols continued to fill many nights and days, but the introduction of the helicopter brought a new facet to an old activity of the Marine Branch.

All aircrew were required to take training courses in sea survival with new equipment in the form of fully covered dinghies and radio transmitting and location devices. Even Mae Wests were fitted with small water-activated transmitters which could emit a signal over a short range. The device was known as SARAH (Search And Rescue And Homing). Launches and helicopters carried SARAH receivers and buoyant SARAH beacons for practice purposes. Square searching was all but obsolete.

The format of dropping the flyers in the water from a launch then steaming away was virtually unchanged, but the difference came with the pick-up. No longer did the boat pull alongside and break out the scrambling net. Now, the airmen were plucked from their dinghies on the end of a helicopter winch cable. In the early days, the winchman did not normally lower himself on the wire as is the current practice. Given that he was able, the survivor was required to pass a strop over his head, and with arms akimbo wait to be hoisted into the aircraft. He would then be lowered on to the launch where he would be bundled below and treated with a generous tot.

This was not always straightforward, especially in a heavy sea. The trainees would often be seasick long before they leapt overboard and in a very short time could become mentally, if not physically, incapable of following the correct procedures. There were further difficulties in lowering the airman to the heaving launch, for the winch wire had a tendency to swing in a wide arc beneath the chopper. Early SAR helicopters were not *that* controllable and the combination of a short winch wire and a surging launch often contrived to bring the aircraft dangerously close to the boat's mast. The first MBC to reach out and grab the dangling 'survivor' was virtually guaranteed a substantial electric shock caused by the different electrical potential betwixt launch and helicopter.

The sailors were sometimes called upon to demonstrate the art of 'chopper dangling' to new aircrew. Just to show what fun it all was, the helicopter pilots would add a few extra touches. A favourite trick was to fly directly at the speeding launch, swinging the dangling man so close to the mast that his reflex action was to fold his legs to protect his vitals.

A more serious demonstration was in the use of the Robinson stretcher. One of the boat's crew would be strapped in this cross between full-length strait-jacket and splint which was designed to allow the manhandling of a severely injured person, and is still in use today. Once strapped in, it was impossible to make the slightest movement, and then to be hoisted by a helicopter was the essence of total dependence on others.

The early SAR helicopters were more suited to rescue operations over the land than over the sea. Their range and duration were limited compared with the later Wessex and Sea King. They were difficult to control in high winds, were not able to fly at night or in poor visibility and they relied mostly on visual or 'dead reckoning' navigation. Because of their size and engine power, their carrying capacity was limited and their short-drop winch wires could only be operated from inside the aircraft.

The latter half of the 1960s saw the helicopter's ascendancy in the sea rescue role, but meanwhile the sailors accepted that in high winds, poor visibility or just plain filthy weather, they were still very much in the front line. They needed to update their ageing fleet to do the job properly.

The 'Hants and Dorsets' had outlived all expectations. The first of the class, HSL (later RTTL) 2552, had entered the service in 1943 and served in 15 different ASRUs and MCUs at home and overseas until her disposal from 1113 MCU Holyhead in April 1958. The last of the class to be constructed, HSL (RTTL) 2746, had arrived in March 1946 at Fanara. From here she was moved to 1153 MCU at Morphou Bay, Xeros, Cyprus. During the 1950s, the launch was employed in action against EOKA terrorists and with her sister ship, RTTL 2713, she carried out many successful interceptions of arms smugglers. The longest serving 'Hants and Dorset' was HSL (RTTL) 2743, which was withdrawn from service at Holyhead in October 1962 after an eventful 17 years.

Of the 90 'Hants and Dorsets' built, only one had been lost to enemy action (HSL 2598, Algiers, November 1943) and one was sunk by a 'friendly' attack by the US Air Force in March 1944 (HSL 2706, Great Yarmouth). Several were damaged in the course of their service lives and written off charge as a result. One of these was RTTL 2555.

In May 1950, RTTL 2555, whilst on passage to Alness in Scotland, put in to the MCU at Blyth. After refuelling, the launch was moored alongside other Blyth boats for the night and the crew prepared themselves for an evening ashore.

From the sickbay the Cox'n saw sparks near the tankspace bulkhead, but was unable to act before he was blown backwards by exploding petrol fumes. The skipper, who was in his cabin below, escaped through a hole which had been blown in the side. In seconds the launch was ablaze. The base staff dragged the burning boat away from its neigh-bours and attacked the fire with hand extinguishers, but the flames were not finally doused until the boat sank. Amazingly, the fuel in the tanks had not caught fire, only the fumes. After beaching, the hull split open and all the petrol leaked into the harbour, causing a further hazard. RTTL 2555 was scrapped. The Cox'n Flight Sergeant Sparkes (sic) suffered from delayed concussion.

By 1950, the proposals for the replacement of the 'Hants and Dorsets' were with the MCPC. Of all the tenders received, those from Vosper emerged as the most feasible, and the design followed closely the lines and the layout of the 'Hants and Dorset'. This was not altogether surprising for when the BPBC had closed down in 1946, George Selman advised Vosper's design team.

The new boat, the RTTL Mk IA, was the same length at 68 ft, but the beam was broadened to 19ft ⅞ in, with a proportionately wider timber superstructure. The construction was still double-diagonal planking on timber frames. In general appearance, the new launch was much bulkier than the 'Hants and Dorset', which now became known as the RTTL Mk I. The sides of the new hull did not taper as much towards the after end, thus the transom was much wider. Not only did this increase the space below deck, but it also provided an increased planing surface aft to give greater lift to the hull.

Atop the deckhouse was a large aluminum tripod mast which carried a Decca radar scanner and the various UHF, VHF, R/T and W/T aerials. There were also footholds and grab rails to enable lookouts to ascend the mast.

Unfortunately, the first Vosper boats to enter service between 1953–5, were merely sheep in wolves' clothing. They were grossly under-powered and painfully slow to plane. Even with 'dry' boats (ie before the hulls had soaked) and in ideal conditions, the maximum speed was barely 24 knots compared with the 28 knots of a 'Hants and Dorset' in full service trim. Once alginate slime had fouled the bottoms and the hulls had absorbed water, the new boats struggled to cruise above planing speed. These bigger, heavier boats were still powered by Napier Sea Lion engines! Neither the Air Force nor Vosper had intended it so, but delays with development of the chosen Rolls-Royce Sea Griffons and their Mathway hydraulic gearboxes had obliged the RAF to use the Napiers as an interim measure.

In other respects, the new RTTLs showed promise. The crews' quarters and the sickbays were comparatively cavernous, although the latter were still restricted by a skipper's cabin. The engineers gained a lot of space in the beamier after section where the layout of the engines had been reversed, in that the centre engine drove direct to the centre shaft and the wing engines drove through Vee-drives. In the tank compartment forward of the engine room, fuel capacity was increased from 1,800 to 2,300 gallons.

By 1959, the Napier engines were removed, the boats were stripped to the basic hulls and retro-fitted with two Sea Griffons. Their maximum speed was then in excess of 38 knots. After conversion, which might be better described as transformation, the Mk IAs were designated Mk IB. The first of these compromise boats was RTTL 2747 and three more followed, Nos 2748, 2749 and 2750.

While development work on the Mathway gearboxes continued, Vosper produced five more boats with the old Lion engines. These were 2751, 2752, 2753, 2754 and 2755 which were different yet again. A new parallel-sided deckhouse was constructed from aluminium. The Master's cabin was sensibly placed behind the conning bridge and the Wireless Operator was relegated to a poky cabin on the starboard side. The new deckhouse incorporated a sliding door for exterior access to the wheelhouse from the port side. Unlike the earlier boats, there was no internal alleyway from the after deck. To get to the wheelhouse from the engine room or wireless cabin, there was a choice between walking forward via the side deck, or threading through the sickbay and crew's quarters and climbing a vertical ladder to enter through a hatch in the wheelhouse floor. Neither route was particularly difficult when the launch was at rest or in moderate seas, but at high speed and in bad weather both could be extremely hazardous.

The five boats with the combination of aluminium deckhouse and

Napier engines were known to the sailors as Mk 'IIA' and after their conversion to Sea Griffons as Mk 'IIB'. These designations were never used officially because all the 'ali-top' launches became Sea Griffon-powered ultimately, and were documented only as Mk IIs.

The plot was further complicated when in 1956, while the Mk IA and 'IIA' boats were still labouring on with their outdated machinery, RTTL 2756 emerged from the factory as the first complete Sea Griffon-powered Mk II boat.

The sailors now had a mixture of 'Hants and Dorsets' with three Napiers, Vosper 'wooden tops' with three Napiers, Vosper 'ali-tops' with Napiers, and an 'ali-top' with Griffons! The sailors were themselves confused, but it got worse.

There was no clear prototype of the Vosper Mk II, although drawings and scantlings existed before 1955. Arguably, the *actual* prototype was RTTL 2756, but the prototype drawings depicted a Mk II boat with the number 2762E (E for Experimental), and when its sea trials began this was the number painted on the hull. In fact, 2762E was a one-off. It was built entirely from aluminium, the only timber being in the teak deck planking. Even before the boat was launched, it was realized that the number 2762 clashed with a German D-boat in RAF service (see page 180). After the acceptance trials, the number was changed to 2772E.

Because of its light construction, RTTL 2772E was the fastest of all the (sic) Mk II launches and in its early days was reputed to have achieved around 52 knots. It remained in service for many years, but was the subject of constant monitoring for the effects of sea water and electrolytic corrosion on the hull. Eventually, the hull deteriorated and had to be skinned with traditional double-diagonal planking. This modification, among others, slowed the boat to a more or less standard Mk II performance and it finally had its 'E' designation removed.

By the early 1960s, all the Mk IA launches had been converted to Mk IB by Vosper, and most of the Mk II series (and 2772E) were in service. Only the remaining hybrids, 2751–5, were still struggling with Napier power units.

The Marine Craft Maintenance Unit at Calshot, and after 1961 at Mount Batten, took on the job of converting these to full Mk II specification. With components provided by Vosper, Rolls-Royce and other suppliers, RAF boatwrights, fitters and electricians embarked on this complex task. They succeeded in completing each conversion much quicker than the builders had, and at a lower cost. After the conversion programme, the following craft were all listed as Mk II launches. RTTLs 2751–61 and 2767–72.

The Mk IB and Mk II RTTLs were modern, powerful, responsive and exciting. With the twin Sea Griffon engines developing 1,700 hp at 2,750 rpm each, the wooden hulled boats could cruise between 32 and 36 knots and achieve over 40 knots in emergencies. At low speeds they required skilful handling. The *slowest* speed with both engines in gear at idling rpm was over 10 knots, thus the slightest error by the helmsman could have an expensive outcome.

The speeds which could be attained by the various types of RTTLs were always somewhat subjective if the launch speedometers were to be believed. Competition between crews to have the 'fastest boat on the unit' often put pressure on the engineers to squeeze that little bit extra from the engines. When every tuning trick had been tried, the fitters would pull the Chernikeef log out of its mounting and put a little bit of additional twist on the impeller blades. The speedometer would then show an immediate gain of a knot or two. This invariably satisfied the skipper until the next calibration run over a measured mile, at which time the boat had usually completed a major service and was light and 'dry'.

The Sea Griffon RTTLs had a number of problems compared with their 'Hants and Dorset' predecessors. The first concerned the three aluminium fuel tanks. These were prone to split, filling the bilges with 120 octane Avgas. A redesigned five-tank system was introduced, with each tank cascover-sheathed with an epoxy-type coating. Fuel capacity was reduced to 2,220 gallons, but the problem did not recur.

The second problem was created by the Plessey cartridge starters fitted to the main engines. Despite many built-in safety devices, the cartridges did not always align correctly, but instead discharged with an impressive jet of flame into the engine room. The flash was followed by acrid ammoniac and cordite fumes and clouds of smoke which were frequently responsible for the engineers abandoning the engine room in record time. The starters gave no prior warning of an imminent failure. One moment they worked, then suddenly they didn't. There were also difficulties restarting hot engines, or even cold engines, in a hot climate. In some foreign climes, a pre-dawn start was preferable to the alternative of vainly banging off multiple cartridges after sun-up. There were many immobile RTTLs with seething skippers and impatient, jeering deckhands counting aloud in chorus as red-faced engineers fired cartridge after cartridge, praying for just one of the 48 spark plugs to bring the engines to life. Some fitters acquired the mystical art of balancing the fuel priming so precisely as to achieve a first time start, whatever the ambient conditions. These rare souls were known as 'one-shot wonders'. The real show-offs could start up two engines simultaneously, and were held in awe by their peers.

A few years and many thousands of cartridges later, it was discovered that the cartridges supplied had been of the wrong type in the first place! None the less, the principle of the system was questionable, and many sailors were convinced that someone among the specifiers had a shareholding in the Plessey Company.

The third and most significant fault with the new boats manifested itself over a period of time, when severe cracking of frames and outer skin began to appear under the starboard chines of several launches. The problem was principally due to the fact that both propellers rotated in the same anti-clockwise direction while the hull tried to rotate clockwise in response to the torque effect. At the speeds attainable, the starboard chine was effectively slamming into rock-hard water.

Urgent trials were conducted to compare the angle of attack of the Mk II launches with that of the veteran Mk Is. It was found that the newer boats tended to a bow-high attitude which meant that the deep vee section of the forefoot was above the water and not cutting into it to soften and divide the waves as it should. Adjustable trim tabs were attached to the transom to deflect the nose of the craft downwards, but although the test was successful the trim tabs created handling difficulties in following seas.

A fixed angle trimming wedge was fitted under the rear hull instead, which also helped the launch to rise on to the plane more efficiently. The boat used for the investigative trials was RTTL 2757, which now resides at the RAF Museum, Hendon. The wedge can still be seen above the rudders.

Although wedging helped to reduce the pounding, the torque reaction could not be eliminated altogether (except by changing the rotation of one of the Vee-drives which, presumably, was not practical). The RTTLs were strengthened internally, but eventually a third outer skin was fitted to all the boats to the detriment of speed.

Despite the delays and setbacks, the Sea Griffon-powered boats were the flagships of the RAF fleet from the mid 1950s to the early 1970s. Although only 21 of the type were deployed throughout the world, they epitomized the post-war Marine Branch more than any other type of vessel.

Besides the Mk2 RTTLs, other new boats were to lend credence to the comments about 'Daddy's yacht'. The ageing 60 ft pinnaces were gradually phased out during the 1950s, although P 1196 remained at 1107 MCU Newhaven until 1966, and P 1198 continued in Seletar until 1967. These versatile craft, with their three Perkins S6M diesels, had performed outstandingly in a variety of roles for more than 20 years. They had so endeared themselves to the sailors, that it was believed no replacement design could equal them. Groves and Gutteridge's new 63 ft pinnaces were, however, worthy successors. The hull lines were similar to the earlier type, but an angular aluminium wheelhouse/radio cabin raised the profile. Below decks, the accommodation was beautifully fitted out and the engine rooms with their twin 200 hp Rolls-Royce C6SFLM diesels were an engineer's dream. The new pinnaces were able to steam at a respectable 16–17 knots, even in adverse weather conditions. The serials began with P 1371 in 1955 and ended with P 1392 10 years later. The last two boats had turbocharged engines in place of the earlier supercharged type.

Another new craft which was included in the RAFs decision to switch to Rolls-Royce power units was the Thornycroft-designed 43 ft. RSL Mk

II. Here there was a marked contrast with the 41½ ft RSL Mk I (ex-seaplane tender). The new boats were solidly built, crew kindly and comfortable craft which were admirably suited to spending many hours at sea on range safety work. Twin C6SFLMs diesels propelled the boats up to 20 knots, and although they were slower than the earlier craft they were better in a seaway. In common with the Mk II RTTLs and the 63 ft pinnaces, they shared traditional double-diagonal planked hulls with aluminium superstructures. The prototype 43 ft RSL was numbered 1640 and continued sequentially to the last in the series, 1668.

For a period between 1955 and 1961 the RAF operated five unusual boats in Germany (which acounted for the gap in the RTTL serial numbers). Boats 2762–6 were known only as 'D-boats'. These German-built 96 ft launches were of welded steel construction with twin Maybach diesel engines. The design was very similar to the compromise round bilge shape of the wartime E-boats, with the result that the D-boats were both swift and sea kindly.

They were located at List on the German island of Sylt off the Danish coast and were engaged in the principal tasks of range safety, stand-by flying and weather reporting for the RAF station at nearby Westerland. D-boats were popular with their crews and they performed both reliably and well in the extremes of climatic conditions that prevailed. Throughout their time with the RAF they were partly manned by Germans and were eventually handed over to the new Luftwaffe in 1961.

There was a natural enthusiasm throughout the Marine Branch for all the new craft and a spirit of optimism was engendered by their arrival at the various units, but behind it all the 'proper' RAF was in trouble.

In 1952 the RAF operated about 6,400 aircraft, a post-war peak. Within a few years, there was a substantial reduction of aeroplanes in the belief that the Air Force of the future would consist mostly of missiles. Along with many other tradesmen, some Marine technicians were encouraged to re-muster for work on Thor and Bloodhound rockets. They little knew that they were venturing into the wilderness, for when the programme eventually collapsed the Marine Branch was unable to take them all back. It was known as 'the misguided missile scheme'.

Despite the introduction of the V-bomber force and the new Hunters and Lightnings which replaced the Hornet, Meteor, Vampire and Sabre fighters, the RAF was rapidly getting smaller. In the mid-1960s there were only 2,500 operational aircraft: by 1973, when the Royal Navy had once more moved front stage with Polaris submarines, unofficial estimates showed barely 600.

These cuts all affected the mariners indirectly, but none so acutely as when the last Sunderlands of Coastal Command departed from Pembroke Dock for Seletar in 1956. The Malayan crisis kept them operating from there until they were so short of spares that they had to be taken out of service. An era had ended. The demise of the Sunderlands and the failure of the Princess flying boat project, finally snapped the link which had forged the origins of the Marine Branch in 1918. Those sailors who had spent most of their careers with flying boats were bereft. For the first time in almost 40 years, the bomb scows, refuellers, flare path dinghies and ferry boats were lying redundant at their moorings.

Consequently, redundancies hit the sailors too. The sum of all the new front line Rolls-Royce launches to enter service was only 72; far fewer than those which were retired. The closure of the flying boat bases and a dozen or so smaller MCUs; the hand-over of many overseas units as ex-Empire nations achieved independence; technical progress with helicopters; all were events which left the Marine Branch over-manned.

Qualified Master Coxswains, who would have enjoyed the rank of Warrant Officer in other trades, served as Senior Aircraftman, while many First Class Cox'ns had no hope of promotion. The Fitters and Boatwrights who had elected for the technician ladder fared much better, but those who had chosen the command structure were condemned to stagnation.

Recruiting was stopped. Various schemes to supplement 'natural wastage' with redundancy packages and invitations to change to other trades were brought in as an attempt to reduce manpower levels. Some enterprising MBCs fooled the system by re-mustering to Boatwright or Marine Fitter! The fee for purchase-release was reduced, and certain tradesmen were banned from 'signing on'. This was a bitter blow to many potential 'lifers'.

Paradoxically, even as the NCOs and other ranks were being encouraged to leave, promotions and retirements left the Branch short-handed for skippers once more. Masters and Extra Masters were sought from the Merchant Navy, but although the campaign was partly successful the Air Force was unable to compete with the rewards offered by the merchant service. Once again, the Cox'ns were largely overlooked.

Marine Fitters and Boatwrights were granted an official conduit to commissions when the new technician ladder came into effect. SNCOs, on attaining a qualifying length of service and armed with suitable recommendations, were able to apply. The scheme worked admirably, with the result that the Marine Branch technical prowess excelled, thanks to these highly skilled officers. However, there was still the quirky probability of a 'tour' with MT or Balloons.

The contractions and the recruiting freezes did have the positive effect of concentrating the minds of those sailors still serving. The standard of professionalism reached a high point that exceeded precepts. By the middle of the 1960s, just about everyone was so highly qualified that chevrons and rings abounded. It was a case of all Chiefs and no Indians, which in any other branch of the Air Force might have constituted an embarrassment. The sailors disregarded the semantics and got on with the job.

Whilst the Branch was shrinking, the surfeit of sailors was offset to a small extent by two vessels which required relays of crews larger than any other RAF craft. The Service had always operated ships in some form; from the early floating docks, drifters and concrete lighters, through the seaplane/ASR depot ships and barges of the war, to civilian manned moorings vessels. This time the sailors went truly deep-sea when they took over ex-Royal Navy Offshore Fleet Minesweepers, HMS *Bridport* and HMS *Bridlington*. Both had been taken out of reserve from West Hartlepool and prepared for their role under the RAF ensign during 1946–7.

The ships were 'Bangor' class anti-submarine/minesweepers which had served with distinction since they were launched from Denny's of Dumbarton in February 1940. Their overall length was 162 ft, their beam 28 ft and they drew 9½ ft. Two Harland & Wolff 2,000 hp diesels propelled each of the 600 ton vessels.

All the weaponry and wartime appendages were removed and they were repainted in pale grey and white. Each ships' complement was 48 men including four officers, just over half the size of the naval crews that had manned them.

For the RAF crewmen, working the ships proved to be an experience far removed from the closeness of the RTTLs and pinnaces. Lines of demarcation between officers and men were as clear cut as those in the RN. The RAF sailors joked among themselves about reverting to 'wooden men and iron ships'. Life aboard was uncomfortable, hammocks being very much in evidence and space at a premium. The only consolation lay in the thought of how much worse it must have been when the Navy squeezed 80 men below.

The men who were selected to command the 'Brids' were Squadron Leaders of the 'old school'. The majority of them were from the pre-war RAFO group of HSL Masters: men like E. Hardie of HSL 107 in Malta, 'Black Jack' Hillman of HSL 110 in Basra, 'Gerry' Fitzgerald-Lombard of HSL 105 in Singapore, H. P. Dainty, A. T. Cooper, J. D. Loughnan and G. F. Coates, among others. Perhaps some pre-war Merchant and Royal Navy instincts still lingered on with some of the Captains, for ex-crew members all have their stories of 'Pseudo Blighs,' or 'Bucko Mates', and of sadistic SNCO Bosuns. These tales do not extend to 'lashings at the gratings' or 'keelhauling', but there are recollections of men being 'thrown in the brig' for quite minor misdemeanours! Whatever hardship legends surrounded the 'Brids', the sailors who served in them now regard them with pride and nostalgia.

The two ships fulfilled a variety of vital roles before they were scrapped in 1958. They were severally operated in connection with the Berlin Air Lift between May 1948 and June of the following year. HMAFV *Bridport* under the command of Squadron Leader Hardie stood by as rescue ship under the air corridors. Both ships spent many days at sea on NATO anti-submarine exercises and frequently sailed with the Royal Navy to carry out torpedo recovery duties.

In 1955, HMAFV *Bridlington* sailed to Gan in the southernmost group of the Maldive Islands, 30 miles from the Equator. Her voyage took her to Gibraltar, Malta, through the Suez Canal to Aden and thence to Colombo. Whilst on passage through the Mediterranean, she established a Marine Branch 'first and only' when she rescued two escapees from the French Foreign Legion who were adrift in a small open boat.

The purpose of the voyage was to take a survey team and their equipment to Gan island. A PSP (Pierced Steel Plank) runway had been laid across the 1¼ by ¾ mile coral outcrop during the war, but now Britain had found a new use for the old base. The independence of India, the Pakistans, Burma and, shortly, Ceylon effectively removed secure air routes for trooping to the Far East. More important, the plans for the 'nuclear umbrella' of the V-bomber force meant that the essential staging posts for fuel, armaments and servicing should ideally be on sovereign soil. Cyprus, Masirah and the British possessions in the Maldives suited this purpose admirably.

After arrival at Gan, HMAFV *Bridlington* worked for some weeks at ferrying supplies back and forth across the 600 miles of ocean between Gan and Ceylon. When the runway was back in use, the supply train was taken over by Singapore-based Sunderlands and RNZAF Bristol Freighter aircraft from the Sinhalese airfield of Katunayake. Heavy equipment was taken by merchant ships from the UK. Shortly after HMAFV *Bridlington* returned to the UK, streaming her paying off pennant, other RAF sailors were outward bound to operate the landing craft and support vessels for the new staging point.

The two minesweepers were laid up in Devonport until they were scrapped in 1958. There were sighs of relief from the sailors who had not served on them and some sadness in the hearts of those who had. Many of the tasks they had pioneered were to be resumed by another generation of steel HMAFVs almost 10 years later.

# Chapter 19

# Here today,
# Gan tomorrow

*For several years overseas bases outnumbered those in the UK.*

Khaki drill bush jackets and No 1 overseas dress uniforms, with their bright red flashes, were withdrawn in stages during the 1950s, but the traditional and often 'customized' KD shirts, shorts and trousers had lingered. KD was synonymous with romantic Empire locations such as China Bay, Trincomalee, Kalafrana, Alexandria, Cocos, Rangoon and scores of other far away places. When KD was replaced, the new name chosen was SCP. It stood for 'Stone Coloured Polyester', and had all the romanticism of a mail order catalogue.

As the UK MCUs were reduced in number, the sailors found themselves wearing KD or SCP on ever more frequent overseas 'tours'. The normal duration was two years if accompanied (ie with wife and family), or one year if unaccompanied. For many of those who had few qualifying points for Married Quarters, most 'tours' were unaccompanied anyway, at least for some of the time. The busiest overseas base was at RAF Seletar, Singapore, where a Marine Craft Maintenance unit provided repair facilities for the whole of FEAF, while 1124 MCU supplied SAR, target-towing, sonar practice and weapons recovery. The unit worked closely with Shackletons and helicopters from nearby Changi airfield.

On Boxing Day 1962, the crew of RTTL 2755 under the command of Flight Lieutenant Chandler found themselves in trouble and were forced to take advantage of a 205 Squadron Shackleton, a helicopter from 66 SAR Squadron, an MCU pinnace and the Maintenance Unit, all at one go!

The launch had sailed for Borneo after a rebel uprising in Brunei and its task was an anti-piracy patrol in the South China Sea. Whilst on passage, it collided with a floating object and was holed below the waterline. Despite the efforts of Chief Technician George Parsons, a Boatwright who was aboard, the inflow of water could not be stemmed. The

Wireless Operator sent an SOS, but back in Seletar this was confused with a routine position report, so no alarm was given.

Fortunately, the launch was seen by a Transport Command Hastings which alerted the base and circled until the Shackleton arrived. When the 'Crash Call' was received, all but a few personnel were away for Christmas, but a scratch crew was assembled and a pinnace set sail immediately. At Changi, a brand new Belvedere helicopter was being air tested, and although the winch gear had not yet been installed it took off and made for the distressed launch. By this time the RTTL was well down in the water, and there was a danger of the engine room bulkheads giving way.

When the Belvedere arrived it was decided that all but three of the crew should be taken off. This was an extremely hazardous operation as in the absence of a winch and strop each member had to climb a knotted rope and pull himself aboard, but everyone made it, albeit with badly lacerated hands.

A lengthy tow in unpleasant conditions, with Corporal Paddy Blair at the controls of the pinnace, eventually brought RTTL 2755 to Seletar. The launch was awash to within a foot of the gunwhales. The Maintenance Unit repaired the RTTL, fitted an Oerlikon cannon, and it was dispatched once more on anti-piracy patrols.

In 1966 the unit began training locally recruited crews and 1124 MCU was finally disbanded on 1 October 1970. Pinnace 1385 was returned to the UK, the old pinnace P 1198 was sold, and RTTLs 2750 and 2755, along with RSL 1652, were transferred to the Singapore Armed Forces Maritime Command.

The most popular units for the families were at Kai Tak in Hong Kong and Glugor on Penang Island. Kai Tak was closed down in January 1967 after many years of stand-by flying off the end of the runway, and many effective rescues. Like so many other units, the work was seceded in favour of helicopters and locally manned marine craft.

Before its closure in March 1970, 1125 MCU at Glugor had a coloured history. The unit had first been established in 1945 as 231 ASRU, becoming an MCS in the designation changes of 1946. At that time, the unit was based on the RAF depot barge *Hataili* which had provided a base for a mobile ASRU during the Burma advance. When *Hataili* and her sister ship *Henzarda* were returned to their owners after the war, a permanent unit was established at Penang. The change to MCU status became effective in 1955.

The 1125 MCU boats provided seaborne survival training, range safety and SAR services for the Royal Australian Air Force base at Butterworth and during the Malaya/Indonesia fracas, they carried out anti-smuggling and anti-terrorist patrols.

On the evening of Saturday 23 July 1966, RAAF Butterworth advised the MCU that three men in a ski-boat had failed to return from a day trip to an island 20 miles north of Penang. One of the men should have been dropped off in Penang before the others returned to the Butterworth Yacht Club. They were long overdue and it was getting dark.

With the daunting prospect of more than 80 square miles of waters to search, two RSLs were prepared for sea. Before they sailed, they received word that one of the men had been picked up by a Malay fishing boat, but the inscrutable fishermen had finished tending their traps before taking the survivor ashore. The man claimed that the boat had sunk near a wreck buoy and that he had swum against strong tidal currents for over an hour before reaching the fishermen. His two companions had been swept seaward. To the would-be rescuers the clue about the wreck buoy was useful. A well-known local seamark, known as the Russian Wreck, was a Russian ship which had been sunk by the German cruiser *Emden* in the Great War.

Within 20 minutes of receiving the 'Crash Call', RSLs 1645 and 1656 were on their way. They fanned out down tide and began a weaving search on an exceptionally calm sea. The night was dark and searchlights were necessary. At intervals, the boats stopped engines to listen out. The sailors were disturbed to notice a profusion of poisonous jellyfish and sea snakes on the still surface.

A Shackleton from RAF Changi arrived in the small hours when the search was shifted northwards in response to a tide change. In the light of flares dropped from the 'Shack' even the smallest piece of jetsam stood out from the oily surface. The launch crews found themselves pursuing many false leads, often rowing ashore in rubber boats to check the foreshore.

In the morning, RSL 1652 joined the search while helicopters and fixed wing aircraft from Butterworth added support. On the shore, a unit of the RAF Regiment walked some 30 miles of beach and swamp along the coast. At sea, a flotilla of small high speed boats of the Royal Malaysian Customs service helped with the difficult inshore sectors.

On the Sunday evening, some flotsam and two ski rope handles were found, but there was no sign of any survivors. The search was suspended overnight and recommenced at dawn. On the Monday, a body was found. Another was washed ashore two days later. It was a miserable end to all the exhausting efforts, but at least every possible attempt had been made.

RAF Gan on Addu Atoll in the Maldive Islands was an unaccompanied posting to which many of the sailors returned again and again. An oft-repeated saying was 'Here today, Gan tomorrow'. The Marine Craft Section operated tugs, landing craft and dumb barges to offload supplies which came in by sea. Whenever a merchant ship called at Gan, it hove-to outside the lagoon to await a pilot to guide it through the narrows to the inner anchorage. This was the job of the Marine Officers, who amazed many a ship's Captain by lending a whole new meaning to the definition of RAF pilot.

The first landing craft were elderly LCMs (Landing Craft Mechanized) with American Graymarine or Hudson Invader engines. These were eventually replaced with purpose-built LCGPs (Landing Craft General Purpose) with the RAFs standard Rolls-Royce diesels. Pinnace 1374 and a marine tender were the only conventional craft.

The sailors lived in palm frond huts, toiletted in 'thunder boxes' on the beach, and in their spare time watched films in the Astra cinema, drank chilled Tiger beer in the ramshackle NAAFI or Scuba dived in the lagoon. They caught the occasional dose of 'the screamers', contracted coral sores, tinea, and prickly heat, and were eaten alive by mosquitoes. The disease which the insects carried was the gruesome elephantiasis and there were plenty of Maldivians who were walking examples of this unpleasant ailment. One day in 1960, the combined effects of repellent spraying and an offshore gale rid the atoll of mosquitoes for good.

In 1959, the resentful Independent Government of the Maldives in the north of the island chain, elected to invade the RAF base by sea. The invasion vessels were sailing 'bugaloes', a kind of lateen rigged galleon which carried several 'dhonies', a 'dhoni' being a cross between a war canoe and a Viking longship. While the British Government indulged in diplomatic intercourse, the RAF shipped out two RTTLs as motor gunboats. The Commanding Officer chosen for the job was veteran HSL Master and CO of 1113 MCU, Holyhead, Flight Lieutenant Bernard Saunders. With him went a group of volunteers. Saunders flew out to the island ahead of the crews, almost coming to grief when his Transport Command Hastings crashed on the runway.

Newly converted to Griffon engines, Mk IB RTTLs 2747 and 2748 duly arrived and were fitted with Bren guns either side of the foredeck, but before the sailors had any real practice at firing them, Saunders received instructions to remove the guns 'for fear of intimidating the natives'. When the 'invasion' did take place, it was quite a frightening affair. The score or so dhonies were all manned by fierce-looking islanders, paddling furiously and chanting in unison, egged on by wailing 'witch doctors'. The landing craft with their ramps lowered proved more of a deterent than the RTTLs, but the attack was averted, and Bernard Saunders rightly received the credit for handling a potentially nasty business.

Thereafter, the RN destroyer HMS *Cavalier* was the first of several which were based there from time to time, and no further incidents occurred. Aerial defence and search and rescue were fulfilled by Shackletons of 205 Squadron, while the two RTTLs were retained to provide surface coverage.

The first major search and rescue triumph of the 1960s also belonged to Saunders and the MCS at Gan. In March 1960, an RAF Hastings with 20 men aboard crashed into the sea whilst on final approach during a monsoon. It crashed 1½ miles to the south east of the airstrip in treacherous shoals. Eighteen of the complement took to a dinghy and were picked up by RTTL 2748 in the hands of Saunders and his Cox'n,

Sergeant Dickie Denman, while two others who had drifted away from the Hastings were recovered by P 1374. Ironically, the passengers on the aircraft were all Royal Navy personnel.

The staging post on Gan was developed during the 1960s to provide comfortable living for the personnel and a state-of-the-art hospital and other facilities for both servicemen and itinerant population alike. Many of the islanders, especially those who were seafarers themselves, benefited from the rescue services. RAF Gan was closed in 1976 when trooping to the Far East had dwindled to a mere trickle.

Two and a half thousand miles nearer home, the duties carried out by the Marine Craft Section at RAF Khormaksar, Aden, were typical of the variety which challenged the sailors of the 1960s.

The main tasks were to provide rescue facilities for transport aircraft using the airfield and for the Hunter squadrons supporting ground troops in the tribal warfare of the Radfan. Besides an RTTL, pinnace and RSL deployed from a jetty on the Ma'ala/Crater road, the sailors operated a landing craft known as a Z-boat (of which more later), and an LCA (Landing Craft Assault). The Z was later sailed to the distant island staging post of Masirah.

There were some significant 'firsts' at Khormaksar, one of which demonstrated the potential of the first all-weather SAR helicopter.

One night in 1963 a Royal Navy Vixen fighter ditched a few miles outside the harbour. An RAF Wessex from Khormaksar rescued the two crew before RTTL 2767 had cleared the port limits. The event became the subject of much discussion among the sailors because it was the first time that a helicopter had effected a rescue at night. The Wessex set a new standard in SAR operations.

The helicopter squadron beat the sailors to it again some weeks later when an Argosy cargo aircraft crashed. The aircraft was practising 'blind' approaches to the runway, got the whole thing wrong and touched down in the inner harbour. It landed in a manner reminiscent of a flying boat, eventually coming to rest in fairly shallow water. The crew were swiftly taken off by a 'chopper' as the RTTL and pinnace raced for the spot.

Not to be outdone, the engineers of the RTTL climbed aboard the Argosy to salvage as many 'black boxes' as possible. The cockpit of the aircraft was awash and the tide fast rising as they struggled to remove a bewildering array of unfamiliar gadgetry. By the time the sea was lapping around the escape hatch above them, Chief Technician Dick Griffiths and Corporal Technician Keith Beardow had retrieved many thousands of pounds worth of avionics gear. With the help of the port engineers, the Argosy was refloated and towed to the MCS slipway under the supervision of Marine Officer, Flight Lieutenant Duncan Gibbons.

A few days later, another Marine Fitter rescued a boy who had been trapped by the tide at the foot of some cliffs. The SAR helicopter was unable to get close enough, and heaving rollers over a shelving bottom prevented P 1380 from reaching the foreshore. Corporal Technician Lionel C. Male volunteered to swim ashore with a line. The extremely dangerous rescue was successfully accomplished and Male received a well-earned Commendation from the AOC.

The Air Officer Commanding Air Forces Middle East for a time was the legendary fighter pilot, Air Vice-Marshal J. E. (Johnnie) Johnson. RTTL, HMAFV 2767 was frequently called upon to act as his official launch. Whenever the Air Vice-Marshal had cause to visit RN or foreign ships, or entertain visiting dignitaries, the crew would don their special 'whites' and carry out the drills and formalities that befitted the occasion.

One unusual voyage which involved the AOC took place in 1964. The sailors regularly visited the British island of Perim situated at the junction of the Red Sea and the Arabian Sea. In its heyday, Perim had been a major watering and coaling station for ships *en route* from the UK via Suez. Technical advances and political changes had left the island as an unwanted, crumbling relic of empire. The RAF sailors, sometimes accompanied by Royal Army Service Corps vessels, took supplies for the poor but loyal islanders.

On one such voyage, the launch embarked a team of boffins who specialized in techniques for sea and desert survival, and who were investigating ways in which the islanders might supplement their livelihood by intensive fishing. They were accompanied by Air Vice-Marshal Johnson. For the two-day duration of the trip, much of the time was spent in experimenting with long-lining off the African coast at which the Air Vice-Marshal showed considerable prowess. For some time afterwards, the launch was nicknamed 'Johnnie's MFV'.

In June of 1966, Flight Lieutenant Whitchurch and the crew of pinnace 1380 featured in one of the RAFs biggest rescues. An Arab dhow was reported sinking 21 miles out from Steamer Point. A Shackleton and an SAR chopper stood by while the pinnace closed the stricken vessel. Whitchurch and Cox'n Sergeant Johnston boarded the dhow and decided to gamble on towing it to port before the water level became critical. With the pumps going full bore, the pinnace towed the sinking ship for over five hours. They barely made it. On board the dhow were 51 passengers.

The mid-1960s were uncomfortable years in the Aden Protectorate. Rival factions fought each other in a terrorist war and, spurred on by the Yemen and Gamal Abdul Nasser of Egypt, the Brits were the target of them all. The Marine Craft Section personnel had their share of close shaves. Even the trusted foreman of the unit's civilian labour force was revealed as a grenade-throwing rebel. He had often earned a few shillings babysitting for some of the sailors' wives! On one occasion, RTTL 2767 came under fire from Yemeni shore batteries in the Red Sea, and on another it was holed by a terrorist bomb whilst on the slipway. A few feet further aft and the bomb would have exploded under the fuel tanks.

Before the final seige in Crater City and the evacuation of Colonel 'Mad Mitch' Mitchell's Argylls, the Khormaksar MCS was disbanded. In 1967, the boats were moved to Masirah and Bahrain and the sailors went home. RTTL 2767 completed the longest non-stop voyage by a Mk II launch; 563 nautical miles in 25 hours.

The land, the vast wealth and the amenities of the ancient British Protectorate of Aden became the Republic of South Yemen. The airfield and the harbour were occupied by the Russians.

At Masirah island, the sailors operated a steel, ex-army landing craft known as a Z-flat or Zebra craft. Z-12 was a shallow-draft assembly of ballast and buoyancy tanks, 145 ft long by 30 ft beam and powered by a pair of National diesels. The after end of the vessel was similar to a small coaster, with bridge, wireless shack, cabins, mess-decks, galley and storage compartments. From the engine room for'ard, it was a huge, flat, landing craft complete with ramp at the bow. The carrying capacity was impressive, 10 or more laden trucks or half a dozen battle tanks. It was normally employed in conveying goods and vehicles from merchant ship to shore, or from the Omani mainland to the island. Maximum speed was in the region of 7 knots.

Between sailings, Z-12 required a great deal of maintenance, for the ravages of salt water and time had taken their toll on both hull and machinery. It was messy work. The iron deck and hull had to be chipped and red-leaded and the winch machinery regularly cleared of sand and salt. The engines were in a sorry state and spare parts were almost non-existent. Rust holes in the bottom of the ship were simply sealed-off with concrete. There was no air-conditioning below, and the decks were hot enough in the daytime to fry eggs — QED. The Z-12's controls were rudimentary, comprising a large wheel and telegraph and one dubious magnetic compass.

Even so, the Masirah Z-craft crew confounded sceptics and carried out a difficult rescue operation in 1964. Under the command of Flight Lieutenant Peter Moulds, Z-12 put to sea at night to rendezvous with a merchant ship and bring ashore a seriously ill seaman. Moulds' seamanship and navigation was exceptional. Besides the paucity of equipment on the ship, the passage through uncharted shoals and shifting sandbanks was unaided by any form of buoyage or channel markers.

Z-craft were also used in the North African port of Tobruk. Here the sailors handled cargo, ferried personnel from ships to shore, transported fresh water for the garrison and assisted with the laying of underwater pipelines and cables. They even helped with wet dinghy drill exercises for nearby RAF El Adem. However, there was a subtle difference in the manner in which the helicopters returned the pilots to the boat. They were not lowered on winch wires — the choppers landed on the deck! Like the sailors of Gan, the Tobruk men also operated tugs and workboats and there were many visiting naval types who were astounded when they discovered that the Port Authority in Tobruk was the RAF.

By 1967, oil deposits had been discovered and an oil terminal and berthing jetty had been built. The face of Libya began to change. In the twilight days of the Tobruk MCS, pinnace 1373 arrived from Malta for SAR duties, but the most unusual recorded rescue was effected by the unit's 24 ft marine tender. Sergeant Anderson and Senior Aircraftman Chase recovered a calf which was determinedly swimming out to sea!

In the Persian Gulf, Britain has continued to maintain a presence at Dahran air base on Bahrain Island. In the 1960s, then as now, the airfield was used jointly by both civil and military aircraft. The Marine Craft Section at nearby Muharraq was employed for the benefit of all-comers, but when a Middle East Airlines 80-seat Caravelle crashed, the sailors were only able to pick up the pieces.

Dahran control lost radio contact with Flight 444 from Beirut as it approached the airfield at 2332 hrs on 17 April 1964. The 'Crash Call' was received by the MCS at 2350 hrs and RTTL 2751 was prepared for sea. The flight path of the airliner had taken it over an area of deadly reefs and skerries through which there was only one tortuous and poorly marked channel. Winds were gusting at gale force and the crew knew that to try and locate the aircraft at night in such conditions was suicidal. The launch sailed at first light, but visibility was down to 200 yds, and despite several attempts to find the entrance to the channel it returned to base.

At 1100 hrs the Caravelle was found by a US Marine Corps helicopter and a Dakota. This time the RTTL entered the channel safely and was able to make a high-speed dash for the wreck which was lying inverted in 2½ fathoms of water. The RTTL's Gemini was launched to search around the wreck, a task which was impeded by the aircraft surging back and forth with the swell. Meanwhile the RTTL searched to the south, where any survivors would have drifted. Neither craft found any signs of life. Over the next three and a half days, while salvage men dismantled the Caravelle, the crews of RTTL 2751 and RSL 1649 performed the grim task of ferrying the bodies ashore.

In the following year, RSL 1649 won a claim to fame while in the hands of Flight Lieutenant Terry Fryirs.

Five members of the Parachute Regiment bought an Arab dhow in Bahrain which they named *Red Wolf* and intended to sail back to the UK. The dhow laid alongside the MCS jetty for some months while the soldiers fitted it out for the voyage and many of their amateur antics provided a source of amusement for the sailors. The paras showed some wisdom in deciding to carry out a couple of proving trips before they tried for the home run. It was on the second of these that the dhow was caught in a storm 40 miles from Muharraq.

Terry Fryirs and his crew set out in a full gale and had to negotiate shoals and sandbanks without radar or other sophisticated aids. At one point the seas were so steep that the launch had to lie a'hull. When Fryirs did find *Red Wolf*, the bilge pump had become blocked with debris and the dhow was sinking. All five paratroopers were suffering from extreme exhaustion and the effects of prolonged seasickness. It took the RSL crew three attempts to go alongside the tossing dhow before they were able to take the men aboard and turn for home.

The dhow incident was the second in which Fryirs had displayed outstanding seamanship that year. The first had occurred in January, when in equally bad conditions he had successfully rendezvoused with a merchant ship to take off a seaman with crushed legs. Once again, the boat spent hours hove-to in mountainous seas, but after a 13-hour round trip the man was landed safely. Fryirs was awarded the MBE for gallantry. Months later, at the annual 'Man of the Year' dinner at London's Savoy Hotel, Terry Fryirs was presented with the award of 'RAF Man of the Year'.

The Marine Craft Section at Muharraq was disbanded at the end of September 1971 and the boats were sold locally, including the ex-Aden RTTL 2767

*Chapter 20*

# If you can't take a joke...

---

*...you shouldn't have joined.*

The Mediterranean was a hotbed of marine activity throughout the 1960s and '70s and a large share of the Middle Eastern rescue work fell to the sailors of 1153 MCU at Limassol, Cyprus. The island is located in the midst of the busy shipping lanes and air routes of the western Mediterranean, with Turkey, Syria, Lebanon, Israel and Egypt all within a few sea miles. Although at various times some were 'hostile shores', when it came to saving lives at sea there were no boundaries.

The biggest rescue of the period was accomplished in July 1963 when an Israeli hydrofoil *Aleigal* went missing with 80 passengers and crew. RTTL 2769 was dispatched under the command of Squadron Leader T. H. 'Mickey' Finn who found the disabled 'foil and towed it safely back to Cyprus. In September, Finn took RTTL 2769 close to Syria to rescue a soldier adrift in an open boat, while Squadron Leader Hardy recovered the boat itself with pinnace P 1383. At this time 1153 MCU was somewhat top heavy with Squadron Leaders and Flight Lieutenants, but Corporal 'Nobby' Clarke kept the flag flying for the ORs when he and his crew of RSL 1657 saved three men who had been missing in a small boat for three days.

Flight Lieutenant Duncan 'Gibby' Gibbons arrived in Cyprus in 1966 and immediately found himself at sea in command of RTTL 2771, speeding to the rescue of the crew of a Greek ship. Eight men were saved from the *Maria* which had sunk in deep water between Cyprus and Lebanon.

Flight Lieutenant C. Clark was not so lucky in September when he skippered HMAFV 2771 during a search for the crew of a capsized Greek ship, MV *Alexis*. Helped by Squadron Leader Phil Greenall in P 1383, an all-night search brought forth only wreckage and a number of dead sheep. Seven members of the ship's crew drifted ashore on a life-raft, but the Captain's wife, two deck boys and a seaman had gone down with the ship.

Another Greek vessel, the *Three Stars* of Piraeus was the focus of an all-out effort in early 1967. On the morning of 17 February, 1153 MCU was alerted to go to the assistance of the ship which was on fire some four miles south-west of Cyprus's most southerly point, Cape Zevghari. First to sail was P 1384 at 0730 hrs under the command of Flight Lieutenant Clark. Flight Lieutenant G. Hubbard and the crew of RTTL 2771 cleared the harbour 30 minutes later. 'Gibby' Gibbons followed in P 1383 after loading a portable fire pump and other fire-fighting equipment.

As the boats approached the ship, a helicopter was winching the crew to safety, leaving the vessel adrift and burning fiercely. Hubbard took the RTTL alongside to windward of the fire where a salvage party comprising Squadron Leader Greenall and deckhands Maddocks and Pollock boarded the ship. The 'fire crew' of Junior Technician Ashbee, Civilian Seaman Ilhan Ahmet, and the Limassol Harbour Master, Captain George Mavroyiangos, led by Gibbons, started to fight the inferno. Meanwhile, Sergeant Johnson and Senior Aircraftman Connolly jumped aboard from P 1384 to attach a towline. In the 25 knot wind and rough sea, pinnace P 1384 struggled to tow the 1,700 ton ship. A second towline was passed to P 1383 and the small convoy made slow headway towards Episkopi Bay.

Later, the Station Fire Officer from RAF Akrotiri and two firemen were lowered by helicopter and helped fight the fire until it was brought under control. By late afternoon the ship was safely anchored and officially handed over to the Harbour Master. The weary RAF sailors returned to base with thoughts of salvage money and 'gongs'. In the aftermath, Duncan Gibbons was awarded the Queen's Commendation for Brave Conduct.

Flight Lieutenant Hubbard and the crew of HMAFV 2769 made international history in August 1968 when they opened a crack in the diplomatic wall that had divided Anglo-Egyptian relationships since the Suez crisis of 1956. The circumstances which sparked off the easing of the tension were horrific.

On 18 August at 2.40 pm, Hubbard was ordered to a position where the wreck of a missing Egyptian-owned Antonov AN 24 airliner had been spotted by an RAF Argosy. The indications were that the aircraft, which was similar to a Fokker Friendship, had broken up. The wreckage was far out to sea and the RTTL took over five hours to reach the position.

When the launch arrived, there were no survivors — only corpses. From 2000 hrs to 2300 hrs the launch crew searched the surrounding area recovering bodies as they went, but the task had to be postponed due to sharks feeding on the cadavers. During the night, the RTTL was joined by P 1378 with Greenall in command. At dawn, the boats resumed the gruesome labour, continuing until 1125 hrs, when the search was finally abandoned. In all, 25 bodies were recovered, all of them bloated; most of them mutilated. They were piled on the tankspace and distributed around the decks of HMAFV 2769 which then turned south towards Egypt while the crew of P 1378 scrubbed down and thankfully headed back to Cyprus.

During the afternoon the hot sun accelerated the decomposition of the corpses. The launch crew were badly affected and had a most uncomfortable six-hour voyage to Alexandria.

A flotilla of Egyptian MTBs had been ordered to accompany the RAF launch into Alexandria, but they missed the rendezvous leaving Hubbard and his crew to enter the port unescorted. As they slowly approached the jetty with their RAF ensign at half-mast, they could see a silent reception committee of dignitaries, reporters and naval officials. While pieces of the airliner and the remains of its passengers were removed, the Governor of Alexandria visited Hubbard aboard the boat and extended an invitation to the crew to spend the night ashore as guests of the Egyptian Government. On the following morning the Egyptian press gave banner headlines to the efforts of the RAF crews.

The British Consul-General noted: 'This was a sad occasion, and the Egyptians felt deep emotion to it... The fact that the Air Sea Rescue Service is an international obligation did not, in the eyes of the Egyptians, detract in any way from their appreciation of the effort. To them, this was a friendly gesture by the British coming to the help of Egypt in distressing circumstances and the expressions of gratitude to the RAF personnel and to me were so profuse as to be almost embarrassing... it has added greatly to our prestige.'

In such a manner, HMAFV 2769 became the first of Her Majesty's ships to visit Egypt after a 12-year period of cool hostility between the two nations.

A few days later, on 11 September, the indomitable trio of Greenall, Hubbard and Gibbons were at sea again achieving another milestone in Marine Craft history. This time, they rescued nine seamen and salvaged an undamaged ship! HMAFV 2769 was sent to the aid of the Greek ship MV *Podromos* in distress 60 miles east of Cyprus. Greenall assumed overall command of the operation and sailed aboard the RTTL with Gibbons as skipper. An Argosy aircraft guided the launch to the ship which was stopped and listing 30 degrees to port with the sea lapping around the main hatches. Four of the ship's crew were in a lifeboat tethered to the stern while five others were gathered on the after deck. The RTTL picked up all the men while Gibbons went aboard the ship with a party of three MBCs to secure a tow line and establish the extent of the damage.

Much to their surprise, they found that there was *no* damage, but the cargo had shifted and caused the pronounced list. Although the ship was rolling heavily in the swell and the port bulwarks were awash, she was otherwise safe and seaworthy. The RTTL tried to tow the vessel from both bows and stern, but the deadweight of the ship combined with the limited towing ability of the launch made this futile.

Greenall radioed for a pinnace and Hubbard set sail with P 1378. By 2040 hrs Gibbons and Hubbard had secured a line, and as soon as the boarding party returned to the RTTL, towing commenced at a painful 3½ knots. After making sure that the pinnace could maintain headway, Greenall and Gibbons returned to base to offload the 'survivors'. Twelve and a half hours later, the pinnace crew secured *Podromos* to the Akrotiri tanker moorings.

Personnel from the Marine Craft Unit checked the ship for stability and mounted a security guard until details of the salvage claim could be sorted out; a writ from the Admiralty High Court was 'nailed' to the mast. Eventually, the MV *Podromos* was returned to her Master on 28 September and was sailed away under her own power.

As far as the sailors were concerned, 1153 MCU was the biggest remaining gem in the battered marine crown. It was the most pleasant of postings with comfortable accommodation and messing, adequate married quarters and an unlimited range of leisure pursuits. Until 15 July 1974 when Archbishop Makarios was ousted by a military coup. Curfews were imposed. Street fighting broke out between rival Cypriot factions in Limassol. Five days later, Turkish forces invaded in the north of the island and an inter-racial war commenced in earnest.

The Marine Craft Unit became caught in a hail of cross-fire between Turkish and Greek Cypriot sectors. Rifle and machine-gun bullets passed over and through the unit buildings, one salvo narrowly missing the CO, Squadron Leader R. J. M. (Mervyn) Manson. The unit's civilian workers deserted, the sailors donned their tin hats and took cover. As Manson later put it, 'The crunch came, literally, when a mortar bomb blew the officers' mess apart.' With the safety of both the personnel and the boats in mind, Manson obtained permission to evacuate the base. The boats' crews calmly boarded the two RTTLs and a pinnace and put to sea, weaving to avoid small arms fire. One unserviceable pinnace, P 1384, had to be left behind.

The flotilla proceeded to Akrotiri and set up a temporary base with abandoned huts, freight containers, deserted yachts and holiday cara-vans for accommodation. Food was provided by the nearby RAF station, which was fast becoming overwhelmed by thousands of civilians and service families who had escaped to the protection of its sovereign ground. Some of the sailors' wives and children had to fight their way from Limassol along roads choked with armed men and refugees. Bullets flew around them as they wended their way from the town to the safety of the RAF airfield.

With increased air activity precipitated by the war, Manson organized the crews into a three-watch system so that in any 24-hour period, two boats were ready to put to sea. His foresight paid off only three days later when the Turkish destroyer *Kocatepe* was sunk accidentally by its own air force 30 miles from Paphos. Two Royal Navy frigates, an RAF supply ship, a Turkish destroyer, No 84 RAF helicopter squadron and

IF YOU CAN'T TAKE A JOKE...

RTTLs 2759 and 2769 were directed to the search area.

While the Turkish destroyer, the British ships and the choppers concentrated on picking up the bulk of the 72 survivors, the two launches were instructed to search the outer fringes. Their high speed enabled them to cover a large area rapidly which, despite the choppy conditions, they did to good effect. Altogether, a dozen 10-man inflatable life-rafts were discovered along with 10 grateful Turkish sailors. One of the emotional survivors insisted on kissing MBC Dave McAusland, who was the recipient of much ribbing after the event!

After two weeks at Akrotiri, the service families were allowed to return to their homes while the sailors took the boats back to the Limassol base, but it was premature. The Turkish army pushed southwards again and the Marine Craft Unit was obliged to move to Akrotiri once more. On the airfield, a massive airlift of holiday-makers, families and other civilians commenced. Cyprus was no longer the most glittering gem in the crown.

When things had calmed down and the Turks had settled behind the Attila line, the RTTLs of 1153 MCU reverted to their former training and range safety duties. Pinnace 1384 was recovered intact, and towed to Akrotiri and slipped, but was badly damaged as it settled on the cradle and was out of action for several weeks. Meanwhile, pinnace P 1385 became fully engaged in bomb disposal activities. Turkish aircraft had dropped large quantities of ordnance during the invasion, much of which had failed to explode. The pinnace was used for recovering weapons from the sea and dumping others in deep water.

Despite the difficulties, Squadron Leader Manson and launch skippers Flight Lieutenants Head, Leech and Duffy with the NCOs and airmen of 1153 MCU had proved once again that the RAF sailors had lost none of their flair for 'bodging' along and maintaining a top class service.

At 1151 MCU Marsaxlokk on the island of Malta, life for the sailors went on much as it did in Cyprus, but without the added complications of war and unrest. Routine training tasks and target-towing were frequently interrupted by those who found themselves in danger at sea. Many of the recipients of the services of 1151 MCU were swimmers, water-skiers or skin-divers on holiday.

Ferrying sick or injured seamen from ship to shore was a recurring task for the Malta sailors. On one occasion in 1967, Flight Lieutenant Ken Bell and his crew reversed the process by steaming 130 miles through gale-riven seas to place a medical team aboard a Norwegian tanker to tend an injured man. The night voyage was extremely hazardous and the whole crew were commended.

The two RTTLs at Marsaxlokk became film stars in 1967, although they were not the first RAF launches to grace the silver screen. In 1944, *For Those in Peril* starring David Farrar was made at the Newhaven ASRU. Ten years later, John Harris' book *The Sea Shall Not Have Them* featured

RTTLs 2759 and 2761 from Felixstowe. In later years it seems that film-makers believed RAF launches were more naval than naval launches. Both *The Man Who Never Was* and *The Silent Enemy* showed RSLs in RAF colours, but manned and flagged in Royal Navy style.

So it was in Malta in 1967, when Mk II RTTLs 2758 and 2768 were borrowed for Christina Films version of *A Twist of Sand*. Once again, the boats sported a white ensign and the crews were rigged out in Naval uniforms. The film *Hellboats* made by Mirisch Films in the following year went all the way. The Malta RTTLs were repainted in Admiralty grey and fitted with dummy guns and torpedo tubes! The crews included a multitude of 'officers' and 'ratings', all of whom were RAF men from 1151 MCU. One of the launch skippers was heard to remark dryly, 'They may have dressed us up like the Grey Funnel Line, but at least we've been promoted!'

It was not only film companies who found that the RN suffered from a dearth of high-speed patrol boats. In the late 1960s, the Navy itself called upon the RAF to help with its training programme. Royal Navy ships operating in the Mediterranean and the Gulf needed to practise anti-fast patrol boat tactics, as such vessels were much in evidence in the navies of potential aggressors. In the absence of their own FPBs, naval units utilized the RTTLs as 'hostile attacking forces'. The RAF sailors had a great time trying to outwit the Navy, and much to everyone's consternation often did so.

In 1972, 1151 MCU was ordered to close down, but after a last minute reprieve the unit stayed operational until 1978. In a moving ceremony, the RTTLs were handed over to the Maltese Government. It was a diamond anniversary. Royal Air Force sailors had been in Malta for 60 years.

RAF North Front in Gibraltar had also served as a maritime base since the earliest days of floatplanes. During the Second World War, No 71 Air Sea Rescue Unit, which was formed in December 1941, earned an enviable reputation. In the two years 1942 and 1943 alone, 74 British, 17 Allied aircrew and five Sunderland flying boats were rescued by HSL 142, 181 and 2582. In the post-war period, smuggling between North Africa and Spain was rife. Many of the activities were run by British adventurers, including the brother of ex-RAF pilot and comedian, Jimmy Edwards. The smugglers were well-equipped, for they had bought ex-MTBs and HSLs and lightened them by stripping all non-essential fittings. Neither the Navy, the RAF nor local Customs, possessed boats which could match their speed. Even as late as 1964, smuggling and piracy continued on a limited scale. On one occasion, a gang of pirates stole a harbour launch which was chased by Flight Lieutenant Smith and the crew of P 1388. The pirates tried to ram the pinnace but suffered a timely engine failure. Deckhands M. Eardley-Stiff and Peter Turton boarded the stolen launch and overpowered them.

The work pattern was much the same as at other Mediterranean bases, but stand-by flying featured high on the list due to the main runway projecting into the sea. Launches were stationed off the end of the overshoot area and some of the sailors were trained as divers to carry out underwater salvage and recovery. In 1975, RAF North Front became 1102 MCU, a number that was re-allocated following the closure of the original unit at Falmouth. The 20-year-old RTTLs 2753 and 2754 were engaged in routines of target-towing, range safety, surveillance, meteorological surveying and FPB exercises.

Since the war, the everyday practice of wearing life-jackets aboard RAF launches had died out. The crews of the wartime ASR Service wore them at all times, but in peacetime the men found Mae Wests and kapok jackets an awkward encumbrance in the confines of a marine craft. Only in circumstances of extreme danger was the order given to don life-jackets. Two inflatable rafts were carried on RTTLs, one for'ard and one aft whilst lifejackets, flares and Sarbes (a derivative of SARAH beacons) were stowed forward. The assumption was that if a launch sank, it would sink stern first due to the weight of the engines. No RTTL had ever been known to nosedive until one Saturday afternoon in January 1976, when a Gibraltar launch prompted a total rethink of safety procedures aboard all RAF vessels.

RTTL 2754 slipped moorings at lunchtime for what was expected to be a routine 10-hour surveillance run to the east of Gibraltar. The CO sailed with Flight Lieutenant George Bell and his crew. A moderate wind was blowing at 10–15 knots from the west. Wind and sea were on the starboard quarter and the launch was able to make a comfortable cruising speed without the usual head-to-sea pounding.

At 1730 hrs, the senior Fitter, Chief Technician John Crouch, hurtled through the wheelhouse door and shouted, 'There's a hole in the port side!' Everyone stared at him in disbelief, but immediately the bows dived steeply and the crew were thrown forward with the sudden deceleration. Within seconds, the foredeck disappeared beneath the waves and the wheelhouse was awash. The Cox'n Flight Sergeant Sammy Johnston, closed the throttles and the five men who were in the wheelhouse clambered over the superstructure to the tankspace. George Bell stayed on the bridge for a few moments before joining the rest of the crew. All nine were safe, amazed that no-one had been trapped below.

The launch seemed to be in imminent danger of sinking. The foredeck, rope locker and the for'ard life-raft were under water and the wheelhouse was half submerged. From the tankspace the men could see the level rising to the top step of the sickbay. The foc'sle and galley were completely flooded. Only the creaking tankspace bulkhead was preventing the launch from sliding below the surface.

Radio contact had been lost in the instant of the disaster. There were no other ships in sight and no land on the horizon. All the life-jackets were inaccessible down below except for five in the wheelhouse and two with the engineers. The pyrotechnics key and the Sarbe equipped life-jackets were in the half-submerged skipper's cabin, whilst the Verey pistol was under water in a locker beneath the instrument panels. The two officers climbed over the superstructure to the bridge and managed, by a series of hasty forays, to retrieve the Sarbe, life-jackets, Verey pistol and pyro-locker key. Meanwhile, Flight Sergeant Johnston and Senior Aircraftman Mick Quigley, MBC, worked their way around the side of the deckhouse to release the forward inflatable from the foredeck. The waves were breaking over their heads as they struggled to operate the quick-release Senhouse slip, but it refused to work and they had to give up. Some time later, the raft broke free and floated away.

The crew had seven life-jackets and one serviceable life-raft between them. They were cold and soaked, but the bulkhead seemed to be holding and the RTTL was not settling any deeper.

Just before dark, a ship was sighted on the horizon heading towards them. The sailors were well aware of the difficulties of spotting men adrift on a choppy sea in twilight so they patiently waited until they could be sure of their flares being seen. Even so, six red rockets and several Verey cartridges were fired before they were spotted. The Greek registered MV *Kapitanikos* lowered a boat which, with some difficulty in the mounting swells, drew alongside. It was decided that all but the two officers and a volunteer (Corporal Mike Wray, Fitter) would be taken off. Johnston took charge of the departing group and was given the job of co-ordinating the rescue and the salvage. The Greeks were extremely reluctant to leave the men behind, but after many reassurances, they left a supply of lifejackets and returned to their ship.

Back at 1102 MCU there was little concern that the hourly position report from RTTL 2754 was missed at 1800 hrs. It happened occasionally for a variety of innocent reasons, but when there was no message at 1900 hrs anxieties began to fester. Shortly afterwards, Flight Sergeant Johnston's first radio message from the *Kapitanikos* was relayed to the Marine Craft Unit, but the sailors were frustratingly impotent, for their reserve pinnace was on the slipway for servicing. Frantically, they rushed to make it seaworthy.

Meanwhile, Royal Navy Shore Patrols set about rounding up the crews of frigate HMS *Keppel* and the tug *Sealyham*, no mean task on a Saturday evening. By midnight, both ships were underway. A salvage party sailed with HMS *Keppel* comprising Flight Lieutenant Cairns, Duty Officer; Flight Sergeant John Kearns, Cox'n; Chief Technician 'Ginger' Thompson, Boatwright; and Corporal Frank McLaughlin, Electrician.

Far out to sea, the three men on the launch had had a distressing night. As *Kapitanikos* steamed away from them, they launched the remaining liferaft in case the RTTL should sink. The raft had inflated upside down and the survival kit was lost, but they elected to spend the night in it. The sea became rougher, with swells rolling along the boat's deck, across the tankspace and over the gunwhales into the dinghy, which pounded against the hull with every wave. The three men were soaked, shivering and seasick. Their only comfort through the long night was the swaying anchor light of the launch.

Soon after dawn, a French cargo ship hove-to close to the wreck and an American Orion aircraft was able to relay its position to *Keppel*. By 0930 hrs the three survivors had been safely taken off by whaler and the RAF salvage crew placed aboard the RTTL to assess the damage.

There was little they could do. The hole in the bow was deep under water and too big for a temporary repair. There was nothing to be gained by using portable pumps. Only the tankspace bulkhead was preventing the boat from sinking and it could have given way at any second. To aid buoyancy and relieve some of the pressure on the bulkhead, a 20-man liferaft was inflated inside the sickbay before the launch was taken in tow stern first.

During the afternoon, the wind strength increased forcing a reduction to a 2 knot crawl. The men on *Keppel* watched helplessly as the RTTL settled deeper when the bulkhead finally gave way. Eventually the stern of the launch dipped, the bows rose, and it slipped silently beneath the waves. The cause of the sinking was never established.

Although HMAFV 2752 was hastily dispatched to replace her, within a few months all Mk II RTTLs were withdrawn from service.

# Chapter 21

# FWE

*The last entry in a ship's log at the end of a voyage was always the three letters
FWE — Finished With Engines.*

By the end of 1972, the original 30 odd marine bases in the British
Isles had been cut to five. Only 1100 MCU Alness, 1102 MCU
Falmouth, 1104 MCU Bridlington and 1113 MCU Holyhead
remained, with the Marine Training and Engineering Squadrons at
Mount Batten and detachments at Gorleston and Tenby. Plans for new
steel and GRP (glass reinforced plastic) boats had been instigated in
1966, but delays with the building programmes meant that the sailors
were obliged to protract the lives of the pinnaces, RSLs and Mk II RTTLs
way beyond their intended obsolescence dates.

The Rolls-Royce pinnaces were the most popular of all the wooden
boats and they had a well-earned reputation for being stable in a
seaway. In a span of over 25 years, no pinnace had ever been lost to
wind and wave, thus the sailors were deeply shocked when a pinnace
foundered in tragic circumstances on 29 September 1969. It was their
biggest peacetime loss.

Pinnace 1386 from 1104 MCU Bridlington was on passage from
Dundee to its home base after two weeks of exercises with helicopters
from RAF Leuchars. The small harbour of Amble was a popular halfway
stopover on the regular return trip to Scotland, and the boat was
well-known to the locals. Amble harbour lies at the estuary of the
Coquet river with its entrance protected by two concrete jetties
extending for more than 100 yds to seaward. About a mile offshore is
Coquet island which is uninhabited apart from a lighthouse keeper. A
treacherous submerged shoal, known as the Pan Bush, extends between
the island and the approach to the harbour entrance.

On this particular day, the launch was due to carry out an evening
helicopter exercise with 202 Squadron from nearby RAF Acklington. The
launch had left Dundee at lunchtime and had made good progress

through a heavy easterly swell. The skipper, Flight Lieutenant Ken Bell, decided that as they were early they would put into the harbour for a while. Ken Bell and Cox'n Sergeant Danny Coutts could see heavy seas breaking over the northen pier and decided to cross the southernmost tip of Pan Bush before swinging to starboard to align the boat with the entrance. High tide ensured more than 3 fathoms of water under the keel. Bell sent MBC Bill Traynor below to tell the rest of the crew to prepare the mooring lines.

In the foc'sle, Sergeant Robert Moore, Fitter, and Deckhand Charlie Chase had just finished their mugs of tea. The youngest member of the crew, 21-year-old MBC David Ashton, was in the adjacent galley washing up. Don Ivil, the Wireless Operator, was in the tiny radio cabin below and for'ard of the wheelhouse with Geoffrey Benson, another Wireless Operator who was due to join the crew in place of Ivil.

The swells were long and deep with 100 ft between crests. Before making the turn for the harbour entrance, Bell and Coutts watched the rollers closely in order to choose their moment. Bell saw a huge sea heading towards the boat on the port side.

'We'll wait for this one before we turn,' he said. The Cox'n nodded.

The pinnace lifted with the wave as expected, then began to heel alarmingly to starboard. Horrified, Bell and Coutts looked down into a sheer 20 ft chasm. The undertow from Pan Bush had swept the water away from beneath the hull.

'Christ,' exclaimed the skipper. 'There's nothing underneath it!' In the same instant, the crest of the freakish wave broke above them and the 62 ton pinnace rolled over.

The local Coastguard, Tom Brown, had been watching a small yacht approach the harbour. From his hut on the foreshore, he could see it having difficulty with the long breakers. He held a 'maroon' flare in his hand, just in case. As the yacht reached the shelter of the south pier, a relieved Brown glanced up to see how the pinnace was progressing. He was just in time to watch it turn turtle. He fired the 'maroon', then immediately called for a helicopter from RAF Acklington. The Coastguard log entry was timed at 1830 hrs.

Around the inner harbour the lifeboat men sprinted for the boatyard. While two men launched the 16 ft inshore rescue boat, others set off up river for the RNLI *Millie Walton*. She sailed at 1839 hrs, five minutes behind the IRB. Meanwhile, the first of several fishing boats headed out of the harbour towards the launch.

Aboard the pinnace, neither Bell nor Coutts had time to grab their life-jackets before they were overwhelmed by surging water. They both struck out instinctively for the surface, but neither of them was able to grasp the hull before being swept away.

Traynor was caught halfway down the companionway between the wheelhouse and the foc'sle. He held on grimly as a wall of water frothed around him and then swam out from under the launch. Like the rest of the crew, he had no life-jacket. The remainder of the sailors were trapped in near-darkness below. Ivil and Benson were in the radio cabin and Moore, Chase and Ashton were in the foc'sle.

When the boat overturned, the men in the crews' quarters became disorientated. Cushions, boxes, loose equipment, pots, pans and other debris rained down on them as they were thrown in a heap on the inverted cabin roof. Water poured in. It was already waist high when Charlie Chase tried to open the grating above the steps to the wheelhouse. It would not budge. He called out for Bob Moore to have a go. The grating was firmly wedged. Much later they recalled that they had been pushing futilely against the boat's bottom boards.

'We'll have to use the for'ard hatch,' said Moore, realizing that the sliding deck hatch was now beneath their feet. He dived down but could not shift it. On the second attempt it moved a little and the trapped men saw a pale green light filtering through. Chase dived and moved the hatch further, but it had become jammed by debris which had cascaded into the well. They dived again and again until the obstruction was cleared and the hatch was fully open. The water level rose dramatically and swirled around the pitching compartment. Bob Moore told the others to dive down and swim up again on the outside of the boat.

'Charlie first, then Dave, and I'll follow behind,' he instructed.

Ashton demurred. 'I can't swim,' he announced. Moore and Chase were appalled.

Chase, a Deckhand of considerable experience and ability, dived through the hatch and surfaced without any problems. When he had gone, Ashton hesitantly lowered himself towards the opening, but panicked when the water reached his face. Moore talked to him firmly but calmly.

'All you've got to do is go down. Once you're through the hatch, you'll automatically go to one side or the other.'

Ashton tried once again. This time, Bob Moore stood on his shoulders and attempted to shove him through, but the youngster stayed rigid and bobbed back into the foc'sle like a cork. He was badly shaken. Moore reasoned with him to keep trying, but Ashton was adamant. He scrambled up as high as he could in the bilge and refused to move. The water level crept upwards.

Reluctantly, Bob Moore dived through the hatch. When he surfaced, there was no-one in sight. He dragged himself on to the upturned hull and gathered his breath. Charlie Chase and Bill Traynor were clinging to one side of the boat. Neither of them knew where the others were. The Sergeant scanned the wave tops, there was no sign of the two Wireless Operators or the Skipper, but he could see Danny Coutts struggling to stay afloat 40 yds away.

The cox'n just managed to gasp, 'I can't go on much longer Bob. Can you help me?'

With the intention of swimming to Coutts, Moore untangled a lifebelt which had become snagged in the boat's handrail, but before he could use it he saw a helicopter heading towards him. In the distance he could just make out the IRB racing to the scene.

From the helicopter, it appeared that Bob Moore was the only survivor of the disaster, but Moore waved it away, pointing to the Cox'n. Winchman Sergeant Alan Jones lowered himself towards the broiling sea. He splashed in alongside Coutts, but with the swell rising and falling more than 20 ft it was impossible to place the strop over the Cox'n's head and shoulders. Coutts was heavier than Jones, but somehow the winchman managed to hang on to him and lift him aboard the chopper.

Meanwhile, the heaving breakers had forced Traynor and Chase to lose their grip on the pinnace, but not before Moore had thrown them the lifebelt. The two Deckhands clung to it as they were washed seaward into the turmoil of Pan Bush. At great risk to themselves, RNLI men Robbie Stewart and Andy Scott steered the tiny IRB towards them and hauled them aboard. They were already suffering from exposure and shock. Chase and Traynor were able to tell the IRB crew that the Skipper was unaccounted for, and that three men were still trapped inside the pinnace. Stewart and Scott asked a fishing boat to radio for divers from the local sub-aqua club. Navy divers from Rosyth were also called, but there was little chance that they could reach Amble in time.

Above the maelstrom, the helicopter searched in vain for signs of Skipper Ken Bell. Despite the violent pitching and the breaking waves, Bob Moore continued to cling precariously to the underside of the launch. He could hear a repetitive tapping from inside the hull. It was Ashton, who by now was pressed right into the vee-bottom of the boat. Water was lapping about his ears and the air gap was a mere 4 in.

Outside, *Millie Walton* closed with the pinnace.

'Have you got an axe?' Bob Moore shouted. 'There are men trapped inside.'

Veteran lifeboat Cox'n Willie Henderson vetoed the idea.

'You'll break the airlock,' he yelled. 'We'll try and right her.'

One of the lifeboat crew, Jimmy Stewart, helped Moore into the lifeboat, then boarded the pinnace again to attach grapnel lines, but the pinnace resisted all efforts to roll her upright. Once more, Jimmy Stewart leapt aboard the tossing hull, this time to secure a tow. The plan now was to right the pinnace with a crane inside the harbour. Stewart could only find a purchase around one of the propeller shafts which meant towing the launch stern first against the drag of the transom and the open wheelhouse. Progress was slow and they had barely reached calmer waters when the tow parted. Stewart jumped aboard for the fourth time and fixed dual ropes to the prop shafts. Once more they crept ahead. It was 1915 hrs, 45 minutes since the launch had foundered. Ashton was still tapping.

The IRB returned with four divers and Henderson ceased towing to give the divers a chance, but the tide had turned and they were unable to enter the launch. Exhausted and frustrated, they gave up and the painful progress towards the harbour resumed.

As the ebb increased, *Millie Walton* struggled to make headway until the fishing boat *Ocean Vanguard* took one of the lines. The tow rope to the fishing boat parted when they were only 100 yd from the harbour bar and the lifeboat carried on alone.

Henderson carefully assessed the seas breaking across the bar and the depth of water over it. There was a chance — just — that the pinnace would clear it if she could be borne over on one of the swells and her mast would break away. The lifeboat Cox'n opened the throttles. *Millie Walton* ploughed forward over the bar in a surge of white water. Behind her, the pinnace's mast dug into the sea bed. The tow ropes parted and the lifeboat, freed from its burden, charged ahead. The rescuers surveyed the scene with dismay. The pinnace was now in a totally inaccessible position and stuck fast. It was a little after eight o'clock and almost dark.

By the light of car headlights, and floodlights rigged by the emergency services, the gathering crowds ashore and the would-be rescuers afloat, watched impotently as the pinnace ground against the bar. Bob Moore, now in caring hands ashore, broke down with remorse at leaving the young deckhand behind. Still suffering from shock and exposure, he was inconsolable.

After an hour, the wreck started to move and the rollers drove it slowly towards the rocky shore where it grounded in shallow water some yards out, held fast by its dangling anchor. At 2130 hrs, the naval diving team arrived and decided to try and reach it from the foreshore. With the aid of other rescuers, the frogmen succeeded in clambering aboard the hull where, above the noise of the crashing surf, they could just hear a tapping sound. Ashton was still alive.

A few minutes after 11.15pm, the hull was breached, and a pale, shaking, staring Dave Ashton was extricated. For almost five hours he had lapsed in and out of consciousness. In the pitch darkness he had been heartened by the scuffling of feet on the hull and the shouts of Moore and Stewart. He had heard the helicopter overhead and the lifeboat alongside. His spirits were further uplifted by the changed motion of the hull under tow, but they had plummeted again when all he could hear for over two hours, was the wracking and grinding of the pinnace on the sea bed. For all he knew, the boat had sunk in deep water. Throughout the ordeal he had remained calm, tapping with his cigarette lighter whenever he could.

Of the four missing men, Ashton was the only survivor. Don Ivil, Geoffrey Benson and Skipper Ken Bell had perished.

During the night, breakers smashed the launch to pieces and wreckage was scattered along the shore in all directions. The surviving crew members of P 1386 gradually returned to their routine work. Danny

Coutts, approaching his 45th birthday was soon due for demob. Bob Moore, Charlie Chase and Bill Traynor forced themselves to resume crew duties.

Within a few weeks, Moore was engineer aboard another pinnace on passage from Bridlington to Plymouth. Whilst he was below in the foc'sle, the launch started to make water and he hurried to inform the Cox'n. Not a word was spoken. The Cox'n took one look at Moore's ashen face and headed straight for nearby Newhaven!

For a time, David Ashton was employed on dinghies and Marine Tenders within the limits of Bridlington harbour, but ultimately he left the Marine Branch.

In the aftermath of the accident, six gallantry awards and several commendations were issued, among them Sergeant Alan Jones received the Queen's Commendation for Valuable Service in the Air. The highest award of all went to Bob Moore, who received the British Empire Medal for Gallantry. Moore, accompanied by his wife Shirley, his children and in-laws, attended an investiture at Buckingham Palace on 28 July 1970.

The sailors' blind faith in the indestructability of the pinnaces had been undermined for all time, although everyone was aware that the Bridlington boat had been lost to a freak wave. None the less, one can speculate on the thoughts of the crew of P 1381 when in 1971 they set out on a rescue mission in seas which had already forced an RTTL to seek shelter.

The occasion was the Annual Royal Navy Regatta for gigs and whalers which was run each year from Plymouth to Fowey in Cornwall. In previous years the RAF sailors had entered their own whaler, and had achieved some spectacular wins, but in 1971 their boat was unserviceable.

When race day dawned on 18 June, there was an overcast sky, drizzle, and a fresh breeze from the south-west. The RN decided to go ahead with the race, but by the time the first hour had passed, the wind had risen to Force 7–8 and the sea became very rough. By noon, the small boats were in serious trouble. Some capsized or broached, while others were swept into the surf off Whitsands Bay and Looe.

A general alarm was put out and RTTL 2757 left Mount Batten to search for survivors. The wind had accelerated to a full south-westerly gale by the time she rounded Rame Head and the launch was unable to make headway against the massive waves. As the RTTL returned to the sanctuary of Plymouth Sound, Flight Lieutenant Bryan Audhlam-Gardiner, Cox'n Flight Sergeant Stewart and their crew, headed for the search area in P 1381.

The seas were confused and mountainous. The pinnace took a bone-shattering pounding and was tossed about like a plastic bottle, but the crew systematically checked several of the upturned boats by the expedient of nudging them over with the bows of the launch. Two hours into the search, they found two men in the water. Both were rescued, one an RN Lieutenant and the other a boy seaman from the training depot, HMS *Raleigh*. The Lieutenant responded to the ministrations of Senior Aircraftman Garson, P 1381's medic, but the youngster was too far gone to save. After a further three hours of quartering the storm-wracked sea, the pinnace was recalled to base. All of the crew received commendations.

For several years, the annual International Offshore Power Boat Races from Cowes to Torquay drew the attention of Mount Batten-based RTTLs as standby rescue craft. In the early 1960s the RAF boats were faster than the racing boats, but the latters' technological developments eventually pushed them to twice, then three times, the speed of the launches.

In the 1970 race, rough conditions knocked out 27 of the 58 starters. Two competitors were rescued by RTTL 2772 and two damaged boats were towed in to Brixham and Portland. In the following year, RTTL 2757 showed her age in the Force 8 gale which bedevilled the event. She was forced to retire from escort duty with one engine, her radar, log and radio all unserviceable. A week later, she was ignominiously towed to Plymouth by the new steel launch, HMAFV *Sea Otter*.

During the tow, the skipper of the RTTL observed, 'This is the way to travel: no noise, no navigation, and a chunk of iron up front to flatten out the waves!' It was an involuntary acknowledgement that the evocative high-speed rescue launches were now *passé*.

Five years later, in November 1977, HMAFV 2757 left Mount Batten for the Port of London where she was craned out of the water and transported to the RAF Museum at Hendon. The last of the legendary HSL breed had become a museum piece.

While some sailors continued to man the diminishing fleet of wooden boats, the remaining years of the Marine Branch were dominated by new 'Iron Ships'. Many mourned the old boats' passing, for when the pinnaces and RSLs were finished, so were the NCO Cox'ns' last chances of an independent command at sea.

# Chapter 22

# You'd better teach me to weld!

*Comment from a Boatwright on hearing of plans for new steel-hulled launches.
The following lines appeared in a Marine Craft Newsletter.*

From Plymouth's hard — to Rosyth's yard
The scene was set — the greatest yet
To change, in Devon — our trade group seven

Way up north — hard by the Forth
A Naval base — has set the pace
To increase in part — the Boatwrights' art

By car they came — to work with flame
These men of wood — to prove they could
Learn a trade — of metallic grade

From the realm — of American elm
To the acrid scene — of acetylene
To get the feel — of molten steel

In Argon's region — with dangers legion
Carburizing, oxidation — overheating, penetration
Terms so Greek — to their world of teak

So give them a chance — with thermal lance
And let them mend — a web-toes bend
And prove to all – their new-found call.

T he sailors were affected by several changes in Air Force structures throughout the 1960s. The technical ladder was revised in 1964 resulting in the ranks of Corporal Technician and Senior Technician being scrapped in favour of straightforward Corporal and Sergeant.

The Junior Technician's single chevron was replaced by a new four-bladed propeller badge and, to their dismay, the Chief Technicians lost their crown. All inverted chevrons were unstitched and sewn back on the 'right way up'. In 1970, eagles were deleted and chevrons reduced in size. Battledress was replaced by a shapeless barathea jacket with zip pockets and the Bridgedale style of 'woolly-poolly' was introduced for everyday wear.

In a move towards Combined Services, the Air Ministry became the Air Department of the Ministry of Defence, and in November 1969 Coastal Command was absorbed into the all-embracing Strike Command.

At Lacon House in London, the Deputy Director of Marine Craft, Group Captain Les Flower, MBE, MM, and his staff were faced with a dilemma. The Marine Branch's commitments had to be maintained in the face of defence cut-backs and closures. By the late 1960s, fewer sailors were clearly going to have to do more work with fewer boats and from a small number of widely spaced units.

The existing pinnaces and RSLs were adequate for the majority of tasks where speed was not essential, but the RTTLs were too limited in range. Flower recalled the Fairmile 'D' type boats he had commanded at the end of the war. With modern construction methods and up-to-date, high-speed diesels, similar craft would be able to stay at sea for long periods and, if purpose-designed from the outset, would meet all the requirements of the new age. In 1965 the Admiralty design department started work on what were to become LRRSCs (Long Range Recovery and Support Craft).

In the interim, three Naval 'Ham' class inshore minesweepers were seconded to the RAF in April 1966. They were 107 ft long by 21 ft beam displacement boats, powered by twin Paxman diesels. By Air Force standards their speed was low at 13¼ knots maximum and 9 knots cruising. HMS *Bottisham*, HMS *Chelsham* and HMS *Hailsham* became HMAFVs 5000, 5001 and 5002 respectively. With typical Marine Branch acuity they were called Interim Recovery Vessels (IRV). These numbers were later transferred to the first three LRRSCs, at which time the IRVs became 5010, 5011 and 5012. They were not popular with the sailors who had been weaned on the dash and excitement of the RTTLs, but they fulfilled their purposes exceptionally well and established lengthy coastal passages as a norm. When the first of the new LRRSCs entered service in 1967, IRVs 5010 and 5011 were returned to the Navy. It was a hasty action, for there were long delays before the next two new craft were completed.

The remaining boat, HMAFV 5012, stayed at 1107 MCU Newhaven as a floating laboratory for the RAE Farnborough until late 1972. During that year she sailed from Newhaven as far as Malta and back, and thence to Campbeltown, the Clyde and the Scilly Isles. On 17 October 1972, her RAF ensign was lowered for the last time and she was handed over to the Royal Corps of Transport. Two weeks later 1107 MCU Newhaven was closed down.

The first of the new LRRSC class, HMAFV *Seal* was named by Lady Grandy, wife of the Chief of Air Staff, Air Chief Marshal Sir John Grandy, at Brooke Marine's boatyard on 2 August 1967. It was a symbolic return to the Lowestoft yard which had built the Brooke motor boats of the 1920s, but now the sounds were of riveting and sandblasting. The smells of resin and newly planed wood had been replaced by the dust and rust of steel work.

HMAFV *Seal* was 120 ft 3 in in length with a 23 ft 6 in beam, and drew just under 6ft. Her two 2,000 hp Paxman Ventura 16YJCM engines gave her a top speed slightly over 24 knots and a continuous cruising speed of 17 knots. Exhaust discharge was via a single funnel. Most impressive of all was her range of 950 nautical miles at 20 knots, or 2,000 miles at 12 knots, on 31 tons of fuel oil. She was a large boat for the RAF, displacing 159 tons compared with the 45 tons of the Mk II RTTL. *Seal* was equipped with the latest navigation aids and communications systems. Power winches and capstans were installed for weapons handling and a large transom door and a roller ramp in the stern allowed for hauling recovered weapons inboard.

Spacious accommodation provided for a crew of 18 who worked a two or three-watch system at sea. Separate cabins were included for the Captain, First Lieutenant, the Cox'n and Chief Engineer with comfortable bunks and mess decks for the rest of the men. For the first time since the demise of *Bridport* and *Bridlington* an RAF vessel carried a full-time cook.

The new boat was placed under the command of Flight Lieutenant Parkin who sailed her into Mount Batten on 7 August 1967. During her trial period of deep-sea sonobuoy exercises, she achieved a 100 per cent recovery rate. Working out of Portrush in Northern Ireland with Shackleton aircraft, some 12,000 pick-ups were made. All that remained was to test her long range reliability and sea-keeping qualities.

In November it was decided that *Seal* would participate in torpedo recovery trials with the Atlantic Undersea Test and Evaluation Centre (AUTEC) at Andros Island in the Bahamas. The trials were due to start on 18 March 1968.

The Engineering Squadron at Mount Batten fitted four 500 gallon Argosy reserve fuel tanks, thereby increasing *Seal's* cruising range to 2,500 miles. Copious stores and spares were loaded aboard, including two tons of bonded goods. Extra radio systems and electronic location equipment were fitted and tested, and deep freezes and dry food storage was added. Meanwhile, the crew underwent medical and dental checks.

On the overcast, sultry morning of 1 February, the LRRSC slipped her moorings and sailed for Lisbon on the first leg of her voyage, a distance of 777 miles which was covered at an average speed of 15.69 knots. The passage was uneventful except for signs of influenza among the crew. Two men were confined to their cots. When *Seal* arrived in Madeira on 7

February, the epidemic had spread. Two of the crew were transferred to a hospital and the launch stayed in Madeira for a week. When she sailed on St Valentine's Day, the weather was warm, the crew had changed into their summer rig, and they enjoyed favourable north-east trade winds during their 1,047 mile run to the Cape Verde Islands. Here, they refuelled and revictualled before setting out on the final transatlantic leg on 19 February.

After six days of steaming, *Seal* made landfall in Barbados on 25 February. The first Atlantic crossing by an RAF launch had been completed without incident.

For five days the crew languished in the West Indies before heading out past the Leeward Islands, Puerto Rico and Cuba for Freeport on Grand Bahama. The 1,516 mile trip took four days. On 6 March, *Seal* arrived at the American Naval Base on the barren Andros Island.

For the next six weeks, the crew worked from dawn to dusk on torpedo recovery using their 21 ft rigid inflatable inshore rescue craft. Although the sun shone from clear skies, the sea was often extremely rough and there were a disconcerting number of sharks and barracudas around. American launches of AUTEC worked with sonobuoys and submarines, aided occasionally by *Seal*, whose more sophisticated search equipment proved both faster and more effective.

The launch departed from Andros on 15 April, Easter Monday. The return voyage via Nassau, Freeport and Bermuda was a round of socializing and preparing the boat for the crossing to the Azores. On 2 May, *Seal* docked in Ponta Delgada. A favourable weather forecast prompted a decision to leave the Azores after only an eight-hour refuelling stop, but the met men were wrong and *Seal* was caught in a full north-westerly gale when only 30 hours out. She tried to lie a'hull without success, but the crew discovered that she was both stable and controllable providing the weather was kept abaft the beam. They made a 350 mile dash for the nearest shelter in the port of Leixoes in Portugal.

Now only a few hours from home, the launch was storm-bound for five days, but at last, on 10 May, she set out on the final run to Plymouth. When she arrived on the following day after averaging 18.01 knots, the crew's wives and girlfriends and the entire base staff were there to greet her. After 101 days and 12,500 miles, she had successfully completed the longest voyage ever to be undertaken by an RAF launch.

Delays and complications of supply plus modifications to specifications meant that it was over two years before *Seal* was joined by LRRSC 5001, *Seagull,* and a further six months before the third boat, LRRSC 5002, *Sea Otter,* was commissioned.

Moves towards more dependency on the Royal Navy had started in 1966 when in April the ships and personnel of Moorings Branch were transferred to the Navy Department. In 1969, all marine stores, spares and rations ceased to be supplied from RAF sources and were hence-forth drawn from the RN. The size of the 'Seal Class' boats placed them beyond the handling capacity of the Engineering Squadron at Mount Batten. From then on, all steel launches had to be serviced in H.M. Naval dockyards. By 1971, even the major servicing and storage of the remaining wooden boats was handed over to dockyard 'mateys'. This facility was located at the Naval Gunboat Yard at Haslar with overall responsibility for the unit in the capable hands of Boatwright Flight Lieutenant Ted Bull.

Like all other Engineering Officers, Ted Bull attended a two–part training course at Mount Batten and the RN Engineering College at Manadon, Plymouth. The subjects covered welded steel and glass fibre craft, naval dockyard procedures and familiarization with Ruston, Paxman and Perkins engines. Similar training for NCO Boatwrights commenced in the following year at both Mount Batten and HMS *Caledonia* in Rosyth.

In January 1970 the Deputy Directorate of Marine Craft (DDMC) became the Directorate of Marine Craft (DMC). This time the revision of the title was a reflection of the reduction in scale of marine operations. At the end of the year, the sailors said a sad farewell to the legendary Les Flower when he retired after 36 years marine service. He had risen from Aircraftman Deckhand to command the Marine Branch, a unique achievement. His replacement was ex-Master Mariner, Group Captain D. T. Beamish, OBE, MMar, AMBIM.

During the changeover period of the two Group Captains, plans were laid for three new types of vessels to replace all the wooden boats. The first was a Mk III RTTL of 73 ft, the second a general service launch of about 60 ft to take over the work of the pinnaces and RSLs, and the third a 24 ft boat to carry out the work of the marine tenders.

The introduction of the new RTTL was the first and most complex task, and as its multi-purpose concept evolved, the GS launch project was cancelled. While *Seal, Seagull, Sea Otter*, IRV 5012 and the tired wooden craft continued, the DMC staff focused on getting the new design into service. There was a great sense of urgency. The future of the Marine Branch depended on it.

The prototype, HMAFV *Spitfire* was built by James and Stone of Brightlingsea in Essex. The steel hull was of semi-displacement configuration and the superstructure of aluminium. Overall length was 72 ft 9 in with a beam of 18 ft 6 in and a draft of 5 ft 4 in. Two Paxman 8YJCM diesel engines of 1,000 hp each were installed to give a designed speed of 24 knots. Two Perkins 4.326 diesels provided auxiliary power for pumps and generators, and a small Lister engine drove the fire pump. The launch was fitted out for one officer and eight crew. Sandwiched between the engine room and the tiller flat at the aft end, a large sickbay doubled as a storage compartment. Above the upper deck, a squared-off superstructure contained wheelhouse, bridge and radio cabin, and extended aft at reduced height over the engine room and sickbay. The electronic aids ranged from a variety of sonar and search devices to the latest radar, radio and navigation equipment. An array of aerials surmounted the lattice type topmast which was just forward of two large side-by-side funnels. On the upper deck on the starboard side, a hydraulic crane took the place of the more customary derrick.

RTTL 4000 HMAFV *Spitfire* was launched in January 1972 and handed over to her first skipper, Flight Lieutenant Cannock, for acceptance trials. In the course of a few months she acted as anchorage control vessel for Naval trials off Falmouth, recovered practice mines, visited the Channel Islands for Operation Sea Splash, an annual parachute drop by the Territorial Army, and towed targets in the North Sea. Whilst on passage for one of these latter details, she encountered her first SAR 'Crash Call'.

When the call was received shortly before midnight on 17 August 1972, skipper Flight Lieutenant Graham Duffy, Cox'n Flight Sergeant Smith, and their crew were hammering *Spitfire* against a north-westerly gale and looking forward to landfall at Gorleston. The sea was very rough and the RTTL was displaying her tendency to ship large wedges of solid water and spray over her bows. When the distressed vessel had been located north of Lowestoft, *Spitfire's* searchlight revealed that it was a sailing yacht, *Genapi Too*. On board were two men, two women and two children. The yacht had suffered an engine breakdown and the tidal stream was gradually pushing it towards treacherous sandbanks. Duffy and his crew succeeded in securing a towline and eased the sailing boat away from danger. Later they towed it safely into Gorleston. A congratulatory letter from HQ 18 Group said: '…it is pleasing to see that *Spitfire* acquitted herself well in her first live SAR incident.'

But all was not as it seemed. *Spitfire* was a disappointment, for experience had revealed some major faults. She did not trim correctly and she was incapable of attaining her designed speed. The launch was returned to the builders where 11 in trim wedges were fitted under the transom to keep her down by the head when underway. This resulted in a speed increase to an acceptable 22 knots, but it also meant that she shipped even more water over the bows. The shape of the stern was modified, and spray chines were added for'ard, but when she went back into service she continued to be a very wet boat. In 1973 she was slipped at James and Stone once more; this time a new stem was fitted and a further 5 ft of flared bow welded in place. It was quite astounding that the hull design could have been so wrong. Whatever the reasons for the errors, those who had watched or experienced *Spitfire* scooping her way through even moderate seas could see that the prow was obviously too short and stubby. Someone once said of the Spitfire aeroplane, 'If it looks right, it is right.' Maybe the same adage should have been applied to its nautical namesake.

The new 'stretched' *Spitfire* was a much better sea boat. During the winter of 1973–4 she was thoroughly tested in the English Channel and the Western Approaches. One morning she was dispatched to recover a wave recording buoy which had broken adrift in a gale to the south of the Eddystone lighthouse. The buoy was located and was still transmitting data of wave heights up to 30 ft. *Spitfire* was able to maintain 20 knots in these conditions without shipping green seas over the bow. At slower speeds some broken water did tumble aboard, but as the report thankfully stated, 'without the well-known vertebrae-collapsing, biscuit-breaking crash of a Mk II RTTL!' After all the frustrating trial and error, the Mk III RTTL was declared to be a winner. The last line of the report summed up the impromptu test: 'Altogether, *Spitfire* is reassuringly seaworthy, and we can all look forward with confidence to accepting lots and lots of these fine craft into service before long.'

It was a badly timed statement. Britain was shrouded in the gloom of the falling pound, multiple strikes, the three-day week, petrol rationing and an outbreak of terrorism in Northern Ireland. In June 1973, Group Captain Beamish warned that the replacement RTTL programme was set back about 20 months. In the following year, a Marine Craft Review to determine the future status and requirements of the Branch was swallowed up in a major Government Defence Review. The sailors were sick of filling in questionnaires about man hours and crewing levels for HMAFVs. There was still no sign of the second Mk III RTTL, and spirits were low.

The three LRRSCs and *Spitfire* were holding their own between periods in dock, but the wooden boats were all but rotting away. At Mount Batten, Warrant Officer Len Lomas did a commendable job cannibalizing older boats to keep the dwindling number of Mk II RTTLs going, but there was a limit to even his creative talent.

The second of the new RTTLs, No 4001 HMAFV *Sunderland*, entered service on 2 April 1976, five years and three months after *Spitfire*. All the lessons learned from the prototype had been incorporated. The funnels were gone, the accommodation and equipment were improved and the hull extended to 80 ft loa. HMAFV *Sunderland* was allocated to 1102 MCU Gibraltar under the command of Flight Lieutenant Mike Tyrell. She was the first RAF launch under 100 ft in length to sail to Gibraltar under her own steam.

On 24 January 1977, No 4002 HMAFV *Stirling* came off the stocks and proceeded to her new base at 1104 MCU Bridlington. No 4003 HMAFV *Halifax* followed in April of the same year to operate with the Marine Squadron and *Spitfire* out of Mount Batten. Although the next boat was scheduled for December 1979 with three others phased at four monthly intervals, industrial disputes, component delays and late delivery of the main engines disrupted the building programme. RTTL 4004 HMAFV *Hampden* did not emerge from the yard until June 1980. She was dispatched to Gibraltar almost immediately to allow *Sunderland* to return to the yard for a refit. No 4005 HMAFV *Hurricane* was launched in September 1980, followed by No 4006 HMAFV *Lancaster* in 1981. The last of the series and, indeed, the last RTTL of any kind to be built for the RAF, was No 4007 HMAFV *Wellington*, which was handed over on 9 July 1981.

When Flight Lieutenant T. R. Bennett took command of *Wellington*, 10 years had passed since the first of the eight keels was laid. It was tempting to recall the time when the British Power Boat Company produced 90 68 ft launches for the RAF in a period of only 28 months!

While awaiting the Mk III RTTLs, the LRRSCs changed the sailors' way of life completely. With longer voyages and prolonged detachments from their bases, they came to regard their ships as 'home'. There were the inevitable changes of personnel within each crew, but in the main the crews became identified with each boat much as was the custom in the Royal Navy.

When 1105 MCU at Portrush was disbanded in March 1971, HMAFV *Seal* was transferred to 1100 MCU at Alness. Most of *Seal*'s crew stayed with the boat, but the crew of Mk II RTTL 2757, which had also been transferred, were either posted or absorbed into the unit. During that summer, *Seal* and *Sea Otter* spent long periods away in the Shetland Isles on NATO exercises. In October, *Seal* became due for a six-week refit. The dockyard took six months to complete the job, during which time *Seagull* sailed from Mount Batten and operated from Alness to the Shetlands in her place. By mid-1971, *Sea Otter* had returned to Mount Batten and departed again for Malta to replace IRV 5012.

By the end of 1971, the first full year of working with all three LRRSCs, the sailors had adjusted to spending long periods at sea and had adapted themselves to the nomadic lifestyle. They had learned to have faith in the boats, all of which had encountered extremes of weather and sea conditions at some time.

The one storm which they found unacceptable was one that blew up ashore in the naval dockyards. Strikes, working to rule and go-slows had been responsible for the disproportionate time that *Seal* and later *Seagull* spent refitting. At one stage the 'mateys' had threatened to 'black' *Seagull* when the crew had warped her ahead a few yards in the dock basin. On another occasion pickets refused the crew entry to the dockyard.

The RAF men wondered how the Royal Navy had been able to tolerate it for so long. They tried to arrange for servicing at other yards by civilian contract, but the rules stated that the Royal Dockyards had the first option. When all RAF forms and documentation were phased out in favour of naval procedures in 1976, it began to seem as though the raising of the white ensign was only a matter of time. However, in 1978 the sailors received the go-ahead to negotiate their own servicing with civilian firms.

Meanwhile, the LRRCs and the RTTLs pursued their routines of NATO exercises, FPB practices and 'Subsunk' training with the RN. Now and again there was some lighter relief from the regular tasks. The RAF launches were often allocated the job of 'guardship' during fleet exercises. This was really a euphemism for keeping Russian ships away. In 1973, *Seal* confronted a 'Riga' class escort vessel which came too close to an exercise in the Firth of Forth. *Seal's* crew went to action stations during the confrontation and the Soviet ship kept a respectful distance thereafter. It was a bit like a bulldog snapping at a bear.

In May 1980 *Sea Otter,* under the command of Flight Lieutenant Gault established a marine craft first as a drug buster. The launch put into Oban whilst on passage to Plymouth from an FPB exercise in the north of Scotland. She was immediately commandeered by the Special Investigations Branch of HM Customs and Excise and used to mount a series of clandestine raids on several island properties in the Firth of Lorn. Over £12,000,000 worth of drugs was recovered.

In the same year, *Sea Otter* escorted the Royal Yacht *Britannia* during HM the Queen Mother's visit to Dover for the unveiling of the ASR and MCS memorial window in St Mary's church. *Halifax* joined the escort flotilla at Dover, and it was both appropriate and poignant that serving RAF sailors were able to honour their predecessors in such an impressive manner.

Compared with earlier years, rescue operations were few and far between. All the boats were utilized for SAR at various times but the onus of this activity was now firmly on the capable RAF and naval helicopter crews. However, there was one aspect of rescue work which the choppers were not able to carry out. Salvaging could only be done by surface craft and the sailors often assisted the RNLI on such tasks.

An outstanding rescue of this type was accomplished when *Sea Otter* took a damaged tug, *Duke of Normandy 2,* under tow in a Force 9 gale in 1977. It was a difficult and dangerous job, but with a lifeboat and a helicopter standing by, *Sea Otter* safely delivered the tug and its crew to Campbeltown. On another less happy occasion *Stirling* was dispatched to stand by the wreck of a Red Arrows' aircraft which had crashed 200 yds off Brighton sea front during a display. The crew were sickened by the ghoulish crowds, some of whom even tried to filch pieces of the wreckage for souvenirs.

None of the latter day SAR incidents equalled the originality of a search carried out by *Seal* in the North Sea in 1972. She had been engaged in night target-towing exercises with Buccaneers from RAF Honington. After completing the exercise, the Wireless Operator, Bob Symons, sent an 'Off Task' signal, but to his surprise was told that an aircraft had been seen to crash in the area which *Seal* had just vacated. A helicopter was scrambled and a search began. After a couple of fruitless hours, the chopper was diverted to another location and Symons asked for a confirmation of the original position report. When the reply came — 'Flares were seen' — the penny dropped. An ocean weather ship had seen *Seal's* splash target and the parachute flares, thus assuming that an aircraft had crashed. *Seal* had been searching for herself!

In 1971 the RAF received its first all-GRP, motor boat, but this replacement for the marine tender was also subjected to delays. Based on a well-tried Cheverton Workboat hull, the new Ferry Boat prototype,

No 2000, was 24 ft long with two cabins and a central cockpit. Beneath the midships boarding deck, a Perkins 75 hp 6.354 engine generated a speed of 10 knots. Various modifications were applied to the boat and not until 1977 did the final 27 ft version enter service.

The enforced economies of the early 1970s and restrictions on the use of the fuel-gobbling Mk II RTTLs prompted the DMC to invest in two special craft which had their origins in the past.

The highly successful armoured target boats of the 1930s and the less than successful remote control HSLs in the post-war period led to the adoption of small, radio-controlled, high-speed target launches. The 18 ft GRP *Sea Flash* speedboats could be operated for 4 to 6 hours from distances up to 12,000 yd (6.8 miles or 10.9 km), at speeds between 20 and 35 knots. In one respect they represented a major breakaway from both RAF and naval purchasing tradition. The specified engines were of foreign manufacture. Their six-cylinder, 170 hp Volvo AQ170/200 petrol engines with outdrive units were of a special type pioneered by the Swedish manufacturer. *Sea Flash* boats were used extensively by Mount Batten on FPB and surface gunnery exercises with HMS *Cambridge.*

Another small boat which proved effective was the 21 ft 'Atlantic' Class rigid inflatable known as IRC (Inshore Rescue Craft). These boats were carried by the LRRSCs for use in weapons recovery, but like their RNLI counterparts they were invaluable for the job which their title suggested. One of these, IRC 54, made a name for itself in only a few weeks whilst at Tenby in South Wales. The first pick-up was achieved by Senior Aircraftmen Wheeler and Badham, when they saved the life of an 11-year-old boy who was drowning after trusting to a toy inflatable. Shortly afterwards, Senior Aircraftman Munro rescued a nine-year-old from rocks near St Catherines Point. Two days later, Senior Aircraftman Mathews and Junior Technician Moss retrieved four skin-divers whose boat had drifted on to skerries. Wheeler and Mathews were at it again after a fortnight when they rescued a 13-year-old who had fallen down Monkstone Cliffs. Wheeler had to climb the cliffs in order to bring the teenager down safely. Mathews, Badham and Wheeler all received commendations.

A recurring nightmare which accompanied the acquisition of new craft was that of balancing the manning levels. The establishment of marine personnel had only once achieved equilibrium in the post-war period. Most of the time, the sailors lurched between either a surfeit in some if not all ranks and trades, and a deficit. The smallness of the Marine Branch brought an esoteric inflexibility in numbers. There were barely 5,000 sailors in the peak period of 1944, a figure which was more than halved in the peacetime peak of the 1950s. By the late '70s, under the command of Group Captain J. N. Burgess, there were only a handful of men operating a score of seagoing boats.

When the numbers were reassessed in 1972, it was discovered that there were too many senior Boatwrights and Marine Fitters and a shortage of MBCs. A wave of incentives was offered to persuade SNCOs to accept redundancy in 1973 and 1974, a scheme which worked rather too well, whilst the Training Squadron reinstated courses for MBC recruits. At the same time, many of the more experienced skippers were leaving and the shortfall was not being helped by continued detachments to non-marine operations.

By 1975, the pendulum had partly swung the other way, for there was hardly an SNCO to be seen, but the Branch was still having difficulty in attracting officers with Extra Masters' Certificates. As was the case 10 years earlier, RAF pay and prospects could not compete with those of the Merchant Service.

In 1976, many of the remaining Flight Lieutenants were promoted to Squadron Leader at the very time that the service lacked junior officers. Marine Officers were still being sent on 'tours' with Balloons and MT, and now other alternatives had been added, including training posts at RAF Swinderby and RAF Henlow and at the Parachute School at Hullavington.

In 1977 there were some outspoken views in favour of recalling officers from these other duties, but the problem was resolved in an untypical manner. Entry standards were relaxed, and for the first time ever commissions were available to Master Coxswains of the rank of Sergeant and below. This concession had a useful outcome, but in 1978, with the establishment remaining unfilled, the conditions for direct entry officers were lowered to include men with a First or Second Mate (foreign-going) ticket. Within 12 months, eight new officers had joined the Branch.

To help resolve the shortages in the lower ranks, a new scheme of recruitment was introduced. The aim was to achieve 25 per cent manning by men residing in each unit's locality. These 'locals' would not be subject to postings and detachments and would, in effect, commute daily to their regular place of work like civilians.

Soon after Group Captain J. E. Williams took over as DMC in 1980, he faced further serious problems with technical manning. In 1981, the trade of Marine Fitter became Marine Technician in accordance with changes in the 'proper' RAF. At the same time, the trade of Marine Mechanic was suspended and the rank of Chief Technician discontinued. Prospective engineering sailors only had to attend a 46-week General Technician's course at RAF St Athan, followed by familiarization training 'on the job'! It was rationalization gone mad and it marked the demise of the highly trained, specialist marine engineers. Two years later, the trade of Boatwright was made obsolete.

The last Director of Marine Craft, Group Captain J. S. Fosh, CBE, inherited a pale shadow of a Branch that had once been thriving and vital. Shortages of spares for the boats and a dearth of qualified and experienced men to crew and maintain them were matters for concern. The job still had to be done, but the blunting of the tools was the legacy of financial stringency. Those who had been largely responsible for cutting budgets to a level where only inefficiency could ensue then took the next logical step in the familiar process. They studied the accounts, scratched their heads and opted for privatization.

On 4 May 1984, Fosh received a directive from the Ministry of Defence to commence the winding-up of the Marine Branch. In February 1986 the essential RAF marine support tasks were delegated to a civilian ship management company. Eleven seagoing vessels and one harbour craft were redesignated AFVs and handed over to civilian captains and crews.

At Lacon House a contract monitoring cell of RAF sailors was set up under the command of veteran skipper Wing Commander George Bell. The cell reverted to the old title of Deputy Directorate of Marine Craft.

The Marine Branch was officially disbanded at midnight on 31 March 1986. A few of the younger sailors felt sadness and resignation but most of the more experienced hands were delighted. They had shed their RAF uniforms to become the select civilian crews of the AFVs.

Well, where else would the contractors have found men of the right calibre?

# Epilogue

*In the wake*

After the disbandment of the Marine Branch, the DDMC continued to watch over contractual arrangements for the launches until the office was itself disbanded in February 1991. The last sailors to serve in the RAF were Marine Officer Wing Commander Bryan Audhlam-Gardiner, MMar; Technical Officer Squadron Leader Bob Moore, BEM and Marine Technicians Warrant Officer Reg Nash and Flight Sergeant Ron Dorre. MOD Navy has now taken over and the launches, no longer HMAFVs, carry neither the RAF ensign nor the Union Jack, but continue to serve the Air Force which spawned the maritime branch 75 years ago.

Every year ex-RAF seafarers hold a series of reunions under the auspices of either the Marine Officers' Association, which is open to officers who served after 1947, or the Air Sea Rescue and Marine Craft Section Club, which is open to any ex-RAF sailor.

ASR/MCS Club annual dinners, branch meetings, informal get-togethers and bi-annual newsletters, keep the shipmates in touch. This organization, which was formed in 1951, has always retained its 'Club' status, and perhaps that is how it should be.

Sailors in the RAF were members of a very exclusive club indeed.

# Glossary

| | |
|---|---|
| AB | Able Seaman, Royal Navy. |
| ABL | Airborne Lifeboat. |
| AC | Aircraftman. |
| AC/H | Aircrafthand. |
| A'hull | Boat stopped with drogues streamed to keep head-to-sea. |
| AOC-in-C | Air Officer Commanding in Chief. |
| ASR | Air Sea Rescue, sometimes printed A/SR. |
| Astro-navigation | Navigation by the stars. |
| ATB | Armoured Target Boat. |
| AUTEC | Atlantic Undersea Test and Evaluation Centre. |
| Barrico | Small coopered barrel, also 'breaker.' |
| BEF | British Expeditionary Force. |
| Bf 109 | German Messerschmitt fighter. |
| BG | Bombardment Group of the USAAF. |
| BPBC | British Power Boat Company. |
| Carley float | Solid cork life-raft similar in appearance to a rubber dinghy. |
| CAS | Chief of Air Staff. |
| Cavitation | Air bubbles forming on propeller surfaces causing it to lose 'grip'. Recently discovered to be related to sound waves. |
| C/B | Carpenter/Boatbuilder. |
| Ch Tech | Chief Technician, a rank equivalent to Flight Sergeant. |
| Chernikeef log | Device for recording speed through the water via an impeller protruding beneath the hull and electrical impulses. |
| Chine | The 'corner' between the side of the hull and the bottom. |
| CMB | Coastal Motor Boat. |

| | |
|---|---|
| CO | Commanding Officer. |
| Coaming | The raised rim around a cockpit or hold. |
| COE | Combined Operations Executive. |
| Conning | Controlling a vessel via verbal instructions to the helmsman. |
| CPBC | Canadian Power Boat Company. |
| Cpl | Corporal. |
| Cpl Tech. | Technician rank equivalent to corporal. |
| Dan buoy | Small floating marker with a weighted sinker, usually with a pennant on top. |
| DDMC | Deputy Director (or Directorate) of Marine Craft. |
| Deckhead | The underside of a deck or the roof of a cabin. |
| DI | Drill Instructor. |
| D of ASR | Director (or Directorate) of Air Sea Rescue. |
| DGAS | Director (or Directorate) of Air Safety. |
| DMC | Director (or Directorate) of Marine Craft. |
| Dumb | Without engines, eg dumb dinghy. |
| ERS | Emergency Rescue Squadron. |
| ETO | European Theatre of Operations. |
| FAA | Fleet Air Arm. |
| F/DP | Fitter/Driver Petrol. |
| FEAF | Far East Air Force. |
| Fitter 2E | Aircraft engine fitter. |
| Flt Lt | Flight Lieutenant. |
| F/O | Flying Officer. |
| Focs'le | Forecastle, the forward accommodation below the main deck. |
| FPB | Fast Patrol Boat. |
| Freeboard | The height of the side of a hull above the waterline. |
| Fw 190 | German Focke-Wulf fighter. |
| F Sgt | Flight Sergeant. |
| FWE | Finished With Engines, the last entry in a ship's log at the end of a voyage. |
| GOC | General Officer Commanding (Army). |
| GP | General purpose. |
| Gp Capt | Group Captain. |
| GPO | General Post Office. |
| GS | General Service. |
| Gunwhales | The top edge of a hull side. |
| Helm loading | Resistance of water pressure on rudder(s) when steering. |
| HMAFV | His (or Her) Majesty's Air Force Vessel. |
| HMS | His (or Her) Majesty's Ship. |
| HSL | High Speed Launch. |
| IDC | Imperial Defence Committee. |
| IRB | Inshore Rescue Boat. |
| IRV | Interim Recovery Vessel. |

| | |
|---|---|
| Jury sail | Improvized sails or rig. |
| LAC | Leading Aircraftman. |
| LCA | Landing Craft Assault. |
| LCGP | Landing Craft General Purpose. |
| LCM | Landing Craft Mechanized. |
| LOA | Length over all. |
| LRRC | Long Range Rescue Craft. |
| LRRSC | Long Range Recovery and Support Craft. |
| MAEE | Marine Aircraft Experimental Establishment. |
| MASB | Motor Anti-Submarine Boat. |
| Mayday | Voice (R/T) distress call from the French M'*aidez*, 'help me'. |
| MBC | Motor Boat Crew. |
| MCPC | Marine Craft Policy Committee. |
| MCS | Marine Craft Section. |
| MCTS | Marine Craft Training School. |
| MCU | Marine Craft Unit. |
| MGB | Motor Gun Boat. |
| ML | Motor Launch. |
| MT | Mechanized Transport. |
| MT | Marine Tender. |
| MTB | Motor Torpedo Boat. |
| NCO | Non-Commissioned Officer. |
| N/O | Nursing Orderly. |
| OC | Officer Commanding. |
| Paddlewheel effect | Sideways movement of a boat at slow speed due to propeller rotation. |
| P/O | Pilot Officer, RAF, or Petty Officer, RN. |
| Pram dinghy | Small boat with snub-nose. |
| Propeller slip | The difference between the theoretical forward movement of a rotating screw and the *actual* movement in the liquid. |
| PSP | Pierced Steel Plank. |
| PT | Physical Training. |
| Pulpit | Safety framework at bows of a boat. |
| Pushpit | Safety framework at stern. |
| Quarters | The port and starboard stern sectors of a boat. |
| RAAF | Royal Australian Air Force. |
| RAE | Royal Aircraft Establishment. |
| RAFO | Reserve of Air Force Officers. |
| RAFVR | Royal Air Force Volunteer Reserve. |
| RCAF | Royal Canadian Air Force. |
| RCN | Royal Canadian Navy. |
| RD/F | Radio Direction Finding. |
| RFA | Royal Fleet Auxiliary. |
| RFC | Royal Flying Corps. |
| RML | Rescue Motor Launch. |

| | |
|---|---|
| RNAS | Royal Naval Air Service. |
| RNLI | Royal National Lifeboat Institute. |
| RNR | Royal Navy Reserve. |
| RNVR | Royal Navy Volunteer Reserve. |
| RSL | Range Safety Launch. |
| R/T | Radio Telephony, voice communication. |
| RTB | Return to base. |
| RTTL | Rescue/Target-Towing Launch. |
| SAAF | South African Air Force. |
| SAC | Senior Aircraftman. |
| Samson post | Strong wooden post for attaching towing cables. |
| SAR | Search And Rescue. |
| SARAH | Search And Rescue And Homing. |
| SBF | Stand By Flying. |
| Seenotdienst | German Rescue Service. |
| Scow | Shallow-draft vessel for conveying bombs, etc. |
| SD | Special Duties. |
| SGB | Steam Gun Boat. |
| Sheer | The curvature of a deck seen from abeam. |
| Sgt | Sergeant. |
| S Ldr | Squadron Leader. |
| SNCO | Senior Non-Commissioned Officer. |
| SNO | Senior Naval Officer. |
| SOS | Distress signal via morse code, 'Save Our Souls'. |
| SP | Service Police (RAF), or Shore Patrol (RN). |
| Square search | A search pattern starting at the last known position and covering the area by a series of 90° turns to complete an ever-widening concentric square. |
| ST | Seaplane tender. |
| Stanchion | Vertical support or rail. |
| Snr Tech | Senior Technician, rank equivalent to Sergeant. |
| Strakes | Fore and aft external hull members. |
| SWO | Station Warrant Officer. |
| Top hamper | Excess weight and bulk above the deck. |
| Transom | The (usually flat) stern panel. |
| Trenchard Brats | Nickname for apprentices and boy entrants. |
| TS | Troop ship. |
| UHF | Ultra High Frequency. |
| USAAF | United States Army Air Force. |
| VHF | Very High Frequency. |
| W Cdr | Wing Commander. |
| WO | Warrant Officer. |
| W/Op | Wireless Operator. Also W/OM for Wireless Operator Marine. |
| W/T | Wireless Telegraphy, via morse code. |

# Bibliography

Allward, M. *Seaplanes and Flying Boats* (Moorland, 1981)
Arnold-Forster, M. *The World at War* (Wm Collins, 1974)
Atkin, R. *Dieppe 1942, The Jubilee Disaster* (MacMillan, 1980)
Blackman, E. *Airman at the Helm* (K. Mason, 1979)
Bowman, M. *B 24 Liberator* (Patrick Stephens Ltd, 1989)
Bowyer, C. *Men of Coastal Command* (William Kimber, 1985)
Bowyer, C. *History of the RAF* (Hamlyn, 1977)
Bowyer, C. *Sunderland at War* (Ian Allen, 1977)
Deighton, L. *Fighter* (Jonathan Cape, 1977)
Du Cane, P. *High Speed Small Craft* (Temple Press, 1951)
Freeman, R. *Mighty Eighth War Diary* (Janes, 1981)
Garnett, D. *The Letters of T. E. Lawrence* (Spring Books, 1964)
Harris, John *A Funny Place to Hold a War* (Hutchinson, 1984)
Jablonski, E. *Flying Fortress* (Doubleday Inc, 1965)
Lawrence, T. E. *The Mint* (Jonathan Cape, 1955)
Lawrence, A. W. *T. E. Lawrence by His Friends* (Jonathan Cape, 1937)
Montgomery-Hyde, H. *Solitary in the Ranks* (Constable, 1977)
Pereira, W. D. *Boat in the Blue* (Line One, 1985)
Pilborough, G. *History of RAF Marine Craft* (Canimpex, 1987)
Plummer, R. *The Ships That Saved an Army* (Patrick Stephens, 1990)
Pritchard, J. *RAF Air Sea Rescue Launches* (W. Waters, 1974)
Ramsey, W. *The Battle of Britain Then and Now* (After The Battle, 1980)
Ramsey, W. *The Blitz Then and Now* (After The Battle, 1987)
Rance, A. *Fast Boats and Flying Boats* (Ensign, 1989)
Rendall, I. *Reaching for the Skies* (BBC Books, 1988)
Scott, P. *The Battle of the Narrow Seas* (Country Life, 1945)
Taylor, J. W. R. and Munson, K. *History of Aviation* (New English Library, 1975)
Willis, S. and Hollis, B. *Military Airfields* (Enthusiasts Publications, 1987)
Wilson, J. *Lawrence of Arabia* (Wm Heinemann, 1989)

*Appendix*

# A selection of RAF Marine Craft drawings

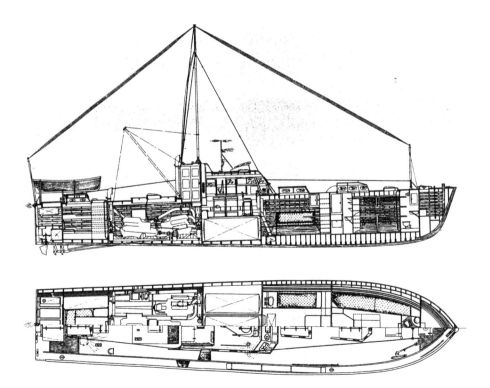

General arrangement drawing of '100 Class' HSL dated June 1938.

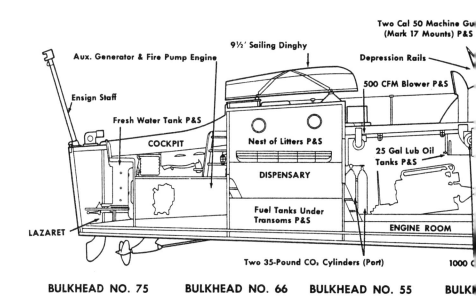

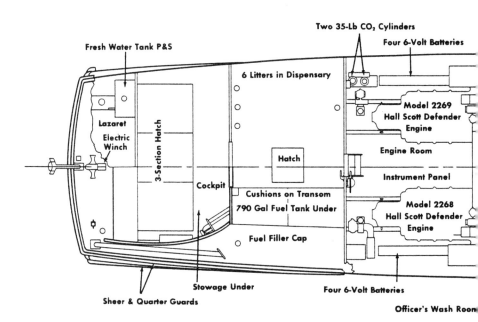

Accommodation layout of 63 ft Series 3 'Miami' (USA).

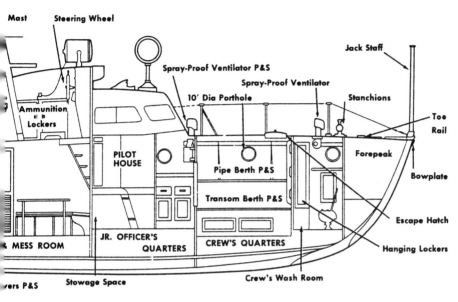

Mast
Steering Wheel
Jack Staff
Spray-Proof Ventilator P&S
Spray-Proof Ventilator
10' Dia Porthole
Stanchions
Ammunition Lockers
Toe Rail
PILOT HOUSE
Pipe Berth P&S
Forepeak
Bowplate
Transom Berth P&S
Escape Hatch
MESS ROOM
JR. OFFICER'S QUARTERS
CREW'S QUARTERS
Hanging Lockers
ers P&S
Stowage Space
Crew's Wash Room

42     BULKHEAD NO. 28     BULKHEAD NO. 18     BULKHEAD NO. 4

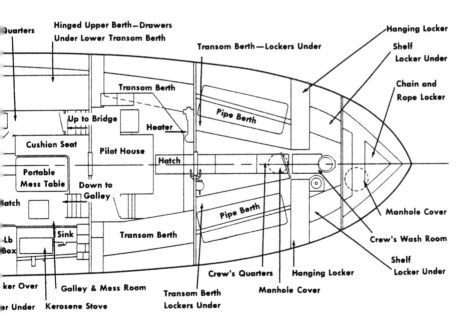

Quarters
Hinged Upper Berth—Drawers Under Lower Transom Berth
Transom Berth—Lockers Under
Hanging Locker
Shelf
Locker Under
Transom Berth
Chain and Rope Locker
Pipe Berth
Up to Bridge
Heater
Cushion Seat
Pilot House
Hatch
Portable Mess Table
Down to Galley
Manhole Cover
atch
Sink
Transom Berth
Pipe Berth
Crew's Wash Room
Lb Box
Shelf
Locker Under
ker Over
Galley & Mess Room
Crew's Quarters
Hanging Locker
r Under
Kerosene Stove
Transom Berth Lockers Under
Manhole Cover

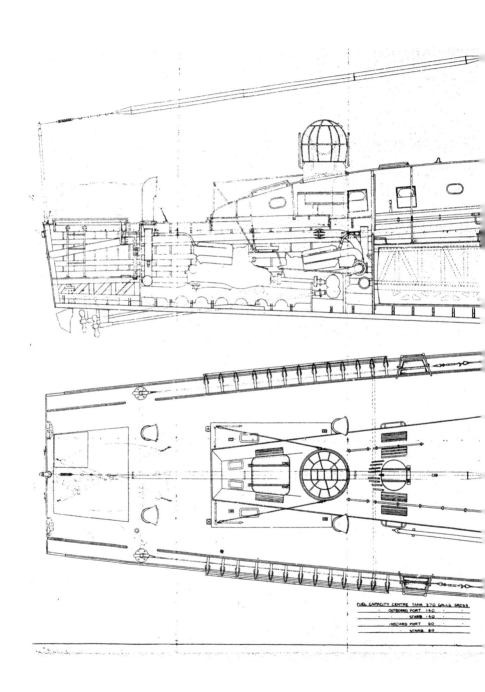

BPBC Type 2 HSL, the 'Whaleback'.

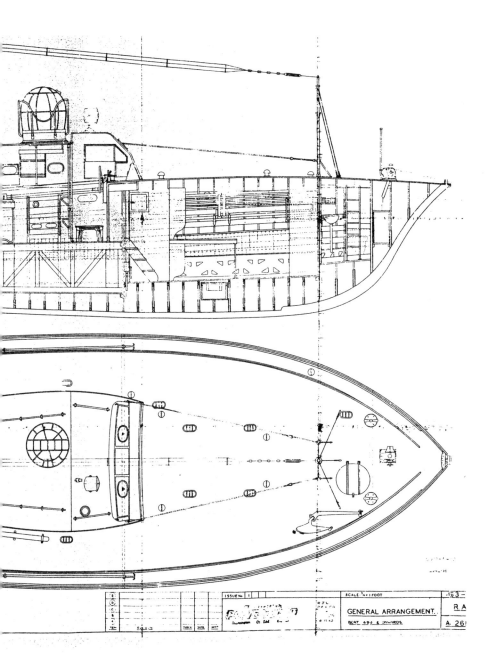

GENERAL ARRANGEMENT.

BOAT 490 & ONWARDS

SCALE ¼"=1FOOT

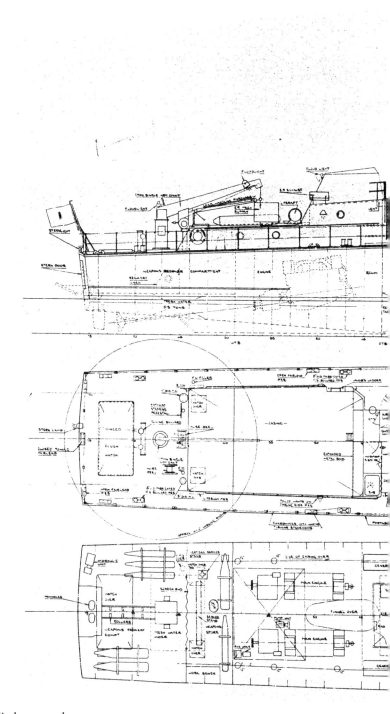

Layout of 'Seal' class vessel.

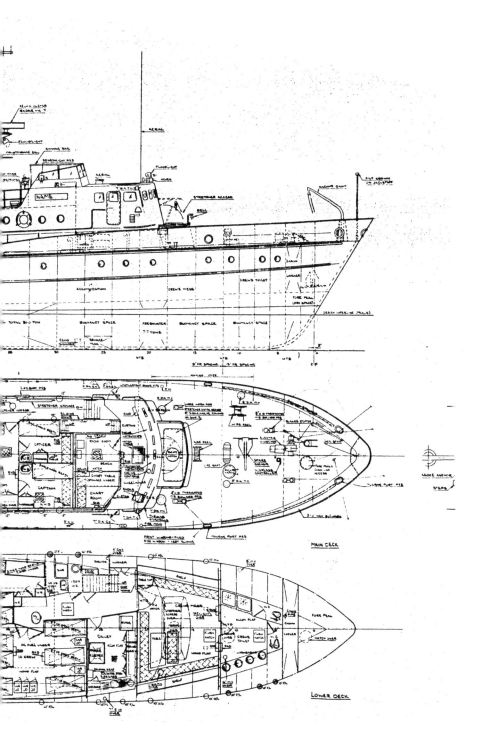

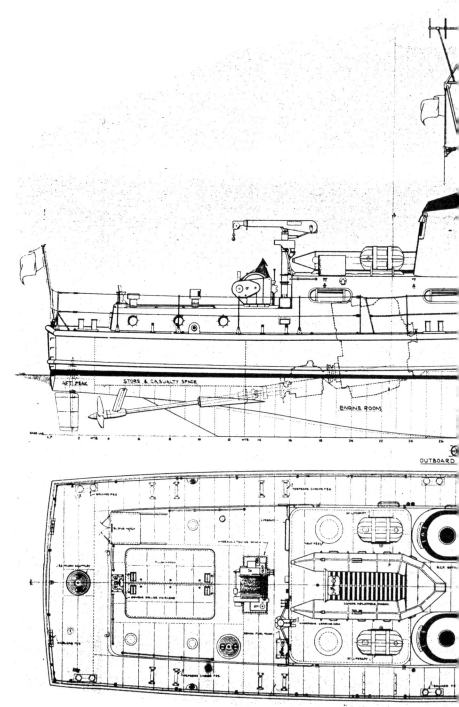

Drawing of HMAFV *Spitfire* showing the stubby bow.

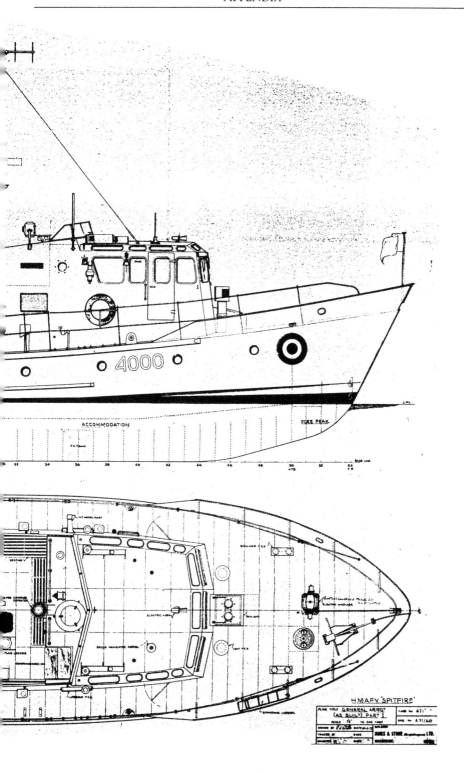

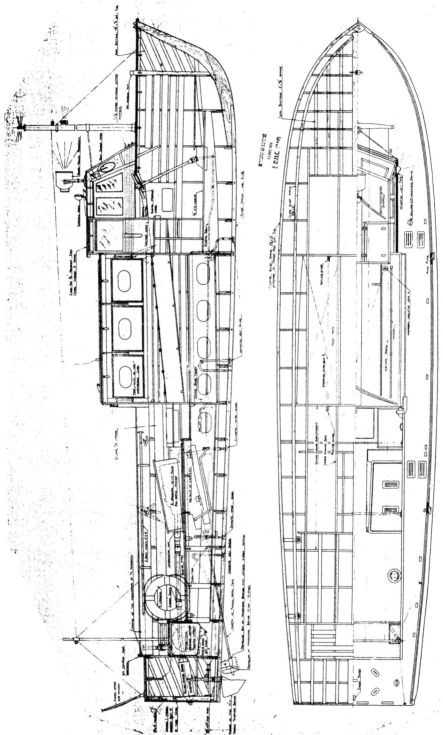

The simple construction and layout of the '200' class seaplane tender.

# Index

# INDEX

Duffy, G. Flt Lt 197,214
Dunning, E. S Cdr (RN) 16
Durnford-Slater Lt (Army) 90

Eardley-Stiff, M. SAC 198
Edwards, J. F Sgt 157
Ely, E. 15
Esmonde, E. Lt Cdr (RN) 84
Evans Flt Lt 159

Farnsworth Flt Lt 159
Felloch Cpl 95
Field, H. F Sgt 137–9
Finn, T. S Ldr 193
Finucane, B. W Cdr 85–6
Fitzgerald-Lombard, G. S Ldr 182
Flower, L. Cpl 60–3,94,210
Forster, E.M. 38
Fosh, J. Gp Capt 219
Fox, Uffa 136
Fryirs, T. Flt Lt 191–2

Garret, W. F/O 145
Garson SAC 208
Gault Flt Lt 217
Gibbons, D. Flt Lt 188,193–6
Gibson, G. W Cdr 136
Good LAC 92
Gort, Lord F Mar (Army) 59,63
Grandy, Sir J. ACM 211
Graves, R. 35
Greenall, P. S Ldr 193–6
Greenhalgh Cpl 92
Griffiths, R. Ch Tech 188
Guinness, Sir A. Flt Lt 147

Haig, Earl D. F Mar (Army) 160
Haines, E. S Ldr 146
Haldane, Lord 13
Hardie, E. F/O 152,182
Hardy S Ldr 193
Harris Sgt (USAAF) 135
Harris, J. Cpl 161,197
Hawkins F/O 159
Head Flt Lt 197
Henderson, W. 205–6
Hermitage LAC 95
Heward Cpl 41
Hill, A.J. 158
Hill, J. 158
Hill, J. F/O 92
Hillman S Ldr 182
Hoare, Sir S. 36–40
Hodgson Lt (RNVR) 86
Holmes, G. Lt Col (RFC) 17
Hornell, D. Flt Lt 144
Houston, Lady L. 34
Howe, C. Capt (RN) 69,75
Hubbard, G. Flt Lt 194–6
Hugget, A. Flt Lt 142–3
Hunt LAC 61

Ivil, D. 202–7

Jinman, W. Flt Lt 13,40,42,44
Johnson Sgt 194
Johnson, J.E. AVM 189
Johnston, S. F Sgt 199
Jones, A. Sgt 205–7

Kearns, J. Flt Lt 199
Kernohan A/C 61
King George VI 154,169
Kinnaird, A. F Sgt 163
Kraft LAC 93

Lang, J. P/O 94,157
Lawrence, T. Lt Col (Army) 31,33,35–45
Lawson Cpl 61
Leech Flt Lt 197
Legge F/O 159
Lloyd-George, D. 16

Lockwood LAC 61
Lockwood, G. Flt Lt 146
Lomas, L. W/O 215
Loughnan, J. S Ldr 182
Lovat, Lord Lt Col (Army) 90
Low Sgt 145
Lund-Lack, G. S Ldr 158

Maddocks, A. SAC 194
Male, L. Cpl Tech 189
Manson, R.J.M. S Ldr 196–7
Mathews SAC 218
Mavroyiangos Capt (Gr) 194
McAusland, D. SAC 197
McIntosh F/O 154
McLaughlin F Sgt 161
McLaughlin, F. Cpl 200
Mitchell, 'Mad Mitch' Col (Army) 190
Mitchell, R. 31,33–4
Monti, G. 33
Moore, R. Flt Lt 162
Moore, R.F. Sgt 202–7
Morgan, W. LAC 85
Morrison, D. P/O (RCAF) 93
Moss LAC 93
Moss J/T 218
Motyer LAC 86
Moulds, P. Flt Lt 190
Mountbatten, Lord L. Adml (RN) 89–96
Munro SAC 218

Nathan, A. Maj (Army) 39
Newall, Sir C. 69
Nicholls F/O 154
Norrington, H. Flt Lt 52
Noy Cpl 92

Osborne, F. Sgt 92

Page, E. P/O 60
Parham, E. Cpl 158
Parkin Flt Lt 211
Parsons, G. Ch Tech 184
Pollock SAC 194
Pound, Sir D. Adml (RN) 89
Power Adml (RN) 76
Power Flt Lt 159
Pring A/C 86
Pumphrey Lt Cdr (RN) 84

Quigley, M. SAC 200
Quill, J. 34

Ramsey Adml (RN) 59
Richards P/O 159
Rider, C. Cpl 33
Robb Lt (RN) 136
Roberts Gen (Army) 90
Roberts Cpl 159
Rogers, J. F/O 158
Roosevelt, F.D. 77
Ross, J.H. Pvte (Army) 35
Rudd, H. W Cdr 169
Rutland, F. Flt Cdr (RN) 15

Salmond, Sir G. AVM 44
Salmond, Sir J. M of RAF 31,75,89–96
Samson, C. Lt (RN) 15
Sandford, G. AB (RN) 86
Sassoon, Sir P. 44
Saunders, B. Flt Lt 187
Scarrat, A. LAC 85
Schneider, J. 31
Scott, A. 205–6
Scott, P. Lt Cdr (RN) 95
Scott-Paine, H. 40–54,72,76
Selman, G. 72–76,130–6,149,175
Shakeri F/O 85–6
Shaw, Charlotte 37–45
Shaw, T.E. A/C 32–3,35–45,65
Sikorsky, I. 171

Slater, L. S Ldr 32
Smart, B, Flt S-Lt (RN) 15
Smeed, G. A/C 163
Smith Flt Lt 198
Smith F Sgt 214
Smith, S. W Cdr 33–45
Sparkes F Sgt 175
Spencer, R. P/O 63
Spurr, E. 45
Staines Cpl 41
Stainforth Flt Lt 33
Stephens Sgt 94
Stephenson, R. A/C 94
Stewart F Sgt 207
Stewart, J. 205–6
Stewart, L. Lt (USAAF) 134
Stewart, R. 205–7
Strever Lt (SAAF) 155
Sutton, A. A/C 94
Swann, Sir O. AVM 36
Swenson, D. Lt (USAAF) 134–5
Sykes, F. Maj (Army) 13
Symons, R. 217

Thompson Ch Tech 200
Thompson, Lord 39–40
Traynor, W. SAC 202–7
Trenchard, Sir H. M of RAF 16,30–1, 34–45
Turton, P. SAC 198
Tyrell, M. Flt Lt 215

Waghorn Flt Lt 33
Wake-Walker Adml (RN) 63
Walters, W. F/O 85–6
Waring Gp Capt 136
Waring F/O 153
Watson, E. Flt Lt 146
Webster Flt Lt 32
Webster, C. Cpl 60
Wheeler SAC 218
White A/C 61
Wilkins LAC 93
Williams Lt (RN) 86
Williams, J. Gp Capt 219
Winstone, D. 154
Wooton LAC 61
Worsley Flt Lt 32
Wray, M. Cpl 200

VESSELS:
*(All RTTLs and larger craft were entitled to the designation HMAFV after 1947. In this index, craft type has been prioritized and HMAFV used only where it appears as such in the text or when it refers to a 'named' vessel.)*
Admirals Barge 51
Airborne Lifeboat 136–7
*Aleigal* 193
AMC No. 3 60
*Aquarius* 44
ASR Float 70
*Aster* 20
ATB 43

*Biscuit* 39–45
Brooke 20–32,40,46,154,211

CMB 32,47
Compass Barge 21
Concrete Lighter 21
Cox & Kings 20
Customs Launch 51

D-Boats 177,180
De Jinn 20
Docking Lighter 21,32
*Duke of Normandy* 2 217

E-Boat 70,74,78,84